KILLING

THE

KILLERS

KILLING
THE
KILLERS

THE SECRET WAR AGAINST
TERRORISTS

BILL O'REILLY
AND
MARTIN DUGARD

ST. MARTIN'S PRESS
NEW YORK

First published in the United States by St. Martin's Press, an imprint of
St. Martin's Publishing Group

KILLING THE KILLERS. Copyright © 2022 by Bill O'Reilly and Martin Dugard.
All rights reserved. Printed in the United States of America. For information,
address St. Martin's Publishing Group, 120 Broadway, New York, NY 10271.

www.stmartins.com

Maps by Kate Thorp

Design by Meryl Sussman Levavi

Library of Congress Cataloging-in-Publication Data is available.

ISBN 978-1-250-27925-5 (hardcover)
ISBN 978-1-250-27926-2 (ebook)

Our books may be purchased in bulk for promotional, educational, or business
use. Please contact your local bookseller or the Macmillan Corporate and
Premium Sales Department at 800-221-7945, extension 5442, or by email at
MacmillanSpecialMarkets@macmillan.com.

First Edition 2022

1   3   5   7   9   10   8   6   4   2

*This book is dedicated to the Colaio family
of Manhasset, New York,
who suffered grievously after the 9/11 attack.*

AUTHORS' NOTE

The vast majority of human beings who have been killed or harmed by extremists are innocent Muslims, largely people of goodwill.

KILLING
THE
KILLERS

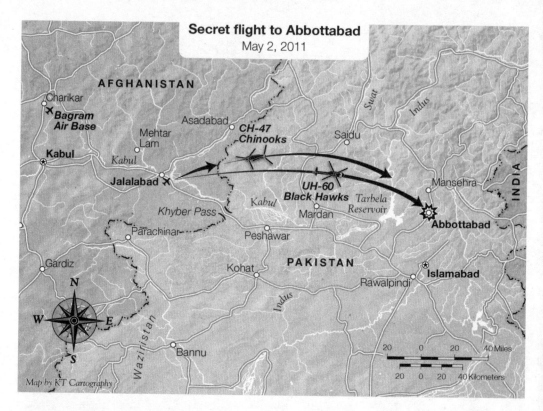

Secret flight to Abbottabad
May 2, 2011

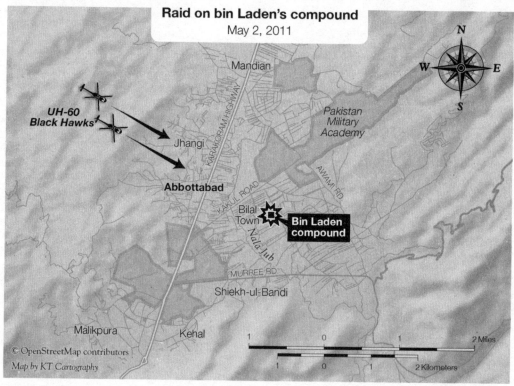

Raid on bin Laden's compound
May 2, 2011

PROLOGUE

MAY 2, 2011
ABBOTTABAD, PAKISTAN
0045 HOURS (12:45 A.M.)

The man with thirty minutes to live sleeps in his beige pajamas.

Meanwhile, two US Army UH-60 Black Hawk helicopters fly low over Pakistani airspace. The moon is a waning crescent. HAC—the helicopter aircraft commander—is up front in the left seat, his copilot to the right. "Chalk One," as the lead bird is known, carries a dozen Navy SEALs on the hard metal floor in the cabin space behind the cockpit. Chalk Two ferries ten SEALs, a Pakistani American CIA translator, and a six-year-old Belgian Malinois dog named Cairo. Like the soldiers, Cairo wears Kevlar body armor and specially fitted night vision goggles.

The fuselage of each bird is painted black. Special metallurgy and heat-suppressing exhaust systems minimize the 60's radar profile. Noise-reducing technology affixed to the tips of the rotors dampens sound. The pilots enhance their aircraft's invisibility by using a flying technique known as "nap of the earth," hugging landscape contours as low to the ground as possible. The fully laden machines travel at a deliberate seventy-five miles per hour.

Death is coming in the darkness.

✦ ✦ ✦

Each member of this special team of SEAL (Sea, Air, Land) commandos remains almost motionless on the floor. The 60s are equipped with crew seats, but it is a matter of pride that SEALs are too tough for such luxury. Many are asleep despite this dangerous mission. Their uniform consists of Crye Precision desert digital camouflage combat pants with a matching pullover shirt designed to be worn under body armor. Pockets along each pant leg contain gear vital to the mission: leather gloves, medical kit, energy bars, extra ammunition.

In case the mission goes wrong, every SEAL carries a few hundred dollars in American currency to buy local assistance and find a way out of Pakistan.

The fighters are navy, but the pilots are army. This is by design. The 60 is flown by both branches of the service, but it is widely acknowledged that army pilots are best in "infil" and "exfil"—infiltration and exfiltration, the dangerous business of landing a helicopter in a battle zone and successfully departing when the mission is over.

Tonight, infil and exfil are life and death.

✦ ✦ ✦

Both Black Hawks took off sixty minutes ago from a secure airfield in Jalalabad, Afghanistan. In support, two larger CH-47 Chinook helicopters flew out fifteen minutes later, loaded with spare fuel for the return journey. The two "Bathtubs," as the Chinooks are nicknamed for their elongated shape, will land at a secret base in Afghanistan close to the Pakistani border, there to await further orders.

The SEALs are headed toward a private compound near the town of Abbottabad, just under two hundred miles away. Locals call it the Waziristan Palace for its enormous size.* Located on Kakul Road, in a middle-class section of Abbottabad known as Bilal Town, the acre-sized facility is surrounded by thick walls ranging in height from ten to eighteen feet tall. Solid steel gates cover each entrance.

---

* Waziristan is a mountainous region of western Pakistan.

Several structures and a large open courtyard for raising animals and growing vegetables fill the space inside.

The plan is for Chalk One to hover low over the courtyard. SEALs on board will invade the compound by sliding down a system of thick ropes attached to a strong point inside the helicopter, known as the FRIES—fast rope insertion/extraction system. "Fast-roping" greatly resembles a fire pole descent—thus the leather gloves each man carries. Once on the ground, they will spread out and begin their search for tonight's target.

Meanwhile, Chalk Two will land just outside the compound walls. Cairo the dog, his SEAL handler, Will Chesney, the CIA interpreter, and a small sniper team will disembark to provide perimeter security. They will seek out any approaching force or anyone trying to escape. One squad of SEALs will remain on board Chalk Two at this time, then be flown into the compound, where they will fast-rope onto the flat rooftop of the three-story main house.

Unloaded, both helicopters will then fly to a designated location to await the order to return and pick up the combatants. Total time on the ground will be no more than forty minutes.

✦ ✦ ✦

There are several buildings to infiltrate, but the main house is of greatest interest. It is thought that "the Pacer," as the tall figure whom satellite cameras so often photograph strolling the grounds is called, lives in this structure. The SEALs will enter the residence seeking this man. If he chooses to come along peacefully, he will be bound and escorted into a helicopter for a flight to captivity.

Should the homeowner prefer to fight, he will be shot dead. The weapon of choice for these SEALs varies by man, whether it be the Heckler & Koch HK416 assault rifle, FN Mark 48 machine gun, or the H&K MP7 machine pistol that fires an armor-piercing cartridge. In addition, each man wears a holstered pistol. And no SEAL is ever comfortable unless he is carrying a very long and very sharp fixed-blade knife.

This April 1998 file photo shows Osama bin Laden in Afghanistan.

✦ ✦ ✦

The target on this warm, humid night is the notorious killer Osama bin Laden, the fifty-four-year-old terrorist mastermind of the 9/11 attacks on New York and Washington, DC. Formally named Osama bin Mohammed bin Awad bin Laden, he is six foot five, with a long black-and-gray beard. Saudi Arabian by birth, the terrorist was born the son of a billionaire who died in a plane crash when Osama was just ten.* Bin Laden is known to be frugal and soft-spoken but a

---

* The father, Mohammed bin Awad bin Laden, was the wealthiest nonroyal person in Saudi Arabia. He made his billions in construction, as the official "royal builder" of Saudi Arabia, running an organization now known as the Saudi Binladin Group. He fathered fifty-two children by twenty-two wives. Osama bin Laden inherited $30 million of his father's $5 billion fortune.

strict father to the estimated twenty-six children he has fathered with his many wives.

The terrorist is the most wanted man in the world. People everywhere know his face; there is nowhere he can go without being recognized. Raised in a world of privilege, he is driven by a deep hatred for America. Bin Laden has turned his back on the peaceful tenets of the Muslim religion, preferring to live a life dedicated to killing US citizens. This has come at a cost: he spends his life on the run, taking extreme precautions to avoid being apprehended. But even from this remote hideaway, bin Laden controls a vast terror network. Extremists rally to his cause, and his message of hate does not fall on deaf ears in the world of the jihadi.

Most of all, bin Laden is a murderer. In addition to the almost three thousand innocent people killed on 9/11, he has used his considerable wealth to lead the terrorist organization al-Qaeda—"the Foundation"—in numerous deadly attacks around the world since 1998. In August 1996, bin Laden declared a holy war, a jihad, against America, operating from a hidden refuge in Afghanistan. For the past ten years, the most well-equipped intelligence agencies on the planet have hunted bin Laden, but he has been elusive. There have been numerous alleged sightings of the man, all of which have led nowhere.

Tonight will be different.

✦ ✦ ✦

The CIA has confirmed that Osama bin Laden, his children, and his many wives have occupied the Abbottabad compound since 2005. Interrogation of al-Qaeda detainees at the US-run Guantánamo Bay prison in Cuba revealed the name of a bin Laden courier known as Abu Ahmed al-Kuwaiti, real name Ibrahim Saeed Ahmed. In 2007, officials learned that this messenger was living in Abbottabad under an alias; careful tracking of Ahmed's movements led the CIA to believe he might be sheltering bin Laden. US intelligence officials sought to confirm this hunch by obtaining a blood sample from one of the many children whom satellite photos showed to be living in the compound. These same images revealed the first intriguing images of the Pacer.

A Pakistan army soldier stands on top of the house where it is believed al-Qaeda leader Osama bin Laden lived in Abbottabad, Pakistan, on Monday, May 2, 2011.

Pakistani doctor Shakil Afridi, considered the top physician in the nearby Khyber tribal regions, was recruited by the CIA to set up a vaccine clinic in Abbottabad. He had previously worked on several US-funded vaccination programs in Pakistan and willingly agreed. Afridi was not told the name of the target. Unbeknownst to the doctor, any blood samples that could be acquired would be compared with DNA known to belong to bin Laden to confirm a match. The operation was successful.*

After the verification of bin Laden's location, the American military and the CIA developed "Operation Neptune Spear."† Several different tactics were discussed, including a stealth bomber dropping munitions on the compound or a drone-fired missile. But none of those actions would confirm the truth about whether Osama bin

---

* Dr. Afridi was arrested by Pakistani authorities on May 23, 2011. He is currently serving a twenty-three year sentence in a Punjab prison. Presidents Obama, Trump, and Biden have been unable to secure his release.

† Operation Neptune Spear was so named because of the trident, the official insignia of the Navy SEALs. The trident is the spear used by the Roman sea god Neptune.

Laden was alive or dead. So the decision was made to send in SEAL teams to do the work.

But the strategy is a high-risk gamble. The SEALs have all volunteered to travel into Pakistan without permission from its government, knowing full well that a Pakistani military headquarters is just two miles from the compound. Should they be captured alive, each SEAL is guaranteed hours of the most heinous torture before being executed, most likely by beheading, in a dank jail cell. Thus, the TOT—time on target—must be as short as possible.

There are so many things that can go wrong. The twin-engine UH-60 carries 1,200 pounds of fuel in each of its two tanks. That's enough gas for ninety minutes of flying. Add in another 1,200-pound auxiliary tank, heavy stealth technology, and the combined weight of the men, and these aircraft are at the very end of their technical flying ability. Simply put: they might not have enough gas to get home. And "getting home" in this case means flying back into Afghanistan over the rugged Hindu Kush, some of the most difficult terrain on earth.

But for pilots and SEALs alike, many years of training have been preparation for a scenario just like this: neutralizing a sworn enemy, one who has killed not just in America but all over the globe for two decades.

Osama bin Laden is *the* most important target in the world.

✦ ✦ ✦

Three minutes until the drop. The pilots close in rapidly. The sound of their rotors will be audible to those in the compound when the helicopters are two minutes out. The residence has been heavily surveilled, but even after months of planning, questions remain. Nobody knows if the walls or rooftops are booby-trapped, whether an underground escape tunnel will allow the occupants to flee into the night, or how quickly the nearby Pakistani military will respond to the incursion. But already, there is good news: no activity has been sighted anywhere in the area, a sign that the American pilots have successfully flown beneath the radar.

Now they need to maintain that cloak of invisibility.

Darkness helps. Power outages are common in this Pakistani garrison town, and on this hot night, Abbottabad is bathed in total darkness. All light in both helicopters is suppressed. The SEALs make last-minute personal equipment checks. The assault is about to begin.

The code name of the target: Geronimo.

✦ ✦ ✦

Osama bin Laden is asleep, his fourth wife, Amal, at his side. There are bars and curtains with yellow flowers on his windows. Barbed wire rings the compound. Before going to bed at 11:00 p.m., the undisputed leader of the al-Qaeda terrorist network ate dinner. Bin Laden prefers bread, dates, and honey; he rarely eats meat. The terrorist also does not use utensils, preferring to eat with his right hand, in the manner of the prophet Muhammad.

Bin Laden's two-year-old son, Hussein, also sleeps in the room. No one pays attention to the power outage. These occurrences are so frequent they are no longer a cause for concern.

The terrorist, his wife, and his child prayed together before bed. Osama bin Laden sleeps just two to three hours a night. He is an anxious man, often lying awake in the darkness waiting for morning to come or taking sleeping pills when he cannot calm himself. But tonight is restful. So while her husband slumbers, it is Amal who hears the rotors of approaching helicopters.

✦ ✦ ✦

"Mr. President," an aide tells Barack Obama, "this is going to take a while. You might not want to sit here and watch the whole thing unfold."

President Obama is in the basement of the White House's West Wing, in the intelligence command post known as the Situation Room. The time is shortly before 4:00 p.m. A large television screen airs a live feed of the mission in Pakistan, transmitted from drones capable of circling as high as fifty thousand feet. The unmanned aircraft is invisible to the naked eye and is capable of remaining over the target for many hours at a time.

President Barack Obama and Vice President Joe Biden, along with members of the national security team, receive an update on the mission against Osama bin Laden in the Situation Room of the White House, May 1, 2011. Please note: a classified document seen in this photograph has been obscured.

Operation Neptune Spear combines the efforts of the civilian CIA and military Joint Special Operations Command (JSOC). So a similar viewing is taking place in a seventh-floor conference room at Central Intelligence Agency headquarters in Langley, Virginia, watched by agency director Leon Panetta, who has dedicated almost a year to this risky venture. Panetta is in direct contact with mission commander Admiral William McRaven at the SEALs' departure base in Jalalabad.

But seeing the president depart causes others to follow him, into the office of a military adviser. The room is cramped, but that does not stop people from crowding into it, much to Obama's dismay.

Barack Obama wears a white golf shirt and blue windbreaker bearing the presidential emblem. Though knowing full well the operation would proceed tonight, he intentionally played golf earlier, to avoid a departure from his normal Sunday routine. Being president means having your every movement and word scrutinized. Obama did not want to hint toward tonight's operation in any way.

A long conference table covered with open laptops and various drinks fills the center of the small space. Vice President Joe Biden is openly nervous. He and Defense Secretary Robert Gates, who is also present, are ambivalent about the mission. Both men have been asking many questions about its viability, still remembering the 1980 American debacle in the Iranian desert, when eight US servicemen were killed and six aircraft destroyed after a botched effort to rescue American hostages. That incident damaged the presidency of Jimmy Carter beyond repair. There was also Somalia, in 1993, where a Black Hawk helicopter was shot down, resulting in the deaths of eighteen Americans. That incident still is vividly remembered by the public because of a bestselling book and a subsequent Hollywood movie.

Failure tonight would be a disaster far worse than Iran or Somalia. And President Obama would take much of the heat.

Wearing a brown blazer, Secretary of State Hillary Clinton enters the room and takes a seat next to Secretary Gates. Antony Blinken, destined one day to become future president Joe Biden's secretary of state, stands in the doorway. There is very little talking. The air is thick with tension.*

Everything is going according to plan.

Until it doesn't.

✦ ✦ ✦

Chalk One hovers over the Waziristan Palace, SEALs poised to fast-rope out the open doors. Suddenly, the eighteen-foot-high stone compound walls and hot night air contribute to a dangerous condition known as "vortex ring state," which prevents the helicopter rotors from producing lift. Simultaneously, the tail of the 60 bounces atop the compound wall. Lack of lift pitches the helicopter forward

---

* Blinken served as national security adviser to Vice President Biden at the time.

and down toward the ground. The tail wheel acts as a pivot point, forcing the Black Hawk to tilt sharply to the right.

The main rotors dig hard into the loose soil of a vegetable garden. Pilot and copilot strain against their seat belts, helmets and harnesses holding them fast to their cockpit seats. In the cabin behind them, the unbelted SEALs pitch forward, falling onto one another. They struggle to remain inside the helicopter. Slipping out the open doors into the spinning blades would be a horrific way to die.

Events unfold quickly. The pilots immediately shut down the Black Hawk's two engines. SEALs, many slightly injured, scramble to exit, guns at the ready. The crash has been anything but silent, and the invaders prepare for incoming fire from the compound.

Outside, Chalk Two lands in a field, but takes off the instant the SEALs and Cairo jump out. The dog is immediately let off his leash to search for threats. He has been in combat before and knows the difference between a helpless infant and a lethal terrorist.

The original task of these operators was perimeter defense, but now they move to blow the walls and enter the compound, not knowing the fate of their comrades in the crashed helicopter.

The invading SEALs now see bin Laden's safe house for the first time. They have practiced on a life-sized version at a secret location in North Carolina. But this is the real thing.

"We opened the doors, and I looked out," SEAL operator Robert O'Neill will remember. Seeing the high walls and knowing what must be done to complete the mission successfully, O'Neill thought, "This is some serious Navy SEAL shit we're going to do."

✦ ✦ ✦

Osama bin Laden is now awake. A loud, bright explosion shakes the house as he crouches on the bedroom floor; the sound of the crashing helicopter cuts through the night with a noise so loud that a witness will later call it a "noise of magnitude I have never heard before." Baby Hussein cries. Amal tries to turn on a light, forgetting about the power outage.

Raid on bin Laden's compound
May 2, 2011

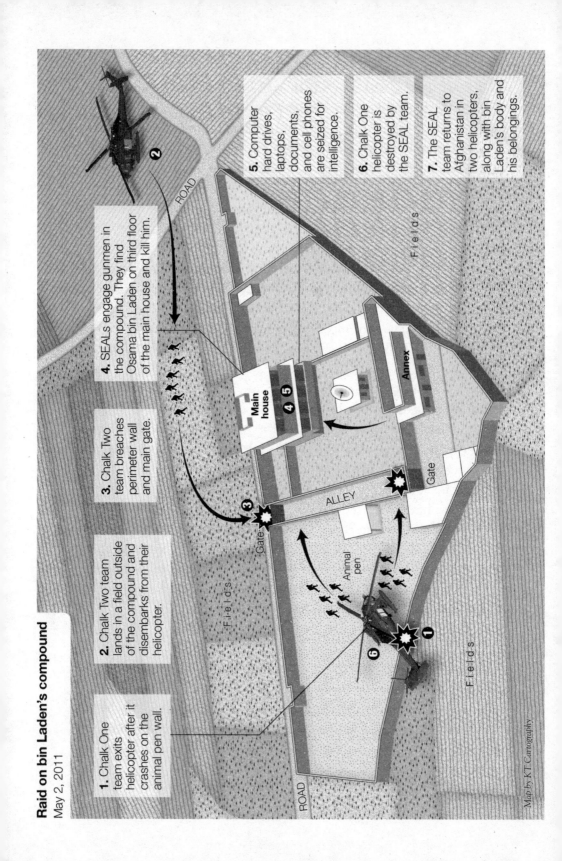

1. Chalk One team exits helicopter after it crashes on the animal pen wall.

2. Chalk Two team lands in a field outside of the compound and disembarks from their helicopter.

3. Chalk Two team breaches perimeter wall and main gate.

4. SEALs engage gunmen in the compound. They find Osama bin Laden on third floor of the main house and kill him.

5. Computer hard drives, laptops, documents, and cell phones are seized for intelligence.

6. Chalk One helicopter is destroyed by the SEAL team.

7. The SEAL team returns to Afghanistan in two helicopters, along with bin Laden's body and his belongings.

ROAD

ROAD

Fields

Fields

F·i·e·l·d·s

Main house

Annex

ALLEY

Gate

Gate

Animal pen

Map by KT Cartography

"No," bin Laden commands. Opening the bedroom door, he screams down the stairs to his son Khalid. "Come up!"*

"Americans are coming!" yells Khalid, running up the stairs in white pajamas, clutching a loaded AK-47 automatic rifle. The crying voices of the many children in the three-story structure echo up and down the stairwell.

Outside, a new explosion rings through the night as SEALs breach the perimeter wall on the north side of the compound. Two bodyguards, brothers Ibrahim Saeed Ahmed and Abrar Ahmed, have sworn loyalty to bin Laden and stand ready to fight. The men are Pakistanis who oversaw the construction of the compound but have long feared that a night like this might come. Several times, they suggested that bin Laden and his extended brood relocate.

After a time, the terrorist reluctantly agreed but asked for postponement of departure until September 2011—the tenth anniversary of the terror attack on America.

Now, five minutes into the SEAL landings, as explosions destroy the big metal doors guarding the compound entrances, Osama bin Laden regrets his decision.

✦ ✦ ✦

"It appears that we have a helicopter down in the animal pen," Admiral McRaven says from Afghanistan over the live video feed. "Backup helicopter on the way."

In fact, McRaven ordered one Chinook to fly to the compound just moments ago.

At CIA headquarters in Virginia, Director Panetta watches the crash of Chalk One with rising fear. A multimillion-dollar helicopter crashes, and it's Black Hawk down all over again.

Maybe.

At the White House, President Obama will recall feeling "an electric kind of fear. A disaster reel played in my head."

The mood in the small conference room is grim. More than a

---

* The authors reviewed the eyewitness testimony from people inside the compound who were not killed. This account is taken directly from transcripts.

dozen of America's top leaders fill the space, anxiously watching the screen. Mr. Obama sits off to the side in a small chair, leaning forward, eyes riveted. Secretary Clinton presses one hand to her face, covering her mouth.

The video feed is a series of monochromatic images. Twenty-four SEALs are now on the ground, with most inside the compound. Explosions and gunshots can be heard clearly as the SEALs apply breaching charges to blast doorways, even as the trapped occupants open fire with AK-47s.

The SEAL weapons are suppressed, making very little noise when they fire. So all audible gunshots are from bin Laden's security team, which now includes twenty-three-year-old Khalid. The team from Chalk One can be seen entering the main house. Others make their way to a small annex known by the code symbol C1 on the SEALs' laminated maps of the compound, secured in their pants pockets.

Suddenly, as the team is about to enter the building, rounds from an AK-47 assault weapon rattle above their heads. Glass shatters, falling onto the crouched Americans. Returning fire, the SEALs shoot into the darkness. There is no response. The firing stops. A woman yells to them, then slowly steps into their sight line. She is holding a baby.

"He is dead," the woman says to the fighters. The SEALs never take their fingers off the trigger, fearing she may be wearing a suicide vest. Slowly, the invaders follow the wife of Ibrahim Saeed Ahmed into a bedroom. There, her husband—the courier for bin Laden who unknowingly led the CIA to this location—lies in the doorway. The floor is thick with his blood, and the SEALs will later remember the room smelling of heating oil. The demise of Saeed Ahmed is not seen by those watching in Washington, Virginia, and Afghanistan; the drone video cannot show the inside of the buildings. So, for twenty long minutes, the feed from space remains silent.

✦ ✦ ✦

Cautiously, the SEALs leave building C1 and cross the compound to the much larger complex mission planners have labeled A1—the main house. The night is far from silent. Children continue to cry. Women are shrieking. A three-man team enters a long hallway with two doors on each side. As the SEALs creep forward, one inhabitant of the residence cautiously leans his head out of the first door on the left. The SEAL walking point immediately fires a single shot.

Unsure if the target is hit, the team moves quickly into the room. Abrar Ahmed lies wounded on the floor, an AK-47 nearby. Suddenly, the bodyguard's wife jumps forward in the darkness, trying to prevent the SEALs from getting to her husband. The Americans have been warned that women in the compound might be armed and that some might even be wearing explosives. The invaders take no chances, opening fire.

Abrar and his wife, Bushra, both die instantly.

It is known that four men occupy the compound. Two are now dead. That leaves Khalid bin Laden and his father, directly upstairs from where the SEALs now stand.

✦ ✦ ✦

In his third-floor bedroom, Osama bin Laden prays. His family is gathered around. "They want me, not you," the terrorist tells two of his wives who have run upstairs to be at his side. There is confusion as some refuse to leave and others have no idea where to go. Americans are in the courtyard, and some SEALs have entered the main house.

Carefully, six SEALs climb to the second floor using a narrow spiral staircase. The steps are tiled. Fighting here will be at close quarters. Every footfall or whining door hinge spells trouble.

The SEALs see the image of a man standing on the stairwell leading to the third floor. He is seeking to conceal himself and does not present much of a target. Believing the individual might be bin Laden's son, the SEAL walking point softly calls out in Arabic: "Khalid, come here."*

The younger bin Laden is confused. Cautiously, he peers out from his hiding spot. He is promptly shot in the chin, the bullet slicing through his brain before exiting out the back of his skull. Khalid

---

* Each SEAL on the mission had a working knowledge of Arabic and Pakistani dialects.

bin Laden falls backward onto the stairs. The SEALs continue their advance, stepping around Khalid, whose white shirt is drenched in blood. His loaded AK-47 is propped against a wall, never fired.

At this point, three of the four males occupying the compound have been eliminated.

Only Geronimo remains.

Two rooms stand at the top of the stairs. A curtain conceals the entrance to one. A man with a long beard pokes his head out; he thinks he is invisible in the darkness. The SEALs immediately open fire. The man withdraws back into the bedroom, but his AK-47 pokes out around the doorjamb.

Two SEALs press their advantage, bounding up the stairs and throwing back the curtain. Two young girls stand in the room. One SEAL tackles them, fearing they are wearing bombs. Terrified, they cry out, having never been touched by a man not of their own family. "Sheikh," one yells toward the man with the beard.

Now comes the stand-off. One SEAL remains, staring into the eyes of Osama bin Laden, who is standing at the foot of the bed. The terrorist's beard is his most prominent feature. His hair is cut short. Amal stands in front of him. Bin Laden keeps his hands on her shoulders, using the mother of his young child, who now sits sobbing just a few feet away, as a human shield. Amal is bleeding from one leg, having taken one of the bullets fired up the stairwell.

Osama bin Laden has had years to prepare for this moment. There is a chance he is wearing a suicide vest, or perhaps concealing a gun or knife, using his wife's torso to prevent the intruders from seeing these weapons. Bin Laden is a man who hates Americans and would have no compunction about blowing himself up to take more American lives in his final act.

The SEAL weighs all these realities.

So it is that Senior Chief Petty Officer Robert O'Neill raises his weapon high, to accommodate bin Laden's height. The barrel is aimed at a spot just over Amal's shoulder. The SEAL does not hesitate. The first bullet cuts a furrow through the top of bin Laden's skull. The second shot is insurance. So is the third. The terrorist's tongue hangs from his mouth as his body goes limp. His head is blown apart.

Other SEALs enter the room, having made their way up the stairs. One by one, they fire into the corpse, payback for those who died on 9/11.

The message is radioed back to Jalalabad and then relayed to Langley and the White House. The acronym for "enemy killed in action" rockets halfway around the world.

"We heard McRaven's and Leon's voices, almost simultaneously, utter the words we'd been waiting to hear," President Obama will write.

"Geronimo, EKIA."

✦ ✦ ✦

There is no celebration. Not yet. Osama bin Laden's corpse is placed in an olive drab body bag, and SEALs carry him to the waiting helicopter outside the compound walls. Inside, the buildings are ransacked for intelligence. Computer hard drives, laptops, thumb drives, documents, and cell phones are seized. This treasure trove of information is the most captured in a single recent raid. Vacuum-sealed piles of opium are discovered beneath bin Laden's bed, the source of his income in the many years since his bank accounts were frozen.

Meanwhile, the explosions have attracted a crowd. Cairo is kept on his leash as the interpreter warns away curious citizens arriving to see the source of the noise. Dogs are considered devilish and filthy in Muslim culture, and the mere presence of a snarling Cairo is enough to deter the crowd.

A Chinook arrives to ferry out operators and captured intelligence. Bin Laden's wives and children will be left behind.* The dead terrorist has two emergency phone numbers and five hundred euros sewn into the fabric of his underwear. Space inside the helicopter carrying Osama bin Laden is so cramped that one SEAL has no

---

* Amal, along with the other wives and children of Osama bin Laden living in the compound at the time of the SEAL mission, were deported to Saudi Arabia after spending a year in a Pakistani detention facility. They remain there to this day. Amal waited until 2017 to reveal her side of the story about the events of the night of the SEAL raid.

choice but to sit atop the body for the flight back to Jalalabad. Photos are taken of bin Laden's face as the first step in authenticating the terrorist's identity.

Inside the compound, the downed UH-60 is blown up to prevent its technology from falling into the hands of the Pakistanis. The bright light and noise of the detonation is so powerful that it can be heard and seen for miles around. A Pakistani military response is surely imminent.

Time to go. The mission is now almost over.

But there is one more danger to overcome. The two US helicopters have a ninety-minute flight back to Afghanistan. A single Pakistani fighter jet could shoot the helicopters from the sky. The SEALs are apprehensive—the journey is especially long.

✦ ✦ ✦

At 5:41 p.m., Eastern time, cheers go up in Washington, DC. This is the moment when both SEAL teams cross safely into Afghanistan. Nine minutes later, they touch down safely at Jalalabad Air Base. US intelligence will later learn that Pakistani authorities had turned off their radar on this hot Sunday night, and that even if there had been advance warning, their fighter pilots were unwilling to fly in the dark.

"Let's see him," Admiral McRaven says as the body bag is removed from the UH-60.

The corpse is dropped onto the cement hangar floor. CIA analysts hastily begin conducting DNA tests to confirm the identity of the body. The sample matches those recently taken from family members. In order to calculate bin Laden's height, one very tall SEAL is ordered to lie down on the floor next to the terrorist's body.*

✦ ✦ ✦

At 11:35 p.m. Eastern, President Barack Obama addresses the nation. In his hastily written speech, he informs the world that the long hunt for Osama bin Laden is over.

---

* In a subsequent conversation, President Obama playfully mocked Admiral McRaven for losing a multimillion-dollar helicopter during the raid, but not having the foresight to purchase a one-dollar tape measure.

CIA director Panetta, who has driven to the White House to share the triumph with the president, leaves shortly after the speech. He is stunned to see crowds lining the sidewalk, cheering this moment of national victory: "USA, USA, USA," they chant.

Panetta will call it one of the best moments of his life.

✦ ✦ ✦

In Afghanistan, the Navy SEALs and their army pilots are reveling in the mission's success, laughing and rehashing the action moment by moment just a few feet from the body of Osama bin Laden. The sense of relief is palpable, with thoughts of the many things that could have gone wrong after the crash of Chalk One in everyone's heads.

This is also a sad moment for Will Chesney, Cairo's handler, who must soon say good-bye to the veteran dog after three years working together. Cairo often sleeps in Chesney's bed and has been his constant companion through that time.*

But the night is not over. Shortly after landing in Jalalabad, the SEALs, Cairo, their harvest of intelligence data, and the body of Osama bin Laden board a C-130 Hercules cargo plane for the flight to Afghanistan's Bagram Air Base—150 miles away. There, they watch President Obama's speech on a big-screen television, clean their weapons, store their gear, and grab a bite. The feeling of elation does not subside. The SEALs will soon continue to Washington, there to meet the president. Each will receive a Silver Star for bravery.†

✦ ✦ ✦

As the SEALs depart for the United States, the body of Osama bin Laden is placed in the hold of a US Navy V-22 Osprey cargo plane and flown to the aircraft carrier USS *Carl Vinson*, in the northern Arabian Sea. The terrorist has been dead less than twelve hours.

---

* Cairo was six years old at the time; the military retires dogs at seven. A little more than a year after the mission, Will Chesney adopted the seventy-pound Cairo, and the two remained together until Cairo's death from cancer in 2015.

† No SEALs were killed or wounded in the raid. Inside the compound, four men and one woman were killed. Two women were wounded.

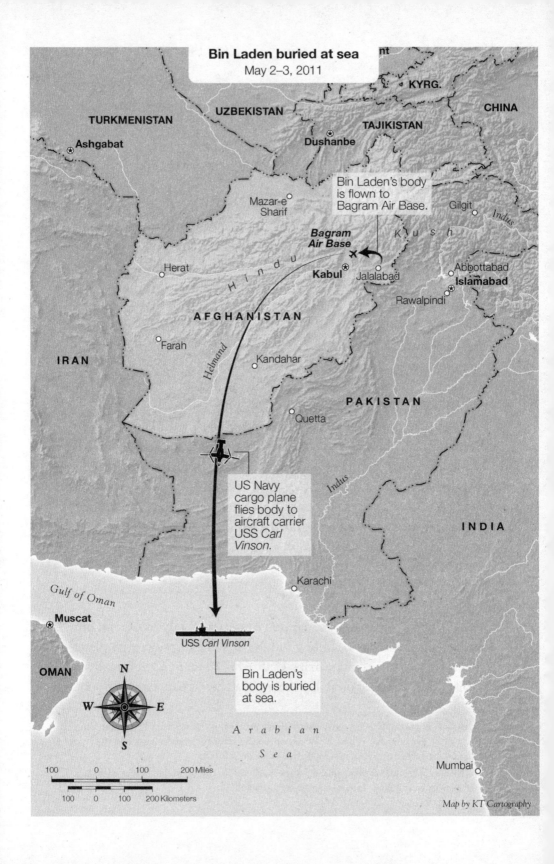

Bin Laden buried at sea
May 2–3, 2011

KYRG.

CHINA

TURKMENISTAN

UZBEKISTAN

TAJIKISTAN

Ashgabat

Dushanbe

Bin Laden's body is flown to Bagram Air Base.

Mazar-e Sharif

Gilgit

Indus

Kush

Hindu

Bagram Air Base

Herat

Kabul

Jalalabad

Abbottabad

Islamabad

Rawalpindi

AFGHANISTAN

Helmand

Farah

IRAN

Kandahar

PAKISTAN

Quetta

INDIA

Indus

US Navy cargo plane flies body to aircraft carrier USS *Carl Vinson*.

Gulf of Oman

Karachi

Muscat

USS *Carl Vinson*

OMAN

Bin Laden's body is buried at sea.

N

W   E

S

A r a b i a n

S e a

Mumbai

| 100 | 0 | 100 | 200 Miles |
| 100 | 0 | 100 | 200 Kilometers |

Map by KT Cartography

Rather than bury bin Laden on land, and have his grave become a shrine for terrorists everywhere, the team will dispatch the corpse at sea, where there is no chance his final resting place will ever be located.

In strict accordance with Islamic law, bin Laden is buried within twenty-four hours of his death. He is washed and shrouded in white cloth. There is no coffin. A US Navy sailor of the Muslim faith witnesses the cleaning and wrapping of the body.

And so it is that Osama bin Laden, wrapped tightly in the cloth, is placed inside a body bag with three hundred pounds of iron chains. The bag, resting on a flat board, is tipped over the side of the *Vinson*, sliding into the depths of the Arabian Sea. There are some eyewitnesses who suggest the body bag holding bin Laden might have been sliced open to allow creatures of the deep easier access to his remains. But that is unconfirmed.

What *is* confirmed is that the heinous mastermind of 9/11 has finally received justice.

But as one killer leaves the stage, many others are anxious to take his place.

There will be no shortage of terror killers in the years to come.

CHAPTER ONE

The condemned man kneels on the rocky ground in an orange jumpsuit. He is emaciated and barefoot, hands cuffed behind his back. The bright sun casts strong shadows. The landscape around him is nothing but beige desert hills—no vegetation, no sign of life. The garish prison garb is intentional, a mocking reminder of the uniform captured terrorists are forced to wear at America's Guantánamo Bay prison.

The executioner is clad in all black, face covered by a balaclava. He stands behind the condemned, right hand gripping his shoulder, left fist clutching a long steel-bladed knife. Both men know that a video crew is recording every word and movement. The desert backdrop offers absolutely no clue to the location of the grisly scene now being filmed.

James Foley is a good man. He stares straight into the camera. His head and face are shaved. Foley is forty and Catholic, raised in New Hampshire, a freelance journalist with a long history of covering war in the Middle East. Almost two years ago, on November 22, 2012, Foley was taken hostage by a Muslim militia while covering the Syrian

Civil War. His hired driver and translator were not kidnapped, but fellow journalist John Cantile was also abducted with Foley.*

It is often said that prostitution is the oldest profession in the world, but in the Middle East that title goes to kidnapping. The motives of terror kidnappers are many, among them seeking to trumpet their atrocities, to influence foreign powers to remove their armed forces, and to convince corporations to do business elsewhere.

But the prime reason is money. Ransom payments raise millions to fund insurgent movements. This "hostage terrorism" makes it almost suicidal for foreign journalists and aid workers to do their jobs in places like Syria. And yet they still come, from nations all around the world, their caution overridden by a desire to find information or save lives in conditions where the term "adventure" does not begin to describe the danger. While some reporters think themselves brave and noble for pursuing this work, many officials from their home countries marvel at their naïveté and label them "useful idiots."

But for James Foley, covering war was his profession, risks and all. "I had done several tours as an embedded reporter with US troops in Iraq and Afghanistan. So, for me, the frontlines felt natural. And I believed it was my job," he has written.

At the time of their kidnappings, James Foley and John Cantile knew the risks of this hostile war zone, both men having previously been taken hostage and subsequently released. Foley was kidnapped in North Africa in 2011, while covering the fall of Libyan strongman Muammar al-Gaddhafi.

"I woke up in a white washed cell, grimed with streaks of either blood or feces, or both. Sun peeked through from a barred window high on the back wall," Foley wrote of his first morning as a hostage in Libya. "I spent the whole day thinking and trying to sleep, my mind wandering between anguish and confusion. I was given rice dishes with no silverware. I ate greedily with my hands."

The journalist spent forty-four days being beaten and mistreated before his release. He went home to New Hampshire afterward,

---

* Foley was working for the French news outlet Agence France-Presse. Cantile was a freelancer who wrote and photographed for, among others, London's *Sunday Telegraph*. Both were abducted from an internet café in northwestern Syria.

speaking openly about his time as a hostage. But despite his experiences, and well knowing the risks, he chose to go back to war again—this time to Syria.

Foley was considered too experienced to let a kidnapping happen again. But while journalists from more established outlets like major television networks always travel with a security detail—usually made up of heavily armed former Special Forces operatives—freelance journalists such as Foley and Cantile cannot afford such a luxury, making them prime targets for kidnappers.

Since being taken hostage, the pair have attempted to escape at least twice. Both failed efforts were immediately followed by extreme torture. They are not the only journalists being held for ransom on this day, but Foley stands out among the captives for his calm demeanor—even fellow hostages will describe his countenance as stoic during his imprisonment. In fact, Foley is considered a leader, sharing the small portion of food given him each day and reenacting scenes from favorite movies to keep spirits high. Along with Foley, there are three other Americans—*Time* magazine journalist Steven Sotloff and two humanitarian workers, Peter Kassig, a former Army Ranger from Indianapolis, and Kayla Mueller, from Prescott, Arizona. The kidnappers are hoping to receive millions in ransom for these individuals.

On one occasion, James Foley did successfully escape, but let himself be recaptured when Cantile was unable to get away, knowing the photographer would be severely beaten for Foley's success.

Now time has run out for the journalist. The only thing that can save him is immediate payment of the terrorists' ransom demand. But 100 million euros—roughly $132 million—will not be forthcoming.

Paying ransom to terrorists is against United States law. Foley's parents are secretly looking for a way to violate this law, but there has not been any payout. As the kidnappers await the ransom, they mentally torture Foley—repeatedly forcing him to don an orange jumpsuit and kneel for his execution, only to have the murder called off at the last moment. Foley has also been ordered to stand against a wall with his arms spread wide as if being crucified. He has been waterboarded, a type of torture which involves pouring liquid into a

American journalist James Foley, who went missing in Syria on November 22, 2012, and was ultimately beheaded by ISIS.

captive's mouth and nose to the point of drowning. The terrorists do not want to kill James Foley, preferring the ransom. But that prospect has dimmed.

One week ago, August 14, 2014, Foley's captors emailed the journalist's parents, stating that the lack of ransom payment would ultimately result in their son's death. In New Hampshire, the elder Foleys cling to hope, believing there is still time to negotiate.

They are wrong.

✦ ✦ ✦

The camera crew filming the kneeling James Foley is highly technical. Grainy footage is a thing of the past for these video experts. A high-definition lens holds the captive and his would-be executioner in perfect focus. There are no shadows on camera, the result of professional lighting meters and filters instead of just the natural illumination of the noonday sun. Precise audio captures every word and sound. The footage, taken on a hill outside what might be the northern Syrian city of Raqqa, will be downloaded and edited with other images and sounds, then packaged in a four-minute-and-forty-second video, ready to be shown worldwide on YouTube.

It is a savage scene of brutality.

"I wish I had more time," Foley says into the camera. "I wish I could have the hope for freedom, to see my family once again."

And then it happens. The knife blade flashes in the desert sun. Foley's executioner grabs the back of the orange jumpsuit to keep his victim from squirming.

The beheading takes ten barbaric seconds. Windpipe, arteries, spine—all severed. There is no lack of blood. The camera records every moment. Millions around the world will soon watch this horrific sight.

The hooded executioner lets go of the orange jumpsuit. Foley's torso falls forward onto the rocky soil. His severed head, face covered in blood, eyes closed, is placed on the small of his back and positioned for the benefit of the lens.

Eventually, after the filming ends, the kidnappers will dispose of James Foley in the desert. His body will never be found.

A single militant group steps forward to claim responsibility. They were once called "al-Qaeda in Iraq" but now go by the name of "the Islamic State in Iraq and Syria." The acronym is the name by which the world will soon know these killers and their vile acts: ISIS.

✦ ✦ ✦

As James Foley lies dead in the dirt, his murderers celebrate their cowardly act. It is done, they claim, for the god of Islam. And many more will die under that belief.

Foley's fellow hostages now know they may meet the same fate as the forty-year-old from New England. And that horror is present every second of every day.

CHAPTER TWO

"**G**ood afternoon, everybody," President Barack Obama greets the gathered members of the press. He stands before a blue backdrop in the Edgartown School cafeteria, the hastily organized press conference interrupting his summer vacation. An American flag is behind him to the right. The presidential seal is affixed to the podium. He spoke with the family of James Foley this morning, offering his condolences.

"Today, the entire world is appalled by the brutal murder of Jim Foley by the terrorist group ISIL," the president begins.

Obama is referring to ISIS, using one of their many acronyms. The use of the "L" refers to "the Islamic State in Iraq and the Levant," a nod to the terrorist organization's growing power throughout not just Syria but the entire Middle East.*

The Islamic State—also known as ISIS, ISIL, or Daesh—emerged

---

* "The Levant" is a historical term dating to 1497, referring to the eastern Mediterranean portions of the Middle East and encompassing Syria, Lebanon, Jordan, Israel, Palestine, and Turkey. The use of this term is a reflection of the Islamic State's intentions of exerting control over this entire region. The word "Levant" refers to the rising of the sun in the Middle East.

from the remnants of al-Qaeda in Iraq (AQI), a local offshoot of al-Qaeda founded by Abu Musab al-Zarqawi in 2004.* This terrorist organization faded into obscurity for several years after the surge of US troops to Iraq in 2007. But the end of the Iraq War and the subsequent withdrawal of most US troops from the region, instigated by President George W. Bush, saw the reemergence of AQI. The group quickly took advantage of growing instability in Iraq and Syria brought on by the US departure to carry out attacks and bolster its ranks, and soon changed its name to "the Islamic State in Iraq and Syria" (ISIS). But that is the English translation. Throughout the Middle East, the terrorists are known by the acronymic Arabic nickname "Daesh."† The acronym sounds similar to other Arabic words meaning both "to trample down or crush" and "bigot," depending upon the conjugation. ISIS detests that label and cuts out the tongue of anyone speaking it aloud.

The United States made an early attempt to halt the terrorist advance. On April 18, 2010, a joint operation of United States and Iraqi forces fired rockets that shattered the ISIS headquarters in Tikrit, Iraq. The subsequent commando raid uncovered intelligence that linked the terrorists with Osama bin Laden, who was still alive at the time.

That American and Iraqi attack caused the Islamic State in Iraq to flee underground. A cleric named Abu Bakr al-Baghdadi was named the group's new leader on May 16, 2010. The Islamic State was once al-Qaeda's representative in Iraq, but that connection was severed upon bin Laden's death. In this way, al-Baghdadi became the most powerful terrorist on earth, simultaneously declaring that he would avenge bin Laden's assassination with one hundred acts of terror. But even as the terrorist organization spread into Syria in 2013,

---

* Not yet forty at the time of his death, al-Zarqawi was of Jordanian birth and had a deep hatred for the United States. He was responsible for the death of American official Laurence Foley in 2002. Al-Zarqawi was killed on June 7, 2006, when the safe house in which he was residing was bombed by a US Air Force F-16.

† The Arabic translation of the ISIS acronym is *al-dowla al-islaamiyya fii-il-i'raaq wa-ash-shaam*. The derogatory term is akin to labeling "Germans as Huns," in the words of national security analyst Evan Kohlmann.

formally becoming the Islamic State in Iraq and Syria, al-Baghdadi was nowhere to be seen.

✦ ✦ ✦

For four years, ISIS's leadership vanished, disappearing so completely that many wondered if it existed at all. This public silence led Iraqi authorities to make claims of al-Baghdadi's death, though all were later found to be false.

But as the brutal death of James Foley can attest, ISIS is back with full ferocity.

Despite the growing threat, President Obama's administration recognizes that it is not politically expedient to send troops into the region to halt the terrorist advance. The majority of Americans are opposed to military involvement in the Middle East. So despite the blatant kidnapping of four Americans, it is still US policy to down-play the ISIS threat.

Making matters even more difficult is the fact that Americans are not allowed to pay ransom to terrorists. So while parents of kidnap victims like James Foley try to find the millions of dollars demanded by the kidnappers, they risk going to jail if they do so. Even more heart-breaking for these helpless family members is that not only do many foreign governments allow the payment of ransom to free their citizens, in many cases it is the government itself that pays for their release.

For Barack Obama, today's speech is a minor embarrassment—just two years ago he thought so little of the militant organization that he referred to ISIS as "the JV team," placing them second in importance behind a weakened al-Qaeda in the terrorist pecking order.* But now the president has no choice but to admit that the organization, led by the forty-three-year-old Iraqi-born thug Abu Bakr al-Baghdadi, is a genuine threat to the lives of free people everywhere.

---

* On January 7, 2014, in an interview later published in the *New Yorker*, President Obama told the magazine's editor, David Remnick, "The analogy we use around here sometimes, and I think is accurate, is if a JV team puts on Laker uniforms, that doesn't make them Kobe Bryant." This effort to downplay the strength of ISIS—which just days before the interview had overtaken Fallujah, site of one of the most hard-won battles by US forces during the war in Iraq—ultimately backfires.

"Let's be clear," says Obama. "They have rampaged across cities and villages, killing innocent, unarmed civilians in cowardly acts of violence. They abduct women and children, and subject them to torture and rape and slavery. They have murdered Muslims—both Sunni and Shia—by the thousands. They target Christians and religious minorities, driving them from their homes, murdering them when they can for no other reason than they practice a different religion."

Obama continues. He is dressed in a blue blazer and light-blue shirt but no tie, having changed out of his more casual golf clothing for this public statement. Outside, the August afternoon is humid and hot, the air smelling of the Atlantic on this small coastal island off Massachusetts.

"The United States of America will continue to do what we must do to protect our people. We will be vigilant and we will be relentless. When people harm Americans, anywhere, we do what's necessary to see that justice is done."

✦ ✦ ✦

Almost seven thousand miles away, Kayla Mueller cannot hear the president's words. The terrified twenty-six-year-old humanitarian worker is being held somewhere in a Syrian terrorist jail—like James Foley, she is a kidnap victim of ISIS. In fact, she knows Foley and was once held in the same compound as her fellow American. The US government is aware of her plight, but the media has only been told that an American aid worker has been kidnapped. Neither her name nor the fact that she is a woman has been made public. The taking of non–Middle Eastern female hostages is rare. Only one other American woman has been kidnapped: Jill Carroll, a freelance writer for the *Christian Science Monitor*, was released after three months, so there is hope for Kayla—even though she has now been held for one year.

Kayla is chained in a room with a rotating number of other female captives. The aid worker has learned to dread the sound of her prison door opening. The squeak of hinges might mean something as simple as a meal being delivered—or it might mean that torture is about to be inflicted.

Or it might mean another brutal rape for one of the women in this dungeon.

Kayla's ISIS captors treat their female hostages as sex slaves, considering it their right under sharia law to force themselves upon the young women. ISIS soldiers regularly defile not only these captives but any female not of the Sunni Muslim faith, often violating girls not even yet in their teens. Thus far, Kayla has been spared because a white female American hostage is quite a prize. Not just any terrorist can claim her for his own.

Indeed, no less than Abu Bakr al-Baghdadi himself has designs on the young aid worker. The ISIS leader is a sadistic bully, an overweight man with a long salt-and-pepper beard, four wives, and a growing lust for his American hostage. He is forty-three and has no concerns about forcing sex upon a woman almost two decades younger. The terrorist believes that Kayla is an infidel and it is his right under sharia law to marry her and take her as his own.

✦ ✦ ✦

Kayla Mueller was once a cheerful brown-haired humanitarian of Christian faith, which she formulated in Prescott. There, her father owns an auto repair business and her mother is a retired nurse. Throughout college at Northern Arizona University, Kayla was active in the campus ministry, then put that faith into action following graduation. Working for a number of relief agencies, Kayla traveled the world, enduring deprivation and hardship for no financial gain. For her, there was no better way to pursue her calling of helping those in need.

Since graduation, the brown-eyed, petite Kayla has served in India, Israel, and then Turkey. She flashed her broad smile often for refugees, offering them hope. There were no politics attached to her desire to help others—Muslims, Hindus, Jews, and fellow Christians all benefited from the food, education, and medical help Kayla's assistance provided. "As long as I live," the young woman once told an Arizona newspaper, "I will not let suffering be normal."

✦ ✦ ✦

It was December 2012 when Kayla Mueller arrived in the Middle East to work with Syrian refugees. Syrian president Bashar al-Assad had begun a brutal crackdown on his own people that included bombings and mass murder, sparking a civil war. As soldiers from countries like Russia flowed in to join the fighting, thousands of Syrian noncombatants fled north into Turkey and claimed refugee status. A group of Muslim terrorists took advantage of the chaos to leave their sanctuary in Iraq and secretly invade Syria in large numbers. The Islamic State of Iraq and Syria has no wish to join the civil war, or to defend Syria from other nations. Its goal is nothing less than capturing these wastelands for itself and then forming a new "caliphate"—a duplication of what happened following the death of the prophet Muhammad in 632 AD.

ISIS always enacts sharia law, a severe religious code dating back to the days of Muhammad, which requires women to cover themselves from head to toe and remain subservient to men at all times. For one and all, male or female, even small crimes like swearing can be punished by forty lashes with a switch that rakes the bare back and leaves lifelong scars. More severe crimes, like theft, can result in a hand being cut off with a sword. Adultery is punishable by death through stoning. But ISIS is not content solely to inflict ancient punishments. It also imposes its own brand of justice in modern ways on the conquered people of Syria and Iraq, using implements like power tools and electric cattle prods.

And, as in the days following the prophet's demise, it is prophesied that the region will be ruled by a caliph granted the name "Abu Bakr"—"the Upright." Thus, the current leader of ISIS is the barbaric Abu Bakr al-Baghdadi. But that name is an affectation. He was born Ibrahim Awad Ibrahim Ali al-Badri al-Samarrai. Fictional or not, his name will soon become synonymous with terror. And the fact that he is a murderer and serial rapist does not seem to bother his followers in the slightest.

✦ ✦ ✦

A little more than a year ago, on August 3, 2013, Kayla Mueller decided to venture from the relative safety of Turkey into ISIS-controlled northern Syria. She is working for the Danish Refugee Council and a group called Support for Life. Based in the small town of Antakya, thirty miles north of the Syrian border, Kayla is restless. More than 2.5 million refugees have fled the war, and the camps are filled to capacity. Like the other aid workers, Kayla performs a multitude of tasks, but she most enjoys playing and painting with the children. Conditions are terrible. Heat, flies, a lack of plumbing and electricity, and the constant sight of human suffering are daily facts of life.

Kayla knows that crossing into Syria is an extreme gamble, but she is curious to see the countryside for herself. Refugees have told her of lush green valleys and verdant hills. They speak of the ancient city of Aleppo, where the once-lovely Queiq River still flows gently—though now the water is filled with the decomposing bodies of those massacred by ISIS. The unfortunates are often executed with their hands behind their backs, tape across the mouth, and a shotgun blast to the head before being shoved into the water to rot.

And yet, on a hot August morning where the temperature reaches ninety-eight degrees, Kayla Mueller believes a journey to this dangerous place is a worthy way to spend a Saturday. She pleads with her boyfriend to let her make the trip. She has been in the slums of India and Palestine, and now she wishes to see with her own eyes the suffering of Syrian refugees displaced by ISIS.

In Syria, kidnapping of foreigners is a daily fact of life. There is no such thing as guaranteed safety. Kayla Mueller knows this. She is also aware that the growing ISIS threat in Aleppo is just a thirty-minute drive on the other side of the Turkish border.

So, nine months into her mission in Turkey, Kayla Mueller gambles with her life. She crosses into Syria, traveling by bus with her Syrian boyfriend, Omar Alkhani, a photographer whose job is providing telecommunications expertise to a group of physicians known as Doctors Without Borders. Kayla's plan is a simple dash over the border to help Omar fix a broken satellite dish at a hospital outside Aleppo. The couple agrees that she will not speak during the journey, for fear of letting those around her know she is American. Then they will sprint back home to Antakya before night falls.

But difficulty installing the equipment means that the long day grows dark before the work is done. Crowds at the border signal a long wait before getting back across. Rather than chance lonely desert roads at night, Mueller and Alkhani elect to wait until morning for their return. Kayla spends the evening speaking to refugee women about their plight.

On August 4, the pair is driven from the improvised surgical center in a vehicle bearing the Doctors Without Borders logo. Their destination is a bus stop. The taxi driver is Syrian and knows the way. Another aid worker from Spain joins them on the short trip.

The four never make it.

On the outskirts of Aleppo, a car full of ISIS fighters, clad all in black, begins following the taxi. They soon force it off the road. The terrorists step out of their vehicle and approach. Their faces are covered, their AK-47 assault rifles at the ready. Mueller and her three companions are taken prisoner. Hoods are placed over their heads. They are driven to a terrorist compound and put in chains. Kayla and her boyfriend are held in separate cells. The two are not allowed to speak with each other, but signal that they are still alive by coughing loudly enough for the other to hear.

At first, ISIS does not announce the kidnappings, or demand a ransom. No outsider knows where they have gone, least of all Kayla's worried parents back home in Arizona.

Temperatures rise into the high nineties, and the victims are granted small amounts of food and water. "Just a little bit," one of the many other prisoners will later recall. "We were starving."

Another kidnap victim will add, "There was so little room [in the cell]. And it was dark, with no power. It was summer and it was so hot."

ISIS maintains several detention facilities to house those they kidnap. To prevent US satellites and drones from discovering their location, Kayla and the others are moved from one confinement another. Meanwhile, in Arizona, her parents try to maintain calm, despite growing panic.

As the days pass, ISIS comes to a decision: the captives will be released, one by one. Among them is Kayla's boyfriend.

But not Kayla Mueller.

She is an "American spy," in the words of ISIS, and is tortured for evidence of her crimes. Her fingernails are ripped out and her head shaved. One cruel ISIS technique specific to the torture of women is known as "the biter," using large tongs with metal jaws to clamp down on female breasts—always administered by a woman, in accordance with Islamic law. Another favored technique is to produce emotional terror by placing severed human heads inside a cage housing a female prisoner.*

This is the life Kayla lives for three long weeks.

Then the email is sent.

Clicking on a link at their home in Arizona, Kayla's parents open a short video. Their daughter, noticeably thinner and sunburned, looks into the camera. Her head is covered by a green hijab. Her lips are pursed and chapped. Her voice is raspy. Terror fills her bloodshot eyes as she speaks.

"My name is Kayla Mueller," she begins. "I need your help.

"I've been here too long and I've been very sick.

"And it's very terrifying here."

That is all. The video image of Kayla remains on the screen, but she speaks no more. Her father, Carl, will remember feeling "catatonic" as he watches his daughter in such unspeakable torment.

But this is just the beginning of the agony that Kayla Mueller will endure.

Three months later, on December 2, 2013, Kayla's recently freed boyfriend, Omar Alkhani, pretending to be her husband, takes the extraordinary step of locating his former ISIS captors in an attempt to free Kayla, who has now been held for four months. He begs for mercy and the release of his "bride." Alkhani is placed in a detention cell with Kayla so that he can see her with his own eyes as he makes this claim. A high judge of the Islamic State stands with them, closely watching the interchange. Kayla is dressed head to toe

---

* ISIS prisons are maintained by the many different arms of its security force: Islamic police, morality police (*hisbah*), security force (*Emni*), and military police. Among the specific methods of torture regularly put into use are lashing, being doused in fuel, the *bisat al-rih* (flying carpet), the *shabeh* (ghost), the German chair, the biter, and the tire. The emphasis is on contorting the body into awkward and vulnerable positions and then either beating or electrocuting the victim.

in a black abaya. Her face is covered at first, but her guards pull back the veil for just a few seconds so Alkhani can confirm her identity. The captors tell Kayla she will not be harmed if she tells the truth.

But she knows this is a lie. Alkhani's brave action actually puts the terrified young American aid worker in a desperate bind. If Kayla acknowledges Omar as her husband after many months of claiming herself single, she will be executed for deceit.

"No, he is not my husband. He is my fiancé," Kayla states.

For the charge of lying, Omar is detained and tortured by ISIS for seven weeks and one day. Among his cellmates during this time are American hostages James Foley and Steven Sotloff.

After fifty days, Omar Alkhani is released without a ransom, while Kayla Mueller remains a prisoner.

The reason is simple: Abu Bakr al-Baghdadi has decided that the time has arrived for his American captive to become his fifth wife. As this sham matrimony is described throughout the ISIS caliphate, Kayla Mueller will be "married by force."

✦ ✦ ✦

The spring of 2014 marks seven months since Kayla Mueller's kidnapping. She is being held along with James Foley and twenty-two other Westerners—Italians, Germans, Danes, French, Spanish, and British. Kayla is the only woman. As a reminder of the fate awaiting them if their ransom is not paid, ISIS decapitates kidnapped Russian engineer Sergey Gorbunov in March and shows the horrified hostages a video of his body.

In April and May, fifteen of the Europeans are released after their ransoms are paid. Like America, the United Kingdom does not negotiate with terrorists. This leaves four Americans and three Britons in ISIS custody. The terrorists also keep hundreds of women from the Yazidi tribe of northern Iraq to use as sex slaves. Kayla is sometimes held with her fellow Westerners but at other times imprisoned with the Yazidi women.

On May 11, emboldened by the many kidnap victims being set free, the Mueller family and relatives of other Americans being held hostage ask for a meeting with President Obama. The request is denied.

Kayla Mueller in Turkey on June 9, 2013.

After two decades of US involvement in ongoing wars in the Middle East, the president has taken a firm stand against any American military involvement in Syria. This precludes a rescue operation.

So while Obama is sympathetic, he believes a meeting with the families will accomplish little. There is also the specter of possible bad press—that could lead to increased pressure for military action.

"This was a clear reluctance to accept facts," one critic of the Obama administration told the authors of this book. "Facts were being adapted to fit the political narrative."

Yet later that month, there are signs of hope. Shortly after the White House rejection, the Mueller family receives a letter from Kayla, smuggled out of Syria by released hostages.

"If you could say I have suffered at all through this whole experience it is only in knowing how much suffering I have put you all through," Kayla writes. "I will never ask you to forgive me as I do not deserve forgiveness.

"By God's will, we will be together again soon," she concludes. "All my everything, Kayla."

✦ ✦ ✦

More hope: just days after receiving Kayla's letter, another contact reaches the Muellers from Syria. This time, it is ISIS sending an email to the Mueller family. The terrorists wish to set Kayla free, exchanging her for a Pakistani woman being held by the Americans for her role in killing US soldiers in Afghanistan. If this demand is impossible, ISIS states, it would instead accept 5 million euros—roughly $7.3 million dollars—for Kayla's release.

To show "proof of life," just as in the video clip sent so many months ago, the terrorists ask the parents to respond with questions to which only Kayla would know the answer.

Carl and Marsha Mueller are weary—and wary. There is no telling whether or not ISIS has any intention of releasing their daughter. "They tortured us with their emails," Carl will recall. "And they reveled in it."

But there is no choice. If the Muellers want to see their daughter again, the game must be played.

The Muellers respond on May 25.

"Music is _____?" they ask.

✦ ✦ ✦

Three days later, in a graduation speech at the United States Military Academy at West Point, President Obama sends a new message to ISIS, toughening his stance. It is just four months since his "JV" comments, and the spread of ISIS power throughout Iraq and Syria now seems unstoppable. The terrorist army is closing in on the Iraqi city of Mosul, yet another instance where a hard-won American victory in the Iraq War is reversed by ISIS advances.

"The most direct threat to America at home and abroad remains terrorism," the president tells the cadets.

However, Obama stops short of promising any confrontation—and is actually hiding a major development. A short time ago, the Joint Special Operations Command (JSOC), the same special warfare group that coordinated the bin Laden mission three years ago, approached the White House about another daring raid. This time, instead of ending the life of a madman, JSOC plans a mission to rescue Kayla Mueller and all the Western hostages from ISIS captivity. New information from an unnamed nation acting as one of America's intelligence partners suggests that the kidnap victims are being held outside the city of Raqqa, one hundred miles south of the Turkish border. There, in an abandoned compound near an oil field, they are under heavy guard.

But this intelligence is thin and dated. By not having a military presence in Syria, the United States lacks the ability to produce the "exquisite intelligence," a term common in the national security community, that could green-light military action. In the absence of hard data, any rescue force is in extreme peril should the situation on the ground have shifted. The chances for failure are high. On the other hand, it is not always possible to know the precise details of every mission. Risks are a part of any raid.

This places President Obama in an uncomfortable situation. He has repeatedly insisted that America will not send its troops into Syria. To do so now would be a complete reversal of his foreign policy. The American public is weary of war. Conflict in Syria, a nation that does not represent a clear threat to the United States, would undermine the gravitas of his administration. Until now, in the words of one senior US official, the White House "did not want to recognize this as a problem they needed to solve."

So the president is conflicted. He can no longer ignore the fact that American lives are at stake. Kayla Mueller, James Foley, Peter Kassig, and Steven Sotloff could be murdered at any time.

Thus, Obama is prepared to green-light a rescue mission. But, as with the bin Laden raid, the odds must be in America's favor. There cannot be another Black Hawk down.

Yet there is major risk in waiting.

Indeed, the measured caution and the White House bureaucracy will eventually doom Kayla Mueller, James Foley, Steven Sotloff, and Peter Kassig.

There are three conditions necessary to launching a successful hostage rescue: proof of life, a grid showing the likely imprisonment location (such as a street or house number), and final approval from the president. The Special Forces operators tasked with any rescue are always on alert, having trained extensively for such scenarios. Yet it is very often the last step—final approval—that holds up the actual mission. The time it takes to move up the chain of command to the president, who must approve all operations into an active hostile war zone, can be hours—or months. And as commandos await orders to launch, restless kidnappers very often move their victims to new locations.

This is on Barack Obama's mind as he wraps up his remarks to the newly commissioned West Point lieutenants. For the first time in public, the president does not rule out commando operations to fight terror. He says quite clearly: "The United States will use military force, unilaterally, if necessary, when our core interests demand it—when our people are threatened, when our livelihood is at stake, or when the security of our allies is in danger. In these circumstances, we still need to ask tough questions about whether our actions are proportional and effective and just. International opinion matters, but America should never ask permission to protect our people, our homeland, and our way of life."

Left unsaid is that an audacious rescue plan is now in the works, designed to penetrate US forces deep into the heart of ISIS-controlled Syria. The level of risk is far beyond that of any hostage rescue attempt in recent memory.* As always, intelligence must be verified. This necessary but laborious process precedes the lightning-quick execution of the mission itself, described by one top administration official as "Slow, slow, slow, slow—BANG!"

The question is, *when* will the president of the United States ride to the rescue?

✦ ✦ ✦

On May 29, ISIS sends an email reply to Arizona: "Music is EVERY-WHERE."

---

* US Special Forces have undertaken a number of hostage rescues since the death of Osama bin Laden in 2011. Perhaps the most successful was that of American aid worker Jessica Buchanan, who was exfiltrated from Somalia by Navy SEALs in 2012. Two attempts were made to free photojournalist Luke Somers, who was being held by al-Qaeda in Yemen in 2013. Somers was shot by his captors as Special Forces entered the compound where he was being held, before the terrorists themselves were gunned down by the US troops. During that same period of time, many European nations were paying large ransoms to free their citizens.

This is the correct response to the question posed by Kayla's parents—something that only Kayla might say.

Even better, another short video clip accompanies the email. The young woman tells her parents that she feels healthy and then repeats the terrorists' demands before the video ends. Unknown to the Muellers, Kayla has recently been moved from a cell so small she could not stretch out, into a bigger room with three other women. Anticipating her release, Kayla has been doing push-ups and other exercises to get strong for the journey home.

But in reality, the Muellers are losing faith in the American government. They desperately want to pay the ransom. Their choices are to go to jail for defying the "no concessions" law or passively to wait for a US rescue operation.

They choose to wait—but grow frustrated by the lack of communication.

"ISIS was being more truthful to us," Marsha Mueller will one day recall.

✦ ✦ ✦

As the summer of 2014 begins to unfold, James Foley, Kayla Mueller, Steven Sotloff, and Peter Kassig are simply helpless. ISIS is becoming more violent and arrogant. America and the world are watching.

But doing little else.*

---

* Steven Sotloff is a thirty-one-year-old American-born journalist, a grandson of Holocaust survivors who also holds Israeli citizenship. He was abducted in Aleppo on August 4, 2013, the same day as Kayla Mueller. Sotloff's Jewish ancestry was not revealed to his captors by the Obama administration for fear the *Time* writer would suffer repercussions. Peter Kassig was twenty-five at the time of his kidnapping on October 1, while delivering food to a refugee camp in eastern Syria. Prior to becoming an aid worker, he served a tour of duty in Iraq as a member of the US Army Rangers.

American journalist Steven Sotloff (center with black helmet) talks to Libyan rebels on the Dafniya front line, fifteen miles west of Misrata, Libya, on June 2, 2011.

CHAPTER THREE

SEPTEMBER 2, 2014
RAQQA, SYRIA
MORNING

The woman with 157 days to live hides her panic.

Sadistic ISIS thugs have just shown Kayla Mueller video of Steven Sotloff's beheading. This comes just three weeks after James Foley suffered the same fate. Kayla well knows that two of the British hostages were also recently beheaded. These were her friends, men with whom she shared her thirteen months of captivity. It is beyond her imagination that they would ever suffer such a horrible fate. Kayla struggles to keep her own fear in check, trying not to think about Mohammed Emwazi, the British-born ISIS soldier who sliced the throats of Foley and Sotloff. But Emwazi is a constant presence in her life, a jailer she sees almost every day. She is well aware that he could appear in her doorway at any time, butcher knife in hand.

Lack of food makes Kayla's dire predicament worse. Today, like every day in captivity, Kayla is hungry. Her jailers do not feed her much. Breakfast is bread and cheese. Dinner is rice or macaroni. She was long ago stripped of her Western clothing and forced to don a long abaya, hijab, and veil.

Despite her plight, Kayla remains strong, even rebellious. She does not back down when Emwazi threatens her. He is fanatical about his radical Muslim ideology and berates Mueller for her Christianity. "If you don't convert to Islam, this will happen to you—we will behead all of you."

Beheading becomes Kayla's greatest fear, preventing her from attempting escape. But each time Emwazi gloats that Kayla must convert to Islam, she quickly fires back, stating that she will never abandon her Christian faith.

In this way, Kayla contains her emotions, hiding her fear and putting forth a veneer of defiance. So far, the ISIS men have not touched her, although they delight in raping the captured Iraqi women. The fact that she is off-limits offers Kayla hope. She thinks this is because she is an American, and has no idea she is being saved for al-Baghdadi.

One other bit of news: there are rumors among the hostages of a failed rescue attempt two months ago by Americans.

What Kayla doesn't know is that those rumors are true.

✦ ✦ ✦

July 3, 2014. Two Black Hawk "Night Stalker" helicopters pass low over the Euphrates River and flare into a hover outside an oil refinery on the edge of Raqqa. It has been four hours since this covert hostage rescue mission went "wheels up" in the neighboring country of Jordan. In almost total darkness, a dozen Delta Force commandos flew over the hostile Syrian desert. Americans are about to fast-rope to the ground, then immediately advance toward their target with guns drawn.

In the skies above, two direct action penetrator helicopters (DAPs), armed with rockets and heavy-caliber machine guns, circle in search of ISIS ground troops. Farther up in the dark nighttime sky, drones survey the surrounding landscape. The United States does not make a habit of penetrating Syrian airspace, so little is known of the country's government air defenses. Even less is understood about the terrorists on the ground, although it is assumed that an armed response will be likely.

The Delta Force rescuers believe the hostages are being held in buildings on the grounds of the refinery. They know this because

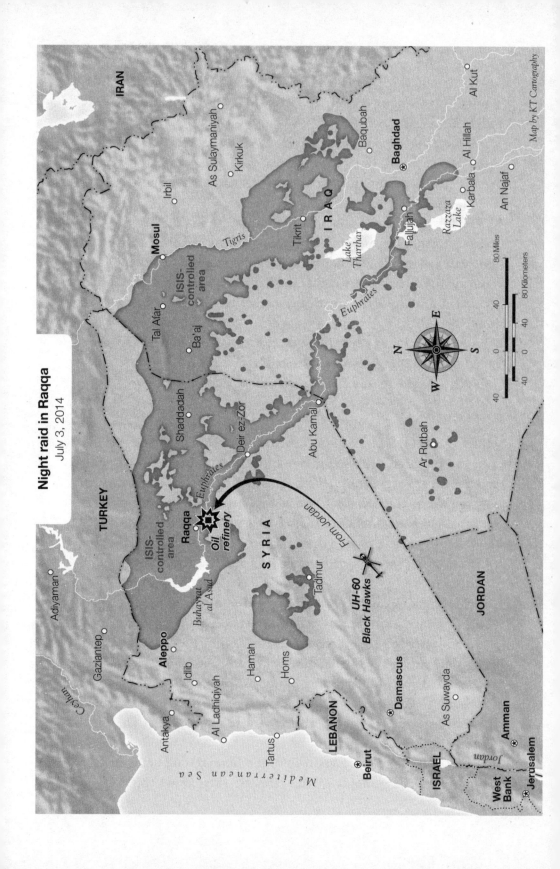

Night raid in Raqqa
July 3, 2014

Danish photojournalist Daniel Rye Ottosen was held here just three weeks ago, before his government paid a $2.3 million ransom for his release. Ottosen returned to Denmark, where he was interviewed by FBI agents on June 22. He told them exact details of the prison in which Kayla Mueller and the other hostages were being held. Based on that information, the White House approved the rescue mission. Special Forces personnel traveled from Fort Bragg, North Carolina, to a secret location in Jordan, where the raid was rehearsed.

Once the operation was set in motion tonight, the four US helicopters encountered vicious winds and hellish sandstorms during the long flight to the refinery target. The exceedingly difficult journey is made worse by the near-certainty of combat.

Shortly after landing, the dozen Delta Force "snake eaters"—as they are often called for their willingness to do anything to complete a mission—are greeted by a wave of automatic-weapons fire. Black-clad ISIS fighters temporarily pin down the Americans.

Temporarily.

Within moments, the terrorists take such heavy casualties from the circling DAPs that they fall back to wait for reinforcements. So many members of ISIS are killed that they never return to confront the Americans. Only one American is wounded in the fighting—helicopter pilot Michael Siler suffers a shattered leg when an ISIS round penetrates his cockpit. Not having the option of landing, seeking medical assistance, or even taking medication for his pain, Siler will fly five more hours without landing until the mission is complete.

The rescuers quickly search the compound. They find evidence that the American hostages were indeed once held there, but an hour of looking for false walls or other hidden rooms turns up nothing.

The Delta Force pilots and soldiers all do their jobs with precision. The intelligence reaped from captured cell phones and computers is enormous. The infiltration and exfiltration of the rescue force without a single loss of American life is a remarkable success, particularly in such a hostile environment.

But the hostages remain in captivity.

✦ ✦ ✦

April 29, 2019: Abu Bakr al-Baghdadi's first video appearance in five years, a month after Islamic State militants were driven out of their last stronghold in Syria.

On July 4, one day after the raid, Abu Bakr al-Baghdadi shows his face for the first time in four years. He is preaching in Mosul's Great Mosque. The ISIS leader is dressed in black robes and matching turban. This public sermon puts to rest any rumors that he is dead or injured. The United States has placed a $10 million bounty on his head, but al-Baghdadi is defiant.

Mosul, Iraq's second largest city, fell to ISIS just one month ago. Its conquest is obviously a great victory for ISIS. This is al-Baghdadi's moment to gloat, particularly in light of yesterday's failed rescue attempt. "Khalifa Ibrahim," as he calls himself, is puffed up and arrogant. The name refers to his self-anointed role as caliph of the Islamic State's conquered territory; it also references the prophet Abraham.*
In his twenty-minute oration, al-Baghdadi declares himself the ruler of all Muslims. He states that slavery is a fact of life—followers of

---

* Al-Baghdadi was selected as caliph by a group known as the Shura Council, a group of religious peers within ISIS. The remainder of the Muslim world outside Iraq and Syria rejected this claim.

Islam belong to Allah, but nonbelievers are destined to become the property of Muslims. This reference to Kayla Mueller and the other American hostages is very much intentional.

Outside, ISIS fighters patrol the boulevards, searching for anyone in violation of Islamic law. Some wave large black flags, and all carry fully loaded AK-47 automatic weapons slung over their shoulders.

"Do jihad in the cause of God, incite the believers, and be patient in the face of this hardship," al-Baghdadi encourages the congregation. "If you knew about the reward and dignity in this world and the hereafter through jihad, then none of you would delay in doing it."

On July 12, 2014, the Islamic State publicly announces that it will murder Kayla Mueller within thirty days unless its ransom demand is met. Carl and Marsha Mueller fly to secretly meet with White House officials about potential ways to save their daughter. They are told little that offers them hope. So it is that the days until the ransom deadline tick down slowly.

The beheadings will begin soon after.

✦ ✦ ✦

Back in Syria, Kayla Mueller is transferred from a prison to a private home an hour away from where the other prisoners are being held. After the beheadings of James Foley and Steven Sotloff, Kayla and Peter Kassig are the only two remaining American hostages. They have been separated. Kayla will never see Peter Kassig again.

The young hostage can definitely feel a change in the behavior of her captors. With two Americans brutally beheaded and videos of the crimes flashing around the world, the United States is finally taking military action against ISIS. But that action is not helping Kayla at the moment.

Kayla is now in the small town of Shaddadah, in the custody of ISIS oil minister Abu Sayyaf and his wife, Umm. The other female captives in the house are the Yazidi women from northern Iraq. Some three thousand of them have been taken hostage and passed around by ISIS terrorists to be raped and abused.

This is when Kayla finally meets Abu Bakr al-Baghdadi, who is a frequent visitor to the Sayyaf home. The ISIS leader likes to stay up until midnight, then sleep until 10:00 a.m. He sometimes talks to the women but prefers to spend hours alone in his room. "Forget your father and your brothers," al-Baghdadi tells the captives. "We have killed them, and we have married off your mothers and sisters. Forget them."

If anything, the increased American pressure leads al-Baghdadi to take an even deeper personal interest in Kayla. He has ordered an email sent to her parents, taunting them about the failed rescue mission. The deadline for ransom payment came and went on August 10, and Kayla is still alive. Four days later, she turned twenty-six. Al-Baghdadi once again uses her as a bargaining chip, emailing her parents that in addition to the $7.2 million in ransom, the US bombardment of ISIS positions must cease in order for her to be released.

Al-Baghdadi wants Kayla to be treated better than the others. Umm Sayyaf is tasked with preparing the aid worker for the caliph's visits, making sure he will be happy with her appearance. "There was a budget for her," she will recall many years later, "pocket money to buy things from the shop. She was a lovely girl, and I liked her. She was very respectful, and I respected her. One thing I would say is that she was very good at hiding her sadness and pain."*

But Umm Sayyaf is no housewife. She is an ISIS warrior, doing a job Islamic law prohibits a man from undertaking. Her task is to procure women for ISIS senior leadership, imprisoning them and listening to their screams as they are raped. She is not beloved by the other women of ISIS, who are deeply irritated that their husbands frequent the Sayyaf household for sex with young women. In late

---

* Abu Sayyaf and his wife, Umm, were among the most senior ISIS leadership. Abu Sayyaf's real name was Fathi Ben Awn Ben Jildi Murad. His role in ISIS was diverting proceeds from oil sales into the continued expansion of the caliphate. On May 15, 2015, Abu was killed during a US raid designed to take both husband and wife captive for purposes of interrogation about hostage locations. Delta Force operatives successfully took Umm Sayyaf alive, as well as so many computers and cell phones that it came to be considered one of the biggest intelligence coups in US history. Umm is Iraqi. She cooperated with the CIA in their quest for information about the location of Abu Bakr al-Baghdadi and was sentenced to death by an Iraqi court. There is a motion to transfer her to the United States, where she will stand trial for the kidnapping and abuse of Kayla Mueller and the many Yazidi women placed under her guard. The issue remains unresolved.

2014, there are nine Yazidi girls in addition to Kayla under Sayyaf's supervision.

There is no place to run for Kayla Mueller, so when al-Baghdadi decides it is time, she is led into his bedroom. "I am going to marry you by force and you are going to be my wife," al-Baghdadi informs the terrified woman. "If you refuse, I will kill you."

So Kayla Mueller submits to the rapes. Each time, she emerges from the bedroom crying. She is given the new name of Iman and told to begin practicing Islam.

She has now been held for sixteen months.

✦ ✦ ✦

Late in November, Kayla is told that Peter Kassig has joined the list of the beheaded. Her spirits plummet. When two of the Yazidis attempt to coax her into joining them for a risky breakout, she declines, reminding them they will be killed if they fail. The young girls attempt the escape anyway and are successful, finding their way to Kurdistan, where US officials question them for intelligence regarding Kayla.

But while the freed women can offer details about Kayla's physical and mental well-being, and even specifics about life inside the home where they were captive, they cannot give the precise location of the home where she is being held.

The truth is, Kayla Mueller has already been moved from the Sayyaf home to al-Baghdadi's own residence in Raqqa. But when one of the caliph's wives violently objects, Kayla is repositioned once again. So it is impossible to pinpoint her location.

But there is some good news for Kayla, as Umm Sayyaf says no harm will come to her. Because she is the new *wife* of al-Baghdadi, she is no longer a captive. Kayla Mueller is now part of the ISIS "family."

✦ ✦ ✦

The search continues.

On January 25, 2015, White House Chief of Staff Denis Mc-Donough appears on ABC News's *This Week*. Interviewer George

Stephanopoulous brings up the issue of kidnap victims in Syria. Without intending to, McDonough breaks the news that an American woman is in ISIS custody.

"As it relates to our hostages, we are obviously continuing to work those matters very, very aggressively. We are sparing no expense and sparing no effort, both in trying to make sure we know where they are and make sure that we're prepared to do anything we must to try to get them home. Kayla's family knows how strongly the president feels about this."

One week later, President Obama appears on the NBC morning show *Today*. This is an unusual step for a sitting president, but with growing pressure to rescue Kayla, Obama has little choice. The United States, he says, is "deploying all the assets that we can, working with all the coalition allies that we can to identify her location, and we are in very close contact with her family, giving them updates."

✦ ✦ ✦

On February 3, a captured Royal Jordanian Air Force fighter pilot shot down while launching missiles on ISIS positions in Syria is placed in a cage and publicly burned alive. Muath Safi Yousef al-Kasasbeh is twenty-six years old, the same age as Kayla.

The video shocks the world, and calls for action against ISIS mount.

✦ ✦ ✦

What happens next is unclear. Jordan launches more air strikes against ISIS-held positions. The date is February 6, 2015.

This is the last day of Kayla Mueller's life. She is not beheaded. Instead, the terrorists say that Syrian bombs kill Kayla Mueller.

The truth is, Kayla Mueller *is* murdered. Umm Sayyaf will later confirm this during questioning after her arrest. She will claim that Kayla knew too much and presented a threat to ISIS leader al-Baghdadi.

Predictably, ISIS boasts about Kayla's death on Twitter. The terrorists then send an email to Kayla's parents. Included in the message is a photograph of Kayla, face bruised and an open wound on her cheek. She lies on her back beneath a shroud.

"May God keep you from any more harm or hurt," Kayla's brother, Eric, tells Kayla as he addresses the crowd at a packed memorial service later that month. His voice trembles. "Only now will you be able to see how much you truly did for the world, by looking down on it."

But there is no burial. Rather than return her body to America, the sadistic al-Baghdadi disposes of Kayla in a hidden location—one that remains secret to this day.

✦ ✦ ✦

"My immediate reaction is heartbreak," President Obama says as news of Kayla's death careens around the world. He has telephoned the Mueller family to offer his condolences. "She was an outstanding young woman and a great spirit. And I think that spirit will live on, the more people learn about her and the more people learn about what she stood for in contrast with the barbaric organization that held her captive.

"But I don't think it's accurate . . . to say the United States government hasn't done everything we could. We devoted enormous resources—and always devote enormous resources to freeing captives or hostages anywhere in the world."

✦ ✦ ✦

On June 24, 2015, four months after Kayla Mueller's death, President Barack Obama officially announces a change in US policy regarding kidnap victims. There will no longer be prosecution for American citizens who raise the money to make ransom payments to terrorists.

CHAPTER FOUR

JULY 17, 2015
GUANTÁNAMO BAY, CUBA
8:00 A.M.

If he is captured, a top secret prison cell awaits Abu Bakr al-Baghdadi.

"The Star-Spangled Banner" echoes across Naval Station Guantánamo Bay, as it does precisely this time every morning. US military personnel immediately stop what they are doing and stand at stiff attention, saluting the nearest American flag, until the anthem is complete. More than five thousand American servicemen and -women, as well as their families, call this Cuban installation home, enjoying all the luxuries of a normal naval base—commissary, McDonald's, child development center, and even hiking at the nearby Hutia Highway trailhead. But just over the hill from the base, on a barren stretch of rocky coastline fronting dark-blue, shark-infested waters, is a stark world of cellblocks, electric fences, and high cement walls surrounded by roll after roll of razor-sharp barbed wire.

This is the notorious Guantánamo Bay detention camp. Abu Bakr al-Baghdadi has been in United States custody before, but that period of incarceration in 2004 is nothing like what awaits him in Cuba.

Now two sailors in pressed white uniforms run the Stars and Stripes up the flagpole. But they stop when the standard is only halfway up. Flying the colors at half-mast is a sign of respect and mourning. And on this summer dawn of glaring sun and balmy trade winds blowing in off the Caribbean, sailors and marines stationed here in Cuba have much to grieve. Yesterday afternoon, in Chattanooga, Tennessee, an ISIS terror attack took lives on American soil. Four marines and a sailor were shot dead when an ISIS killer opened fire at a military recruiting center. The gunman, Mohammad Youssef Abdulazeez, a twenty-four-year-old American citizen of Kuwaiti birth, was then shot dead by officers from the Chattanooga Police Department.

To most Americans, the manners and behavior of terrorism perpetrators are largely unknown. But to the men and women serving a tour of duty at remote Guantánamo Bay, Islamic terrorists are not just the talk of the base but the flesh-and-blood reason Americans are posted to this far-flung location.

The purpose of Guantánamo Bay is detaining and interrogating the world's most dangerous killers—war criminals who have sworn allegiance to men such as al-Baghdadi and bin Laden. The terrorists are treated not just as prisoners but as sources of intelligence about lethal operations.

Some methods of extracting information are simple, like sleep deprivation or standing in place for hours until the monotony becomes a degrading mental exercise. Others, such as the technique known as "waterboarding," make a man believe he is about to die.

"Gitmo" is six thousand miles from the ISIS strongholds in Syria and Iraq and, at this time, houses forty inmates. There has been talk of shutting it down, though that is almost impossible: the men held within these walls are not welcome anywhere on earth. It is a common practice to release those detained at Guantánamo after a period of incarceration, but this is out of the question for some detainees. These hardened terrorists will never reject the global jihad. They are determined to inflict death and destruction, no matter what the cost.

Thus, the Guantánamo Bay detention center is not likely to be shut down anytime soon. United States officials consider the facility a most effective counterterrorism tool—and a place from where there can be no escape.

So it is that when the day comes that US forces capture al-Baghdadi, officials here at Guantánamo will only be too happy to make room for the ISIS butcher.*

✦ ✦ ✦

Guantánamo Bay is the oldest overseas base in the United States Navy. First opened in 1903, the facility was leased from Cuba to serve as a coal depot. The lease was a paltry $2,000 in gold until 1974, when the rent increased to $4,085. Even after Fidel Castro overthrew the Cuban government in 1959, the United States continued to maintain control of the tactically important forty-five square miles on the southeastern corner of Cuba. The base was temporarily abandoned as a safety precaution during the Cuban Missile Crisis of 1962, then immediately reoccupied once the emergency passed. For ninety-nine years, America has maintained control of Gitmo despite acrimony with Communist Cuba.

After the 9/11 terror attacks, President George W. Bush declared a global war on terrorism. US troops entered jihadi strongholds such as Afghanistan to actively take the fight to murderous groups like al-Qaeda and the Taliban. Taking prisoners was inevitable, particularly in a conflict where the enemy constantly lived and worked in the shadows. For their roles in killing Americans, these terrorists fall into a category known as "enemy combatant." Remote Guantánamo Bay, which contained an empty facility that once housed Cuban and Haitian refugees, was the ideal location to confine these radical prisoners.

The first detainees arrived at Guantánamo Bay on January 11,

---

* Guantánamo Bay has housed 731 inmates since 9/11. All but 40 have been repatriated after serving a sentence or transferred to prisons in their homes countries in the Middle East and Africa. Some have been set free. Of the 40 prisoners still remaining in the detention facility, 17 are high-value detainees. Among them are Khalid Sheikh Mohammed and four other men facing capital charges for assisting with the 9/11 attacks by providing training, transportation, or money. Two of the original 20 high-value prisoners—a group nicknamed "worst of the worst"—remain in custody. Ali Hamza al-Bahlul, a Yemeni citizen, is serving a life sentence for his close personal ties to Osama bin Laden. Ridah bin Saleh al-Yazidi, of Tunisia, has actually been cleared for release but refuses to cooperate with officials about a possible new location for resettlement.

2002, just four months after the 9/11 murders. US marines led the twenty new arrivals down the steps of a military cargo plane.

Their citizenship is diverse: Afghani, Saudi Arabian, Pakistani, Algerian, Yemeni, and more. The most dangerous prisoners are known as "high-value detainees," coveted by interrogators because of what they may know. Each "high-value" terrorist is held in solitary confinement. Some are forced to wear headphones and opaque goggles to block out the sight and sounds of other inmates. Each cell has a prayer mat with arrows pointing in the direction of Mecca, the Muslim holy city, where adherents face as they bow and worship Allah five times a day.

Upon his arrival at Guantánamo Bay, Abu Bakr al-Baghdadi will be given a "detainee assessment" to categorize his mental and physical health. This is true for all arrivals. One example reads: "Detainee attended militant training on fitness, pistols, the AK-47 assault rifle, the PK machine gun, and the rocket-propelled grenade (RPG) at the al-Faruq Training Camp [outside Kandahar, Afghanistan] and taught small arms training there."

The report also notes that this individual, Mohammed Ahmad Said al-Adahi, "has a history of depression and schizoaffective personality disorder." *

An essential aspect of each detainee assessment is a history of each prisoner's personal life and career as a terrorist, charting the various campaigns in which they participated. A typical report is ten single-spaced pages, listing places, dates, and names. Known aliases are listed, as are accomplices and employers.

But these complex assessments, loaded with pages of specific documentation and detail, are not easily written. The tight-lipped behavior that allows a recruit to rise through the ranks to terror leadership requires a strict adherence to confidentiality. In short, these detainees are trained not to betray information.

Thus, detainee assessments can only be written with the assistance of complex interrogations.

---

* Schizoaffective personality disorder is marked by severe mood swings, depression, mania, and even hallucinations. It can take the form of bipolar depression.

In almost every instance this ongoing questioning is assisted by the one activity most often connected with life at Guantánamo Bay: "enhanced interrogation."

In truth, there is a revenge factor on the part of some American interrogators. Al-Baghdadi well knows that if he is captured, the United States will spare no painful, shame-inducing technique to extract every last bit of information from the man who raped and murdered Kayla Mueller.

✦ ✦ ✦

The treatment Abu Bakr al-Baghdadi might expect will mirror that of the most famous terrorist already in custody. High-ranking al-Qaeda member Khalid Sheikh Mohammed was captured on March 1, 2003, in the Pakistani city of Rawalpindi. He loathes America, a nation in which he once briefly lived, labeling it a "debauched and racist country." The fifty-year-old Mohammed is not only the "principal architect" of the 9/11 attack, even appearing on Al Jazeera television to celebrate the first anniversary of the mass murder, he also famously beheaded the American journalist Daniel Pearl, who was taken hostage in the city of Karachi.*

After his arrest by the CIA and Pakistani intelligence, "KSM," as the mastermind is known, does not go directly to Guantánamo. Instead, his interrogation begins at a clandestine "black site" in Afghanistan known as the "Salt Pit." There, the terrorist is forced to be naked and subject to sleep deprivation, required to stand for days at a time without being allowed to doze. "Stress positions" are utilized frequently, placing the terrorist in small spaces for prolonged periods of time to induce claustrophobia and discomfort. KSM is beaten and slapped. Cold water is thrown in his face, and loud music is played

---

* Mr. Pearl was a thirty-eight-year-old *Wall Street Journal* reporter serving as the newspaper's South Asia bureau chief in Mumbai, India. He traveled into Pakistan to investigate connections between al-Qaeda and British citizen Richard Reid, known as the "Shoe Bomber" for his attempt to conceal an explosive device inside his shoe for the purpose of blowing up an airliner. It was Khalid Sheikh Mohammed who contrived this unsuccessful terror plot, and who also ordered the kidnapping of Mr. Pearl in the city of Karachi on January 23, 2002. Nine days later, Pearl was beheaded. Video analysis of the veins on the perpetrator's hands show that KSM himself committed the atrocity.

to elevate his sense of disorientation. A hose is inserted into the terrorist's anus through a technique known as "rectal rehydration" that causes him to both urinate frequently and defecate violently.

And that is just the beginning.

Eventually, KSM is flown to black sites in Jordan and Poland, where he is subjected to waterboarding exactly 183 times.* This is a technique once used by the Chinese on American prisoners of war during the Korean conflict in the 1950s. The hands and ankles are immobilized, and a towel placed over the individual's face. The head is tilted backward. Water is then poured onto the cloth, saturating the fabric and slowly working its way into the nostrils and mouth of the captive. It becomes more and more difficult to breathe. Water soon enters the esophagus. The sensation of drowning is induced, and it is common for the interrogated individual to gag uncontrollably.

Khalid Sheikh Mohammed is then moved to another interrogation black site in Romania before finally arriving in Guantánamo Bay. The date is September 2006, more than three years after his capture. All the while, the terrorist resists the torture, refusing to admit his participation in 9/11 and other attacks. Eventually, after four years, KSM breaks. In March 2007, Khalid Sheikh Mohammed finally confesses to planning the 9/11 attacks, as well as several other international acts of terror.†

Now, as the world searches for Abu Bakr al-Baghdadi, KSM remains in Guantánamo. It is twelve years since his capture, and he admits to participating in thirty-one terror plots. Most Gitmo prisoners

---

* On September 6, 2006, President George W. Bush officially acknowledged that the Central Intelligence Agency utilizes secret detention centers to hold and interrogate terror suspects. These prisons are often a stopping-off point on the way to Guantánamo Bay. Suspects held in them have no rights and are subject to torture.

† KSM was tried for the 9/11 killings before a military court in 2008. He refused the right to an attorney, preferring to represent himself. The case was turned over to a civilian court in July 2009, by order of US Attorney General Eric Holder. After significant public uproar against this decision, President Barack Obama signed the National Defense Authorization Act on January 7, 2011, making it illegal to use Department of Defense funds to transport Guantánamo Bay inmates into the United States or to other countries. When the civilian trial began on May 5, 2012, Khalid Sheikh Mohammed refused to answer the judge's questions. A number of motions by the defense delayed the proceedings, which are ongoing to this day.

are incarcerated in communal cellblocks known as Camps 5 and 6. But until April 4, 2021, KSM was held apart from other prisoners in a top secret compound known as Camp 7. Journalists from around the world have visited Guantánamo but were never allowed inside this special section of the prison.*

KSM now inhabits Camp 5, which is modeled after a maximum-security state prison in Bunker Hill, Indiana. It has individual cells, showers, and large outdoor cages for recreation.

If Khalid cooperates, he might be permitted to watch Arab satellite television—albeit with his ankles shackled to the floor in front of his chair. However, if KSM refuses to cooperate, he will not be allowed these privileges. Instead, he will remain alone in his cell.

✦ ✦ ✦

It is impossible to know how much the threat of severe reprisal is affecting the killer al-Baghdadi. What is known is that this self-proclaimed "leader" of the Muslim world is now more arrogant than ever—and a direct threat to much of the world. Al-Baghdadi believes ISIS is winning the jihad. And he sees himself as an Islamic savior.

One who is about to strike again.

---

* Bill O'Reilly has reported from Guantánamo Bay twice.

CHAPTER FIVE

NOVEMBER 13, 2015
SAINT-DENIS, FRANCE
9:16 P.M.

The daughter of the famous journalist Geraldo Rivera is in danger. But she does not know it. Simone Rivera, a twenty-one-year-old Northwestern University exchange student, is spending a semester studying in France. On this Friday night, she is attending a soccer game at the Stade de France—the French national stadium. Simone sits with her roommate and two other friends. The international match between France and Germany is a popular place to be on this chilly autumn evening, and the eighty-thousand-seat stadium is sold out. France wears blue, and Germany white. Even French president François Hollande is in attendance.

Simone Rivera is just days away from finishing her final academic project and flying home for Thanksgiving when the first explosion startles the stadium. The blast occurs outside, along the Avenue Jules Rimet. It is nineteen minutes and thirty-six seconds into the game. The blast is loud enough to be heard over the noise of the crowd. Thinking the explosion is perhaps part of a midgame fireworks display, the audience cheers for a moment and then resumes watching the contest.

Yet Simone feels uneasy.

✦ ✦ ✦

Paris is very aware of terrorism. The city is still grieving over the brutal murders of twelve employees of the satirical magazine *Charlie Hebdo*. The terrorist perpetrators were a group known as al-Qaeda in the Arabian Peninsula, led by ruthless Yemeni terrorist Qasim al-Rimi. That happened ten months ago. A citywide terror alert followed the mass slaying, and soldiers were deployed throughout the area, which is home to 2.1 million people. Shortly after the *Charlie Hebdo* murders, in a related attack, terrorists took nineteen Jewish hostages at a kosher supermarket in Paris, killing four. As in the *Hebdo* situation, the perpetrators were shot dead by police. Later, a massive rally was held in the Place de la République, where Paris mayor Anne Hidalgo condemned the murderers. Fifty-four Muslims who publicly supported the terror attacks were arrested as "apologists."

Simone Rivera follows French news fervently. She knows the people of Paris and Muslim fanatics are at odds. Nearly one million Islamists around the world marched in support of those who killed the *Charlie Hebdo* employees. And militant groups such as al-Qaeda, Boko Haram, and the Taliban all praised the dead terrorists who committed the murders. In fact, more than three quarters of Muslim students in the volatile Seine-Saint-Denis district have voiced allegiance to the killers. "I'll drop you with a Kalashnikov, mate," one student informs a teacher trying to enforce a moment of silence, referencing the AK-47 assault rifle used most often by jihadists.*

✦ ✦ ✦

The terror threat in France is ongoing. Three months ago, French authorities intercepted a thirty-year-old suspect en route to Syria, who

---

* *Charlie Hebdo* ran a caricature drawing of the prophet Muhammad. The Muslim faith prohibits any artistic depiction of their religion's founder, going so far as to call it heretical. Ensuing uproar in the Muslim world forced France to temporarily close embassies in more than twenty countries. The slain cartoonists and magazine staffers were viewed as infidels, and murder is an expected part of global jihad.

told them that attacks on French concert venues were in the planning stages. And just yesterday, Iraqi security forces informed the US-led coalition fighting ISIS in Syria and Iraq that suicide bombers would soon strike a target in the West, location unknown. But, obviously, nonspecific information could not be acted upon.

✦ ✦ ✦

Back inside the stadium, the first explosion mystified the crowd, but the game continues.

Then, ten minutes later, a second blast rocks the night. This time, the fans know something is wrong. Many panic and begin running for the exits.

Unbeknownst to the crowd, a full-blown terror attack is underway. A terrorist, using the alias of twenty-five-year-old Ahmad al-Mohammad, tries to gain entry to the stadium, hoping to slaughter hundreds. But a security guard at Gate D notices the cumbersome vest under his jacket. The Syrian terrorist flees, unable to complete his mission. Seconds later, he explodes the vest, killing himself and an innocent pedestrian outside the stadium.

Another explosion comes when Bilal Hadfi, twenty, blows himself up near Gate H. It will later be confirmed that Hadfi, a Belgian, fought with ISIS in Syria.

Over the stadium loudspeakers, spectators are told to stay calm. Incredibly, the soccer match continues on—the thinking being it is better to keep fans and players inside the stadium than have them run outside into danger. Quickly, Paris police cordon off the area. Then, at 9:53, comes a third explosion, more distant this time. It will later be surmised that a third terror bomber, recognizing that the stadium was now alerted, wandered off in search of a new target. Thus, an explosion takes place inside a McDonald's restaurant on the Rue de la Cokerie, four hundred meters away from the Stade de France. The bomber, a twenty-year-old Frenchman, succeeds in killing only himself.

Simone Rivera realizes that terror now reigns over Paris. "At halftime, we went to get food," she will remember. "They wouldn't let anyone leave the stadium at that point and they weren't telling us anything and they just had a bunch of ambulances and people in uniform starting to look very nervous."

The tension escalates as the game ends. Fans attempting to leave the stadium come face-to-face with armed police officers. Every exit is barricaded.

"No one was telling us what to do," Simone will later recount. "We were all freaking out and then there was one point where we started to break away and then there's this swarm of people running at us and we just all start running in this direction, not knowing where to go and then all the police officers were there with their guns ready."

Simone and her fellow New Yorkers, none of whom speak French, follow instructions to remain in the stadium. Like many fans, they flood onto the field rather than go back to their seats.

Back in New York, Geraldo Rivera hears the news and immediately calls his daughter. But Simone's phone is out of battery. She does not pick up. That night, while reporting on Fox News, Geraldo gets emotional. Holding up a photo of Simone, he tells the audience of her plight. "It's my gorgeous daughter," he says. "She just turned twenty-one years old. She's a straight-A student. She's a wonderful person and a very gentle soul."

Uncertain of his daughter's fate, the veteran journalist then goes off the air and books the next flight to Paris.

✦ ✦ ✦

The night of terror is not yet over.

In fact, it is just beginning.

Even as Simone Rivera and other fans remain trapped for their own safety in the stadium, three terrorists drive through Paris in a small black Spanish sedan. They are armed with Kalashnikov assault rifles. Their targets are the city's soft underbelly: bars, cafés, and restaurants—the sorts of places where people gather in large groups. The assassins focus on the 10th and 11th arrondissements, close to the heart of Paris.

Five minutes after the first stadium explosion, at 9:25 p.m., the three killers get out of the car and spray bullets into restaurants at

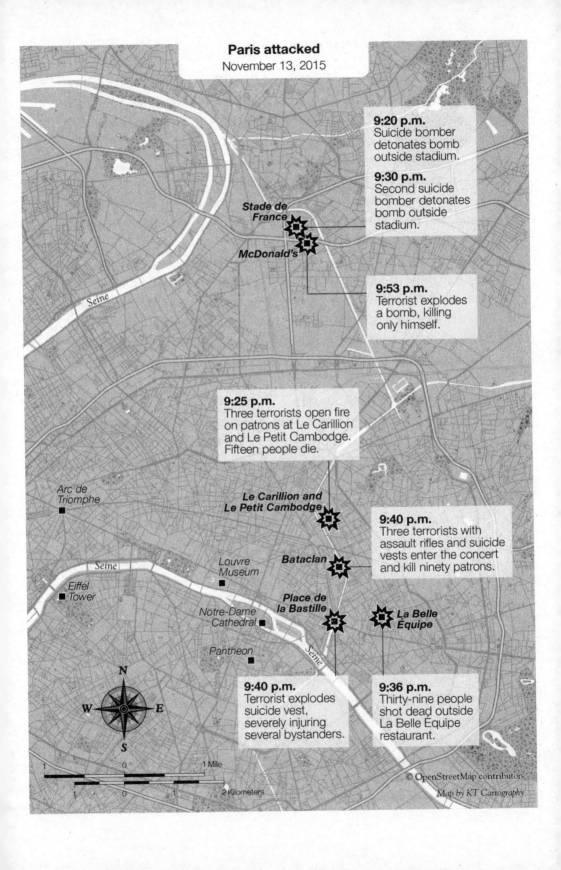

Paris attacked
November 13, 2015

9:20 p.m.
Suicide bomber detonates bomb outside stadium.

9:30 p.m.
Second suicide bomber detonates bomb outside stadium.

9:53 p.m.
Terrorist explodes a bomb, killing only himself.

9:25 p.m.
Three terrorists open fire on patrons at Le Carillon and Le Petit Cambodge. Fifteen people die.

9:40 p.m.
Three terrorists with assault rifles and suicide vests enter the concert and kill ninety patrons.

9:40 p.m.
Terrorist explodes suicide vest, severely injuring several bystanders.

9:36 p.m.
Thirty-nine people shot dead outside La Belle Équipe restaurant.

Stade de France

McDonald's

Arc de Triomphe

Le Carillon and Le Petit Cambodge

Bataclan

Louvre Museum

Eiffel Tower

Seine

Notre-Dame Cathedral

Place de la Bastille

La Belle Équipe

Pantheon

Seine

N
W E
S

1 Mile

2 Kilometers

© OpenStreetMap contributors

Map by KT Cartography

the intersection of Rue Alibert and Rue Bichat. Fifteen people immediately die. Mission accomplished, the terrorists calmly get back into their car and drive to another target. The locations have been preselected—the killers have planned their violence.

It is just a short ride to the next site.

Seven minutes later, at 9:32, five victims are shot outside La Casa Nostra pizza restaurant, and the café Bonne Bière on Rue de la Fontaine. The assassins then hear the sirens of approaching Paris police as they depart for their final destination.

At 9:36, twenty-one more innocent people are shot dead at the La Belle Équipe restaurant. Their mass murder finished, the assassins drive off. The next morning, the car will be found abandoned three miles away in the suburb of Montreuil, still loaded with three assault rifles, five full magazines, and eleven empty magazines. All told, the terrorists fired 330 bullets and murdered thirty-nine people.

But the death does not stop.

In another part of Paris, a terrorist dressed in a hooded sweatshirt sits in a café near the Place de la Bastille. The man is a decoy. His name is Ibrahim Abdeslam, and it was he who rented the black sedan for his terror compatriots. His mother will later talk of the great stress Abdeslam endures in his life. But tonight, his job is to divert police away from the three armed murderers roving the city. Looking at his watch, he knows that his comrades are now most likely trying to escape. Ibrahim Abdeslam stands and screams inside the café. He then explodes his suicide vest, dying instantly. Several patrons and a waitress are badly injured.

Meanwhile, the fleeing terrorist shooters disappear into the night. But five days later, acting on a tip, French police and military units surround an apartment building in the Saint-Denis section of Paris. The stand-off lasts for hours as a pitched battle between the terror suspects and police ensues. Local residents are evacuated amid heavy gunfire. More than five thousand rounds are fired by French authorities during the four-hour siege. When it's all over, three terror suspects are dead, among them Abdelhamid Abaaoud, the mastermind behind the terror plot. The lone police fatality is Diesel, a seven-year-old Belgian Malinois assault dog who was just months away from retirement.*

✦ ✦ ✦

Still, the violence continues on this Friday night, November 13. Another group of terrorist attackers wait inside a rented black Volkswagen Polo outside the Bataclan theater, on the east side of Paris. Three men, all wearing suicide vests and carrying Serbian-made Zastava M70 AKM assault rifles, are ready to kill. Each terrorist is a French citizen. At 9:42 p.m., one of the terrorists sends a simple text: "We're starting."

His phone will later be found to contain a complete map of the Bataclan's interior.

What follows is *the* most horrific of the night's seven terror attacks. As the hard rock band Eagles of Death Metal launches into their song "Kiss the Devil," the three murderers exit the car and spray the crowd gathered on the sidewalk in front of the 1,500-seat venue. The next to die are patrons standing at the bar in the back of the theater. Methodically, the terrorists proceed into the concert hall, shouting "Allahu Akbar"—"God is great." They have practiced this moment and move through the room with military efficiency, making sure to aim for the head and thorax of the concertgoers. One terrorist immediately hastens to block the emergency exit. Any patron seeking to escape through this door will be shot dead.

Hearing gunfire, the band immediately races off the stage and out the back door. The standing-room-only crowd is slaughtered, mowed down as panic fills the hall. The shooters are precise, with one continuing to fire while another reloads; in this way, the killing goes on without pause. Bodies fall from the balcony and lie in heaps on the floor. After a time, some in the crowd take refuge in whatever

---

* Twenty-eight-year-old Abdelhamid Abaaoud was a Belgian of Moroccan ancestry with extensive experience in organizing terror operations. He joined ISIS in 2013, was active in their Syrian fighting, and had a close relationship with Abu Bakr al-Baghdadi. He bragged often about enjoying the spilling of infidels' blood. As a known terrorist, Abaaoud became a suspect within three days of the Paris attacks. Cell phone records proved the connection, leading police to the Saint-Denis apartment block where they later surrounded and shot dead the terror leader.

hiding place they can find. The killers then walk through the stacks of fallen bodies and shoot dead anyone who moans or otherwise appears alive. Ninety concertgoers die. Police reports will also speak of women being molested and bodies being ritually dismembered. The victims are international, hailing from America, Spain, Mexico, Portugal, Britain, Chile, and Belgium, along with France.

After the massacre, one terrorist kills himself by detonating his suicide vest on the stage. The two others remain on the floor, unharmed.

An hour goes by before police enter the building. The surviving terrorists take hostages, but the police sweep in shortly after midnight and rescue all of the captives alive. One terrorist explodes his vest during the gun battle, while the other is shot dead by gendarmes. Police dogs then sniff through the corpses, searching for another possible suicide vest.

All told, 130 people are killed across Paris on this night. President Hollande, who escaped from the soccer stadium at halftime, immediately declares a state of emergency—the first in France since World War II. The country's borders are closed. The search for the terrorist killers intensifies.

"We will lead the fight and we will be ruthless," Hollande will state as ISIS takes credit for the attacks.*

"France is at war."

---

* The full ISIS statement taking credit for the attacks was issued almost immediately after the murders: "In the Name of Allah, the Most Merciful, the Most Beneficent ... In a blessed battle whose causes of success were enabled by Allah, a group of believers from the soldiers of the Caliphate (may Allah strengthen and support it) set out targeting the capital of prostitution and vice, the lead carrier of the cross in Europe—Paris.... Eight brothers equipped with explosive belts and assault rifles attacked precisely chosen targets in the center of the capital of France. These targets included the Stade de France stadium during a soccer match—between the teams of Germany and France, both of which are crusader nations—attended by the imbecile of France (Francois Hollande). The targets included the Bataclan theatre for exhibitions, where hundreds of pagans gathered for a concert of prostitution and vice. There were also simultaneous attacks on other targets in the tenth, eleventh, and eighteenth districts, and elsewhere. Paris was thereby shaken beneath the crusaders' feet, who were constricted by its streets. The result of the attacks was the deaths of no less than two hundred crusaders and the wounding of even more. All praise, grace, and favor belong to Allah."

✦ ✦ ✦

Two days later, one dozen French fighter jets launch air strikes on ISIS targets in Raqqa, Syria. The French have long been a partner in the US-led coalition against ISIS but chose not to actively engage the enemy until the Paris attacks. An ISIS command center, recruitment building, ammunition dump, and training camp are bombarded. In all, thirty bombs are dropped.

Every ISIS target is destroyed.

✦ ✦ ✦

As word spreads about the attacks, hotels, restaurants, and even Paris's underground Métro stations are locked down. Simone Rivera walks the streets with her friends, crying but in control of herself. People are on edge, not knowing if there will be another attack. Many are too frightened to even take a taxi. When Simone and her friends attempt to rent a hotel room, still unsure if more terrorists are on the loose and not wanting to walk across town to their apartments, they are denied.

However, Simone's roommate has now managed to call her mother, who then relays news of their safety to Simone's father. A longtime acquaintance of Rivera's who lives in Paris promises to find the girls and shelter them. After two tense hours, the friend finally catches up to Simone and her friends.

Charles de Gaulle Airport is almost empty as Geraldo Rivera arrives in the morning. The terrorists considered the international facility as a potential target. Soldiers, carrying their automatic weapons at port arms, scrutinize any potential threat. France is experiencing an incredible trauma from the horrific realization that more than a hundred innocent men and women are now dead.

Geraldo and his daughter reestablish cell phone contact and quickly rendezvous.

"Do you want to come home, sweetheart?" he asks Simone.

Fox News cameras record the moment.

"I want to come home."

But as the world now knows, many others will never come home.

CHAPTER SIX

DECEMBER 2, 2015
WASHINGTON, DC
10:09 A.M.

Abu Bakr al-Baghdadi is gathering enemies.

But this time, they are fellow Muslims.

The ISIS threat is being discussed six thousand miles away from the Middle East. The House of Representatives Committee on Foreign Affairs is meeting in Room 2172 of the Rayburn House Office Building. It is almost three weeks since the Paris terror attacks shocked the world, spreading fears of ISIS predation. The men and women in this room have been thoroughly briefed about the Islamic State and well know its lethal ways. Al-Baghdadi has killed more than 1,200 people in terror attacks this year—and this figure does not include the thousands of casualties in Iraq and Syria.

But even though Paris is still very much at the forefront, attention is also being focused on another terrorist organization—one considered far more lethal than al-Baghdadi and his thugs. Today's congressional session will zero in on a fifty-eight-year-old Iranian general named Qasem Soleimani, leader of the largest terrorist outfit in the world: the Islamic Revolutionary Guard Corps.

"Iran and its Islamic Revolutionary Guard have really been on a roll," committee chairman Ed Royce states, setting the tone for the proceedings. "This is the subject of our hearing today . . .

"From nuclear proliferation to support of international terrorism, to human rights abuses, the IRGC has made Iran the global menace it is today. The IRGC is responsible for squashing democracy movements at home, for spreading the Iranian regime's revolutionary ideology abroad, and for sparking turmoil throughout the Middle East. Its forces operate independent of Iran's regular army."

The mysterious leader of the IRGC is the handsome and conniving Soleimani, a former construction worker who has risen through the ranks to become the most feared man in the Middle East. The name "Qasem" means "divider"—and Soleimani has done just that, serving as a divisive presence around the world to further Iranian interests.

"Baghdadi became Baghdadi because he is a reasonably good tactical leader—and a reasonably good figurehead for the ISIS movement," one American politician will point out.

"But Baghdadi is a knucklehead," the official will add. "Soleimani is, in another lifetime, somebody who would run Microsoft. He is brilliant.

"When Baghdadi gets replaced, it's going to be a temporary step backwards. When Soleimani perishes, the loss of leadership and intelligence will be unrecoverable."*

✦ ✦ ✦

The policy of Iran has always been to contain Sunni Muslims living in Iraq. Because the ISIS terrorists are Sunnis, the predominantly Shia nation of Iran sees them as enemies and is not pleased by their success in establishing a caliphate on Iraqi soil.

Nine months ago, in March, General Soleimani launched an attack on the ISIS stronghold of Tikrit. More than twenty thousand Shia military fighters, trained and armed by Iran, pummeled the

---

* This quotation came from a high-ranking government official who spoke with the authors on condition of anonymity.

city—capturing first the suburbs and then working their way into the town center. There was nothing al-Baghdadi's forces could do to stop them.

Tikrit had been in ISIS hands since June 2014. Losing the battle was a huge symbolic blow to the group. The city of a quarter million residents is not large, yet it is the birthplace of former Iraqi dictator Saddam Hussein, one of the most powerful Sunni leaders in modern history. His tomb has already been flattened in the fighting, and his corpse stolen.

In addition to its symbolic significance, Tikrit is tactically important, perched on the banks of the Tigris River, halfway between Baghdad in the south and Mosul in the north. Its capture by a Shia force from Iran has again fueled the centuries-old rivalry between the two sects of the Islamic world.*

In March 2015, al-Baghdadi's soldiers are using the former palaces of Saddam as their headquarters. The ISIS fanatics have also booby-trapped the city, placing bombs and snipers throughout its labyrinth of ancient streets. Roads are mined. As they await the arrival of the Iranian forces, the sky is ablaze from rockets and explosions launched by Soleimani and his soldiers. The Iranians fire Soviet-made weapons. ISIS must overcome long odds to maintain control of Tikrit, as there is every likelihood it will fall; the outmanned ISIS fighters number just four thousand, against twenty thousand Iranians.†

Then, more bad news for the ISIS defenders: Abu Bakr al-Baghdadi is driving toward the western Iraqi town of Ba'aj in a three-vehicle caravan. The region is rugged and wild, a Sunni tribal

---

* Shia and Sunni are Islam's two major denominations; the religion split after the death of the prophet Muhammad in 632 AD over succession issues. The Sunni believed that Abu Bakr, Muhammad's father-in-law, deserved to be named the next Muslim leader. The Shia followed Ali, a cousin and son-in-law of the prophet. The subsequent schism and religious wars between the two factions divide Islam to this day. Both sects adhere to the tradition of sharia law. Up to 90 percent of the world's 1.6 billion Muslims are Sunni. Slightly more than 10 percent, roughly two hundred million people, are Shia; most Shia live in Iran.

† The exact number of men in the elite Quds Force of the IRGC is unknown, but estimates as high as twenty thousand are given.

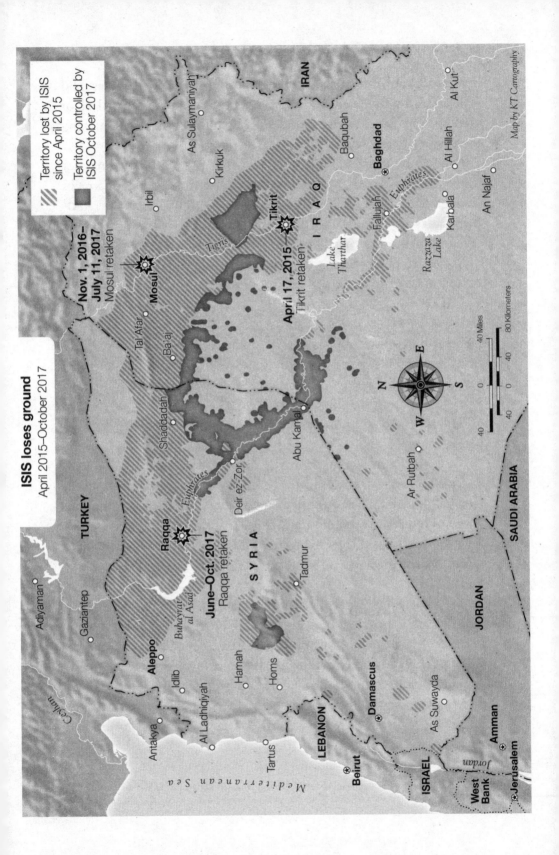

ISIS loses ground
April 2015–October 2017

Territory lost by ISIS since April 2015

Territory controlled by ISIS October 2017

Nov. 1, 2016–July 11, 2017
Mosul retaken

April 17, 2015
Tikrit retaken

June–Oct. 2017
Raqqa retaken

Map by KT Cartography

TURKEY

Adiyaman
Gaziantep
Aleppo
Idlib
Al Ladhiqiyah
Antakya
Tartus

Ceyhan

Mediterranean Sea

LEBANON
Beirut
Damascus
As Suwayda

ISRAEL
West Bank
Jerusalem
Amman

JORDAN

SAUDI ARABIA

S Y R I A

Hamah
Homs
Tadmur

Raqqa
Buhayrat al Asad
Deir ez-Zor
Euphrates
Shaddadah
Abu Kamal

Tal Afar
Ba'aj
Mosul
Tigris
Tikrit

I R A Q

Irbil
Kirkuk
As Sulaymaniyah

IRAN

Baqubah
Baghdad
Fallujah
Al Hillah
Al Kut
Karbala
An Najaf
Euphrates

Lake Tharthar
Razzaza Lake

Ar Rutbah

Jordan

N
W   E
S

40   0   40   80 Kilometers
40   0   40 Miles

homeland known for its smuggling culture. The United States paid little attention to the area during the war with Iraq due to its lack of tactical significance. Therefore, al-Baghdadi thinks he is safe making the journey in daylight.

Suddenly, missiles strike the convoy. An American Predator drone, firing from an altitude five miles above the vehicles, attacks al-Baghdadi. Three of his cohorts are killed, but he survives. Al-Baghdadi's wounds are not life threatening. However, he suffers a severe spinal injury that forces him to hand over day-to-day operational leadership to his top deputy, the Iraqi-born Abu Alaa al-Afri, a charismatic former physics teacher who excels in battle strategy.

✦ ✦ ✦

General Soleimani and his Iranian forces are obviously benefiting from America's stepped-up fight against ISIS. Ironically, after his initial reticence, President Obama has now ordered the US military to wage war from the skies, sending jets to bomb the ISIS-held city of Kirkuk. The operation is conducted in coordination with Turkish Kurd ground forces.

The Tikrit and Kirkuk fronts against the forces of Abu Bakr al-Baghdadi are active simultaneously, less than a hundred miles apart. General Soleimani despises the United States. The feeling is mutual: America refuses to expand its air strikes to Tikrit until Iranian forces leave the battlefield. The Obama administration hopes Iraqi security forces in the region will do some actual fighting and deny Iran credit for the victory.*

General Soleimani's hatred of America escalated when the United States invaded Iraq in 2003 in order to remove Saddam Hussein. Even though the Iranians loathed Saddam, they did provide materials to the Iraqis for use in attacking US forces. Armor-piercing bombs were embedded in roadways by Iranian forces to destroy American vehicles, and rockets were launched at US bases. Soleimani oversaw all of this as his power grew inside the Iranian government.

---

*That did not happen; the Iraqi forces were too weak to confront ISIS.

Soleimani's authority in Iraq is so great that he bullied Iraqi leadership into refusing to let American troops remain in the country. The general has also ordered the construction of a highway from Tehran to Lebanon, by way of Iraq, in order to open a desert link between the two nations for transporting supplies to the terrorist group Hezbollah, whose members are funded and trained by Iran.

Meanwhile, the IRGC leader's actions against American troops have pretty much signed his death warrant, as US intelligence designates the general a top counterterrorism assassination priority.

✦ ✦ ✦

Qasem Soleimani had no military training when he joined the Islamic Revolutionary Guard Corps at the age of twenty-two in 1979. He was quickly ordered to the front during the Iran-Iraq War, dubbed "the Sacred Defense" by the Iranian mullahs. The gruesome confrontation between two neighboring Middle Eastern powers with different religious ideologies impressed upon Soleimani the notion that Iraq must always remain weak, never again to threaten Iran. This philosophy has spilled over: Soleimani is now intent on ensuring not only Iraqi weakness but that of every other nation-state in the region. The general has spent more than three decades expanding Shia power against Sunni rivals such as Iraq and Saudi Arabia, as well as Western powers like the United States.

The rise of Soleimani coincided with Iran's campaign to destabilize the entire Middle East. The general quickly upgraded an elite Iranian unit known as the Quds Force. This organization was charged with defending the nation's Islamic way of life.

For more than 2,500 years, Persia—as Iran was formerly known—was ruled by monarchs. But in 1979, the shah of Iran, sympathetic to Western countries, was overthrown by the ayatollah Ruhollah Khomeini, a fanatical Islamic cleric who quickly militarized the country in order to solidify his power.

Khomeini realized he needed a unique military force all his own to maintain his hold on power. Thus was born the Iranian Revolutionary Guard Corps, formed to serve as a balance between military and religious forces. It was ordered that the traditional Iranian army would protect Iran's borders, and the guard would enforce Islamic tenets within them.

But by 2015, Soleimani's crew has grown to more than 190,000 members and maintains a navy and air force rivaling those of the traditional Iranian forces. And the border is no longer the threshold; the IRGC has expanded its interests to encompass any nation at odds with Iran's interests. In this way, the fundamentalist Islamic clerics who have ruled the nation for almost four decades maintain their tight grip on power, despite growing unrest among those Iranian citizens clamoring for democracy. Soleimani assists in suppressing this resistance, imprisoning, torturing, and even executing voices of dissent.

In 1997, Soleimani was given command of a special intelligence arm of the Revolutionary Guard known as the Quds Force. With this new power, Soleimani became able to wage secret "wars" on a number of fronts. The Quds Force is active throughout Europe, Africa, the Middle East, and the Afghanistan-Pakistan region. Its focus is insurrection through recruitment and training of terror factions—all under the watchful eye of General Qasem Soleimani. The general's forces lent support to Muslim factions in the Bosnian war. In Palestine, Quds offers training and arms to the terror organizations Hamas and Islamic Jihad (which is different from ISIS). Also, to gain greater control in Syria, Soleimani props up the failing regime of key Iranian ally President Bashar al-Assad by flying in Afghanistani and Pakistani fighters to wage war. He supports the Houthi militants in Yemen, who are battling a Saudi Arabian force that has intervened in a domestic conflict.

Finally, using his Quds Force, he is trying to destroy the state of Israel and has set up the Hezbollah terrorist organization in Lebanon for that purpose.* He is also working with the Taliban in Afghanistan to kill Americans in that country.

✦ ✦ ✦

---

* "Quds" is Persian for Jerusalem, a city of signal importance to the Jewish, Christian, and Muslim religions, which Iran has vowed to one day "liberate" from the Jewish people.

Through it all, the general has remained a mysterious sphinx. "Soleimani is the single most powerful operative in the world today," former CIA officer John Maguire stated in 2013, "and no one's ever heard of him."

But, along with his power, the general's desire for self-promotion grows with each success. He actually wrote to General David Petraeus, commander of US forces in Iraq: "I, Qasem Soleimani, control the policy for Iran with respect to Iraq, Lebanon, Gaza, and Afghanistan."

✦ ✦ ✦

Finally, as the battle for Tikrit rages, Qasem Soleimani comes out of the shadows. For the first time, he allows himself to be photographed and to be seen as the face of Iranian power. His image soon graces Twitter and Instagram.

But the general is quirky. He prefers pictures of himself on the battlefield, wearing the fatigues of a soldier but the epaulets of a general. Nothing in the photographs hint at his short five-foot-nine stature, just as the images are unable to capture his habit of rarely raising his voice. Social media takes note of his handsome, unlined face. He presents an image of being religious and kind, alternately appearing stern and impish, ascetic and philosophical. Soleimani is photographed kneeling in prayer in the middle of the desert, midbattle. He affects a gentle smile, his dark eyes hooded by black eyebrows, gray beard neatly trimmed. This vanity campaign is so effective that the visage of General Soleimani soon grows popular not just in Iran but throughout the entire Middle East.

It would seem unlikely to the casual observer that Soleimani would even be capable of terrorism. He lives in Tehran with his wife, rising at four o'clock every morning. He has trouble with his prostate and takes pills for a sore back. Soleimani is a disciplinarian to his five children—three boys and two girls. Sometimes, when the general appears in public, it is not uncommon for citizens to clamor for the privilege of kissing his hand.

Meanwhile, the general is successfully launching a new wave of terror attacks in Somalia, India, and Thailand. Thousands die as a result. And his forces in Tikrit are behaving no differently than ISIS—kidnapping and executing civilians, raping women, setting homes ablaze.

✦ ✦ ✦

In Washington, DC, that December, it is 12:13 p.m. when the Committee on Foreign Affairs adjourns. In the two hours of discussion, Soleimani's name has come up just twice. With ISIS now out of Tikrit, the general has once again disappeared from public view. The congresspeople are told there are even rumors of his death.

So it is that General Qasem Soleimani returns to the shadows, allowing the retreating Abu Bakr al-Baghdadi and ISIS to once again seize the spotlight. This very afternoon, in San Bernardino, California, a married couple of Pakistani heritage, inspired by ISIS, will open fire with assault rifles at a local health department building. Fourteen Americans will be murdered.

Thousands of miles away, both al-Baghdadi and his enemy, Qasem Soleimani, will be highly pleased.

CHAPTER SEVEN

MAY 27, 2016
MOSUL, IRAQ
DAY

The global search for Abu Bakr al-Baghdadi is growing cold.

The ISIS chieftain is still receiving treatment from his wounds of a year ago and is now living in a safe house just miles outside this major city in northern Iraq. Doctors sympathetic to ISIS are still treating him for severe spinal injuries. Al-Baghdadi is thought to have grown paranoid in light of his near-death experience and the rising number of his top advisers killed by US coalition air strikes. President Obama has rescinded a previous promise to not allow American troops to put "boots on the ground" in Syria and Iraq, now secretly ordering an estimated 150 Special Forces operatives stationed in the region to hunt for al-Baghdadi.

More than fifteen senior terrorists have been assassinated, including three of al-Baghdadi's top deputies. Among that number is Abu Alaa al-Afri, who took temporary command after the drone strike. US Army Special Forces cornered al-Afri outside Raqqa in eastern Syria. When asked to surrender, he instead took aim with an assault rifle and was shot dead.*

Yet ISIS thrives. The caliphate is no longer confined to the Middle East, now numbering nine outposts flourishing in distant locations like Nigeria, Libya, and Pakistan. Revenue from kidnappings and captured oil fields is considerable, paying for the arms necessary to wage jihad. Attacks such as the downing of a Russian airliner the previous October, which killed all 224 passengers, as well as terror events in Paris, Brussels, and Tunisia excite the faithful. New recruits pour in from around the world, easily replacing the more than one thousand fighters killed each month—at least fifty of those dying by suicide vest. The Paris attack proved that ISIS could strike anywhere in the world, just as the downing of the Russian Metrojet was the first coordinated attack in the skies.

The Americans could have prevented all this a decade ago, when al-Baghdadi was taken into custody during the Iraq War and held at a US prison known as Camp Bucca. But al-Baghdadi was judged at the time to be a shy man and low-level terrorist. He was released near the end of 2004, then began his slow rise to power.

As the world's most wanted man, Abu Bakr al-Baghdadi rarely sleeps in the same location more than a few nights in a row, frequenting homes in Syria and northern Iraq. The towns of Ba'aj and Tal Afar are personal favorites because the local people not only support him but actively confiscate the cell phones of all residents before his arrival. Coalition intelligence officials are stymied by this cooperation, and reports of al-Baghdadi are scant. What is known is that the ISIS leader travels widely to conceal his location.

However, there is one seat of operations al-Baghdadi favors over all others: Mosul. This large metropolis of 1.6 million was captured

---

* US Special Forces were in Syria as part of a campaign by the Obama administration to permanently defeat ISIS by killing its leaders. This came in response to a terror attack in Brussels that killed thirty-one people. Two helicopters pursued the vehicle carrying al-Afri, hoping to land, arrest, and interrogate the ISIS leader. While al-Afri refused to be taken alive, the cache of intelligence about ISIS seized from the vehicle was substantial.

by ISIS two years ago. Hundreds of thousands of residents fled in advance of the 1,500 ISIS occupiers who routed a much larger but undisciplined Iraqi government force. Those who remain are now subject to a harsh code of punishment and endure growing poverty. But that is not al-Baghdadi's concern. The day will come when Iraqi and Iranian forces will return, so ISIS is busy building defensive barricades, planting land mines, and digging hidden escape tunnels.

During those preparations, ISIS religious police roam the streets, forcing their cultural and religious values on the population. Historic Shia mosques are destroyed as a show of religious force, detonated over the screams of local worshippers. Pro-ISIS religious leaders now rule the city. Perversely, the citizens of Mosul must donate a portion of their income to ISIS to rebuild the very mosques the terrorists blew up.

In addition, women are forced to cover themselves from head to toe, wearing the *khimar* veil to obscure their hair and shoulders. Men who do not enforce this behavior from their wives are flogged. Even gloves are mandatory in the brutal heat, the average summer temperature rising to well over one hundred degrees.

And this is only the beginning: Books are burned. Smoking a cigarette leads to flogging, which is usually inflicted by a power cable, a rope, or even a whip.

Women walking down a street unaccompanied are arrested.

Women entering a taxi alone are arrested.

These female detainees are taken to a police station for torture. Any woman found wearing nail polish has her nails pulled out with pliers. Very often the torture is as simple as a jailer biting into the bare breast of a female prisoner and ripping out a chunk of flesh.

But there is one method of escape—agreeing to marry an ISIS member and going to his bed.

It is not just women who suffer under al-Baghdadi's sadistic reign. Men are skinned alive, their families forced to watch. Young children are beheaded. Citizens are set on fire. Girls and women are taken prisoner and raped.

Theft is punishable by the amputation of a hand.

Christian believers are murdered.

Any man found guilty of adultery is thrown off a building.

Any woman found guilty of adultery is publicly stoned to death.

Citizens are strung up by their feet, then slaughtered like cattle.

When available, a T-55 tank is used to crush lawbreakers under its treads.

But the harshest penalty is reserved for gay people. The Koran condemns the behavior of men in the ancient city of Tel-Afar who engaged in sodomy. But the Islamic holy book does not prescribe a death penalty for such behavior—that judgment is imposed by ISIS. "They hunt them down, one by one," a gay Iraqi man who successfully fled told the British Broadcasting Company. "When they capture people, they go through his phone and his contacts and Facebook friends. They are trying to track down every gay man."

The execution of a gay man is a horrific public spectacle. A hooded executioner reads aloud the charges as two other ISIS fighters, wearing all black, hold the accused on the edge of a roof. Very often the victim will beg to be shot rather than hurled from the precipice. When the charges are read all the way through, the man is thrown to his death. The crowd in the street below often contains small children. The mob cheers. The spectators are encouraged to stone the broken body once it lands, just to ensure that the accused is truly dead. Photos of the corpse are then posted on social media.

"You should see Facebook comments after they post video of the killings," says the gay Iraqi to the BBC. "It's devastating. 'God bless you, ISIS.' 'Amazing news. This is the least gays deserve.' 'The most horrible crime on earth is homosexuality. Good job, ISIS.'"

The videos go out around the world. Yet as harsh as this persecution might be, countless individuals across the globe not only agree with the executions but also want to join ISIS. Many are planning to travel to the Middle East and join al-Baghdadi's army. The ISIS ranks are filled with Muslims from North America and Europe.

Others are keen to impress al-Baghdadi from afar. No city on earth is safe from "lone wolf" ISIS attacks, as the media now dubs the random acts of terror perpetrated by men who plan and execute an act of terror all by themselves.

As Orlando, Florida, is about to find out.

✦ ✦ ✦

It's Latin Night at Pulse, Orlando's largest and most popular gay nightclub. Three hundred patrons, men and women alike, pack the dance floor. It is 2:00 a.m. Befitting the theme, throngs of Puerto Rican, Dominican, and Mexican revelers blend into the crowd. Tequila flows, and Ray Rivera—aka DJ Infinite—spins salsa music on the large open-air patio.

Without warning, a gunman suddenly opens fire with a Sig Sauer MCX assault rifle. He wears a handgun in his waistband. The dance floor is instantly strewn with bodies. The music is loud, but the sound of gunfire is even louder. Patrons race for the exits. "All hell broke loose," DJ Infinite will later recount, "people running for the door."

The music stops.

But the shooting continues. Panic makes it impossible for many to escape. So some barricade themselves in bathroom stalls, which is perhaps the worst place to hide. "I can just remember you can smell the blood," Miguel Leiva, who hid in a restroom, will recall. "All my clothes were full of blood. We were sitting down and there were huge pools of blood."

An off-duty police officer working security at Pulse engages in a gun battle with the shooter. The security guard quickly runs out of bullets and flees. Meanwhile, the killer walks laughing through the pile of bodies, firing his weapons at anything that moves. The assassin is Omar Mateen, twenty-nine, previously investigated by the FBI for an ISIS affiliation. Mateen was born in New York City and has lived in the United States all his life. Mateen is also friends with Moner Mohammad Abu-Salha, an American citizen who carried out a suicide attack for ISIS in Syria. Mateen's ex-wife will later tell authorities that he beat her often, and displayed signs of mental instability.

"In the next few days," he recently posted on Facebook, "you will see attacks from the Islamic State in the USA."

Omar Mateen also shares ISIS's hatred of gay people—and yet he is often found on Grindr, a gay dating app. He sends explicit pictures to men who show interest.

The killer is also a regular at Pulse, where he is often seen trying to pick up gay men.

✦ ✦ ✦

The shooting at Pulse will be the deadliest mass murder to date in American history. Forty-nine people are killed, fifty-three injured. At 2:35 a.m., Omar Mateen calls 911. "I want to let you know, I'm in Orlando and I did the shootings," he tells the operator.

"What's your name?" the dispatcher responds.

"My name is 'I pledge allegiance to Abu Bakr al-Baghdadi of the Islamic State.'"

Mateen hangs up. He reloads. As quiet settles over the bloody dance floor, now piled with bodies, the killer checks Facebook to see if there's a mention of his murders. He phones a friend to brag. As police surround the building, Mateen takes refuge in a bathroom, locking himself inside with several clubgoers whom he now takes hostage.

He texts his wife at 4:00 a.m., asking her if she has heard about the shootings. She responds by saying she loves him.

At 5:00 a.m., three hours into the massacre, Orlando police finally storm the building. The long delay has no explanation. The external wall of the bathroom in which Mateen hides is blasted open with explosives. He emerges from the rubble firing, only to be immediately shot dead.

His hostages, many grievously wounded, survive.

✦ ✦ ✦

The shocking crime in Orlando gives ISIS new status in the terror community. Its global reach is expanding daily through the use of social media to broadcast ISIS atrocities and propaganda. Even as al-Baghdadi remains in hiding, his fanatical followers are killing people all over the world.

"Allah has enabled brother Omar Mateen, one of the soldiers of the caliphate in America, to carry out a raid where he was able to infiltrate a crusaders' gathering at a gay night club," the official ISIS announcement reads.

"Allah enabled him to inflict casualties amongst the filthy crusaders. He killed and injured over a hundred of them. This is the biggest raid to be carried out in America after the raid of Manhattan sixteen years ago. All praise to Allah."

✦ ✦ ✦

The global ISIS terror attacks continue throughout the summer of 2016.

Turkish suicide bombers kill forty people.

In Bangladesh, twenty people are murdered at a restaurant in Dhaka.

In France, a thirty-one-year-old Tunisian man drives a truck through a crowd in Nice, killing eighty-four.

In Germany, a teenager born in Afghanistan wields an axe on a commuter train, injuring five people before being subdued.

And in Russia, a nine-minute YouTube video warns President Vladimir Putin that his nation is next. "Listen, Putin, we will come to Russia and will kill you at your homes. . . . Oh, brothers, carry out jihad and kill and fight them."

Yet unbeknownst to ISIS and al-Baghdadi, the winds are about to change.

CHAPTER EIGHT

JUNE 12, 2016
WHITE HOUSE
WASHINGTON, DC
1:59 P.M.

The massacre in Orlando has embarrassed President Barack Obama. Less than one day after the deadly attack, he stands before a lectern in the James S. Brady Press Briefing Room, broadcasting live on national television. The Pulse murders have shocked America, and the president has no choice but to address the issue. He will call the shooting an "act of terror" and decry the targeting of the gay community.

Anti-Obama media in America have already resurrected his "JV" comments about ISIS made in January 2014. That was two years ago. Since then, the terrorists have declared the formation of a caliphate and have murdered at least 150 Americans in separate attacks.

Today's speech does not mark Obama's first attempt to confront ISIS. Almost a year ago, in July 2015, he warned the nation about the grave terror threat. "This is a long-term campaign," the president stated then, using words that will be eerie in their prescience after the murders at Pulse. "ISIL has been particularly effective at reaching out to—and recruiting—vulnerable people around the world, including here in the United States. . . . The threat of lone wolves or small cells is complex—it's harder to detect and harder to prevent. It's one of the most difficult challenges we face. And preventing these kinds of attacks on American soil is going to require sustained effort."*

However, the American people are in no mood for more rhetoric. They are angry that an ISIS killer could murder so many innocent people, while the terrorists celebrate worldwide. In four days, Mr. Obama will give yet another speech, this time at a memorial in Orlando. But this time, he will try to deflect the issue from ISIS to gun control.

The approach does not work. America is electing a new president in November, and top Republican contender Donald Trump, a real estate magnate from New York City, is publicly blaming Obama for the shootings. "We're led by a man who's not tough, not smart, or he's got something else in mind," Trump will state at a Manchester, New Hampshire, rally. The Republican calls for Mr. Obama to resign immediately, noting that the president refused to use the words "radical Islamic terrorism" in his address to the nation.†

Politics aside, it is clear most American citizens want the president of the United States to punish ISIS.

✦ ✦ ✦

Barack Obama has, in fact, dealt harshly with the murderous group. In the past two years, the United States has spent $7.5 billion in military allocations to battle the caliphate. US forces launched thousands of air strikes in Iraq and Syria and assassinated more than 120 ISIS leaders—all in an attempt to defeat the terror organization.

Despite that, ISIS remains on the offensive.

---

* These remarks were made at the Pentagon on July 6, 2015. The president laid out his "four pillars of US strategy" against ISIS: a systematic campaign of air strikes, increased support for coalition ground forces, enhanced counterterrorism surveillance, and humanitarian assistance for civilians displaced by war.

† Donald Trump has long asserted that Barack Obama was not born in the United States and is actually a practicing Muslim. Obama was raised in a nonpracticing Christian household by his mother and practices Christianity in his adulthood. His estranged father was Muslim (albeit later an atheist), leading to Trump's false assertion that Obama was still a practicing Muslim. Obama's comments that one of his goals as president was to forge "a new partnership based on mutual respect and mutual interests" with the global Muslim community also angered Trump.

An intense man who does not readily accept most criticism, President Obama well understands he must step up the pressure. Knowing the American people are opposed to sending ground troops into the Middle East, he has adopted a two-pronged strategy against ISIS.

The first method is using quick-strike Special Forces—units from the Navy SEALs, Delta Force, and Army Green Berets—to attack strategic targets. With their minimal battlefield footprint and high level of training, Special Forces operators are more effective than large numbers of troops. These elite units are the smallest groups within the US military, allotted just 2 percent of the nation's defense budget.

But they are the most lethal—as Osama bin Laden found out.

✦ ✦ ✦

The second, more controversial aspect of President Obama's antiterrorism policy is the use of drones. Pilotless aircraft, also known as UAV (unmanned aerial vehicles), have been a part of warfare since the seventeenth century, when Austria used unmanned hot-air balloons to bomb Venice. By the early twentieth century, drones were radio-controlled, meaning the operator had to be relatively close to the aircraft to direct it. Today, satellite technology makes it possible to control a drone's flight path from enormous distances. And whereas spy planes like the U-2 and SR-71 Blackbird flew over an area at a high rate of speed, a modern drone can circle high overhead around the clock—sending video that allows intelligence officials to monitor a situation in real time. Also, drones can go where normal soldiers cannot, monitoring rugged mountain ranges and tribal lands to gather intel or carry out an assassination.*

But perhaps the most significant upgrade is that drones can now launch missiles—a development used by the US Air Force and the CIA during the hunt for bin Laden. The Predator and Reaper drones were originally built for surveillance and intelligence gathering. The Predator has a range of 1,200 miles and is operated by a pilot halfway

---

* During the years leading up to World War II, Great Britain experimented with an unmanned biplane controlled by radio from the ground. The name of the aircraft—the de Havilland Queen Bee—and the sound of its engines is where "drones" got their name.

around the world. First introduced during the Clinton administration in the 1990s for use in the former nation of Yugoslavia, they were almost immediately deployed over Afghanistan in the days after 9/11. Now, in addition to bristling with communications gear and cameras, they are armed—capable of firing five-foot-long air-to-ground AGM-114 Hellfire II missiles with ease.* Some experts claim the Predator drone is the greatest new invention to appear on the battlefield since the intercontinental ballistic missile.

President George W. Bush made frequent use of drones during his eight years in office, waging war in both Iraq and Afghanistan. Barack Obama is seen by some as pursuing a less aggressive foreign policy. But the truth is, he has ordered twice as many drone strikes as Bush. By the time Obama leaves office, he will have utilized drones to rain down death from the sky 1,878 times. The reach of their power has expanded to include Yemen and Somalia—nations with which the United States is not at war. The president also keeps a personal "kill list" of deadly terrorists. Targets are separated into "personality" strikes for top leadership and "signature" attacks on training facilities or terrorist compounds.

The current focus of Obama's kill list is the ongoing ISIS expansion into Pakistan and Afghanistan. Mullah Akhtar Mansour, a former Taliban official thought to be joining forces with the Islamic State, was assassinated just one month ago—vaporized on a rural farm road, his Toyota Corolla a flaming wreck after being struck by two Hellfire missiles. The cleric was driving the N-40 national highway in Pakistan. Photographs will show green fields, a dusty highway, and a single mangled vehicle burning alongside the road.

The mission played out to perfection, with US forces electronically intercepting Mansour's location and then sending Reaper drones to first evade Pakistani radar and ultimately kill the terrorist. The assassination was not completely authorized until President Obama gave the go-ahead.

The same fate will soon befall Hafiz Saeed Khan, ISIS commander

---

* The Hellfire weighs roughly a hundred pounds and features an armor-piercing warhead. It can be fired in an air-to-ground or air-to-air capacity.

in Afghanistan and Pakistan. In the wake of his forces engaging the US Army for the first time, a battle that saw three hundred terrorists die and five Americans wounded, intelligence pinpointed Khan as the instigator. The once-senior Taliban leader switched his loyalty to Abu Bakr al-Baghdadi in 2014, marking an uptick in ISIS's power throughout the region. A subsequent suicide bombing at a Pakistani hospital, which killed 74 people, confirmed the expanding reach of the Islamic State. In addition, 80 people were killed and 250 wounded in Kabul, Afghanistan, on July 24—another ISIS suicide attack. All of this is traced back to Hafiz Saeed Khan. On July 26, 2016, Khan is riding in a small station wagon through the Nangarhar province of Afghanistan, a known training center for ISIS fighters. The sun is hot, and Khan feels no threat. All at once, a missile enters the vehicle through the rear hatchback window, blowing Khan into unidentifiable pieces.

The action was personally authorized by President Obama.

✦ ✦ ✦

The average drone strike kills six victims, with targets including motorcycles, sports utility vehicles, cars, homes, and compounds. For this reason, terrorists are often killed while in the presence of their families and friends. This is what happened to the ISIS killer of James Foley, Steven Sotloff, and Peter Kassig.

Nicknamed "Jihadi John" by someone on social media, the Kuwaiti-born British citizen epitomizes the brutal terror outfit in a very personal way.

The brutality of his murders, as well as the fact that he wore a mask and did not offer his name, fascinated many around the world. US intelligence soon learned that Jihadi John was really Mohammed Emwazi, a twenty-seven-year-old terrorist who once dreamed of being an international soccer star.

On November 12, 2015, Emwazi is visiting family and friends in the Syrian city of Raqqa. Unbeknownst to the ISIS killer, three drones—two British and one American—have been tracking his movements for several days. Emwazi's location within the populous city concerns intelligence officials, who do not want civilian casualties. So, it is decided to wait until he departs.

That evening, drones pick up Emwazi exiting a building, accompanied by a friend. Of course, he is oblivious to the fact that his death warrant has been signed.

The US drone, an MQ-9 Reaper with a sixty-six-foot wingspan, launches two Hellfire missiles. Unlike the men he beheaded, who well knew that they would suffer a gruesome death, Emwazi does not suffer—he is dead before he knows the missiles have struck his car. Emwazi's friend is killed as well. There is nothing left of their bodies.

Upon announcing the successful assassination of the much-loathed Jihadi John, the US command will state that he was "evaporated," and the mission "flawless." In fact, American broadcaster Lester Holt of NBC openly showed his enthusiasm for the killing on the air.

But it is a fact that sometimes drones strike the wrong target. Many terrorists have been declared dead, only to reappear quite alive later on. So the American military downplays the action—awaiting confirmation that the ISIS terrorist is, in fact, dead. "It will take time to definitely declare we had success," states a Pentagon spokesman.

Two months later, the world has its answer: ISIS finally acknowledges the death of Mohammed Emwazi.

✦ ✦ ✦

Despite these antiterrorist successes, ISIS still flourishes. And the drones may be part of the reason why, as some mistargeted attacks are giving the jihadists propaganda opportunities.

During President Obama's first days in office, a drone strike accidentally killed tribal elders rather than Taliban fighters in Afghanistan. That rattled Mr. Obama. But he has since come to accept this "collateral damage" as the cost of protecting America. Even so, the Obama administration did not admit to the use of drones until 2012.

✦ ✦ ✦

And so it is that Barack Obama has one hellacious problem on his hands.

"The American people find themselves living in a world plagued with more terrorism than before Obama took office, not less," notes *Foreign Affairs* magazine. "Most worrisome is the emergence in Iraq and Syria of the self-proclaimed Islamic State, whose ability to capture and hold territory, significant financial resources, and impressive strategic acumen make it a threat unlike any other the United States has faced in the contemporary era."

But it's not only the United States that is under siege. Western Europe is a closer battlefield, and easier for ISIS terrorists to access. And a terrible blow is about to be dealt to the biggest target in Europe: London.

CHAPTER NINE

Another day in Europe's third largest city, population about eight million.*

Tourists with jackets zipped all the way up walk onto Westminster Bridge. To their right stand the historic Houses of Parliament and London's iconic timepiece, Big Ben. On the far side of the bridge, across the River Thames, the London Eye towers over the skyline, rising 443 feet in the air. The midafternoon sun is low on the horizon, giving a reflective golden shine to the river and Parliament's windows. None of the fifty-seven tourists walking across the legendary span knows the precise number of closed-circuit surveillance cameras watching their every move. Americans Kurt and Melissa Cochran are photographed meandering slowly, "just being touristy," in Melissa's words, celebrating their twenty-fifth wedding anniversary. The couple from Utah arrived in London just three hours ago.

Westminster Bridge is more than 250 meters long, its seven arches painted the same deep green as the padded benches in the House of

---

* Istanbul is the largest, at fifteen million, followed by Moscow with its eleven million residents.

Commons. The tourists now making their way across it are from more than a dozen nations: America, South Korea, Romania, France, Portugal, and more. They walk in small clusters with their travel companions, taking in some of the most interesting sights in the world.

All feel relatively safe.

They are not.

✦ ✦ ✦

Britain's unique approach to fighting terrorism began with the Irish Republican Army, a group known worldwide as the IRA. For a century, efforts to gain Irish independence from Great Britain have involved acts of terror. Ireland became independent in 1923, but Northern Ireland still remains part of the United Kingdom. The IRA fight for an independent Northern Ireland is the reason for the security cameras and barbed wire surrounding England's most iconic structures, reminding Londoners that mass murder could occur at any time. The IRA is why one-fourth of the world's security devices are employed in the United Kingdom. In addition, Parliament has passed special laws allowing a terror suspect to be imprisoned for twenty-eight days without being charged. Unlike the United States, where such perceived violations of civil liberties often result in a public outcry, many decades of experiencing terror bombings means general acceptance of these measures in Britain. Also, in this country there is no need for official authorization when it comes to executing terrorists. Military groups like the Special Air Service, England's version of the US Army Special Forces units, can legally assassinate on order.

Ireland's battle against British imperialism dates to well before independence, but "the Troubles," as the modern British terror war with the IRA is known, really began in 1969. Riots in Northern Ireland led to the deployment of troops into this disputed corner of the British Empire. Operation Banner, as the incursion was named, would support pro-British Protestant factions and local police—also known as the Royal Ulster Constabulary (RUC).

What began as an intervention became an occupation; British troops would not leave Northern Ireland until 2007, thirty-eight years later. The conflict quickly split along religious lines, with Protestants supporting the RUC and the British military, while Catholics were loyal to the IRA. That paramilitary organization dates back to 1919 and is dedicated to ending British rule in Ireland. Its primary tactics are raids, ambush, and sabotage.

In short, the IRA fights a guerrilla war. It also acts as a de facto police force, punishing child molesters and drug pushers with "knee-capping"—a bullet fired into that joint. Extreme cases will earn the "six-pack," gunshots to the knees, elbows, and ankles that would cripple any human being.

But at least the targets live.

The same cannot be said for those who betray the IRA. Informants are abducted, severely tortured, driven to a remote location with a hood over their head, then shot in the back of the skull. Their bodies—often naked—are dumped in a public place.

The Troubles soon spread to England itself. In one brutal attack, an offshoot group known as the Provisional Irish Republican Army (PIRA) killed and wounded more than two hundred in coordinated raids on British pubs in 1974.

Perhaps the most infamous day in the history of the Irish rebellion, in 1972, would be named "Bloody Sunday" for the enormity of the act—and this time, it wasn't the IRA doing the killing. British troops massacred a group of unarmed civil rights protesters in the city of Derry, murdering fourteen. This brutality against civilians, in full view of the public, only intensified the division between British and Irish.*

In an act of revenge, PIRA members placed a fifty-pound bomb on board the fishing boat of British royal and World War II hero Earl Louis Mountbatten in the summer of 1979. The radio-controlled detonation took place as Mountbatten was piloting his craft out of the harbor in Mullaghmore, in the Republic of Ireland, site of his summer home. The blast immediately severed Mountbatten's legs, but he was alive when pulled from the ocean. The seventy-nine-year-old died shortly afterward, along with three other passengers on the vessel. The murders shocked the world.

---

* The song "Sunday Bloody Sunday," about the Derry massacre, became a hit for the Irish pop group U2 in 1983.

By the end of the British occupation, some three thousand civilians, six hundred soldiers, and three hundred police officers had died. In addition, an estimated thirty thousand Irish and British citizens were wounded. In the long history of Great Britain's military, no campaign lasted longer.

The one positive to come out of the Troubles is the ability of the British government to predict terror attacks. Intelligence gathering and counterterrorism were clumsy in the first days of the Irish campaign, a direct result of a power dispute between the British Army and the RUC. But over the decades, the military, police, and MI5—British domestic security—learned to work together. Their methods of cultivating information and stopping attacks are still in use today.

And they are needed—because ISIS knows London is a prize to be attacked. Britain is home to more than two million Muslims, with almost half of that figure Pakistani. An additional sixteen percent are from Bangladesh, a Muslim nation to the east of India. Followers of Islam account for the majority of terror suspects in the United Kingdom. British authorities have "stop and search" power over anyone, so tension between police and the Muslim community is high.

✦ ✦ ✦

It is 4:00 a.m. on July 7, 2005, a Thursday, as four "home-grown" Muslim extremists don backpacks laden with improvised explosive devices—homemade bombs more commonly called IEDs. Two of the terrorists pause to make a video explaining why they are about to kill people. Thirty-year-old Mohammad Sidique Khan is particularly expressive.

"I and thousands like me are forsaking everything for what we believe. Our drive and motivation doesn't come from tangible commodities that this world has to offer. Our religion is Islam, obedience to the one true God and following the footsteps of the final prophet messenger," says the slight man with the dark-black beard. "Your democratically elected governments continuously perpetuate atrocities against my people all over the world. And your support of them makes you directly responsible, just as I am directly responsible for protecting and avenging my Muslim brothers and sisters."

The would-be assassins travel by rented car from Leeds, four hours north of London. At the town of Luton, they transfer to a train heading into the city, arriving at the King's Cross station at 8:23 a.m. Hundreds of thousands of commuters are using the underground rail system and city buses to get to work. People walk close together through crowded stations, then press tightly into standing-room-only railway cars, lost in their own thoughts.

At King's Cross, the four terrorists split up, heading in different directions. Three board separate trains on the Tube, as the London Underground is also known. Hasib Hussain, eighteen, remains aboveground, waiting to board a double-decker bus. Each target has been preselected for the large number of passengers on board. The movements of these murderers will later be confirmed on closed-circuit television cameras.

The three subway bombs are all detonated at precisely 8:50 a.m. London panics. Survivors are stuck in railway cars, some breaking windows with umbrellas to escape. On the Circle Line train, where the explosion takes place between Liverpool Street and Aldgate, one London resident is partially blinded by a fragment of the bomber's shinbone.

The entire Underground system is shut down by 9:50 a.m.

But not before teenage terrorist Hussain detonates his backpack on the double-decker. The Number 30 bus is traveling through Central London, a place where streets are bumper-to-bumper with vehicles. The sidewalks are also packed with pedestrians. Greek-born bus driver George Psaradakis has been forced to deviate from his normal route due to road closures caused by the Underground bombings. Thirty people got off the bus because of the change, drastically reducing the loss of life when the terror bomb explodes. Lisa French, an employee of a British telephone service, initially sits down next to Hasib Hussain, but there is not enough room for her to open her laptop, due to his large rucksack. So, she moves forward a few seats.

The blast breaks Ms. French's teeth, knocks her unconscious, causes multiple deep cuts and bruises, and punctures her eardrums.

But she lives.

Thirteen other passengers, including Hussain, do not.

Many more would have died were it not for a random stroke

of luck: the route change brought on by the bombings means that the double-decker explosion occurs directly in front of the British Medical Association. A conference is being held inside. At the sound of the explosion, dozens of doctors rush outside and immediately attend to victims, saving countless lives.

Still, fifty-two people are killed in the four bombings. More than seven hundred others are injured. This makes it the largest-ever terror attack on British soil. Images of stunned London commuters in their workday suits and dresses, faces bleeding and white bandages wrapped around their heads, shatter the illusion that Britain's terror problems will end with the cease-fire in Ireland.

In fact, it feels like a new war is beginning.

Which it is.

✦ ✦ ✦

Déjà vu.

Twelve years later, on the afternoon of March 22, 2017, Americans Kurt and Melissa Cochran are almost across the Westminster Bridge on their midafternoon tour of London. They have no idea a brand-new terrorist tactic is just about to be activated—and in a matter of seconds, their lives will never be the same.

Without warning, a rented Hyundai Tucson swerves out of the bus lane. But rather than enter the roadway, the SUV jumps the curb onto the sidewalk and continues accelerating, reaching more than seventy-five miles per hour. Kurt Cochran catches sight of the vehicle from the corner of his eye.

The next morning's papers will call him a hero for what happens next. Instinctively, the fifty-two-year-old musician pushes his wife out of the way, taking the full brunt of the charging vehicle. He is thrown over the bridge's parapet, onto concrete below. Paramedics arrive quickly, but not in time to save him.

Melissa is knocked unconscious. A leg and a rib are broken. The next thing she will remember is being "on the ground, with someone's hand on my head." Melissa Cochran spends a week in a London hospital and then returns to the United States.

Back on the bridge, the Hyundai continues speeding down the

sidewalk, pedestrians flying into the air as they are struck. This is now a scene of carnage, with bodies strewn everywhere. In the span of just thirty seconds, more than fifty people are killed or hurt on the Westminster Bridge.

Retired window cleaner Leslie Rhodes, a seventy-five-year-old described by friends as a "lovely man," dies instantly, as does forty-four-year-old Londoner Aysha Frade, a mother of two on her way to pick up her children.

Romanian tourist Andreea Cristea, thirty-one, who had recently taken a glamorous nighttime photo on the bridge with the Thames and London Eye as a backdrop, cannot get out of the way as the Hyundai barrels closer. Given no choice, Cristea leaps over the side, falling eighty feet into the swift, cold Thames. She is knocked unconscious as she strikes the water. And though the thirty-one-year-old tourist will be rescued from the current by a river cruise boat, she will die at the hospital.

And still the ISIS driver keeps going. The terrorist is using a technique known as "vehicle ramming." That lethal action has become popular around the world for the ease and simplicity with which it can be executed. There is little chance of detection beforehand by law enforcement, no bomb or gun being required. This leads authorities to dub vehicle ramming as the "poor man's weapon of mass destruction." All that's needed is a car, a crowd, and a terrorist unafraid to step on the gas and drive straight at other human beings for as long as he is able. Between 2014 and 2017 there are seventeen such terror attacks, leading to 173 fatalities and 667 injuries.[*]

The Hyundai's driver is Khalid Masood, fifty-two, born in Britain as Adrian Elms. He converted to Islam and changed his name after being sent to prison for selling drugs, where he became radicalized. Masood has made a pilgrimage to Mecca and identifies

---

[*] The tactic of vehicle ramming has now become popular in the United States. Dozens of attacks occur annually, including the one in Charlottesville, Virginia, in 2017. The use of a car to kill was first invented by the Hamas terrorist organization for use against the Israelis, but it is also known that the Soviet Union has long committed murder with vehicles, such as the attempted assassination of General George S. Patton in 1945, as chronicled in *Killing Patton*.

with ISIS. He is old for a terrorist, most of whom are under thirty. Masood believes that he will die a martyr for his faith, feted as he arrives in paradise.

But while Masood's life has been chaotic, filled with drugs and police altercations, his preparation for today's terror attack has been meticulous. Two days ago, he performed reconnaissance on the bridge, walking his kill zone on foot. Mass murders are an act of jihad to Masood, done in accordance with the Koran as opposition to Western coalition forces fighting ISIS in Syria and Iraq.

Eighty-two seconds after his murder spree begins, Masood is shot dead by London police. He has killed six. As he hoped, word of the heinous act travels around the world, enhancing the brutal reputation of ISIS.

✦ ✦ ✦

The terror attack in London gains the attention of a very powerful person. "A great American, Kurt Cochran, was killed in the London terror attack," the recently elected American president, Donald Trump, announces on Twitter. "My prayers and condolences are with his family and friends."

Although ISIS sees the reaction, it does not process it realistically. Abu Bakr al-Baghdadi still believes his terror organization is winning the jihad.

When London mayor Sadiq Khan says the deadly attacks "are part and parcel of living in a great global city," President Trump returns to Twitter.

"You've got to be kidding me," he types. The president's statement infuriates his opponents, who accuse him of using the terror attacks for political gain.

And he may be. But there is no question the United States is changing how it will fight the war on terror.

There is, indeed, a new sheriff in town.

CHAPTER TEN

MAY 21, 2017
RIYADH, SAUDI ARABIA
EVENING

Donald Trump is uneasy.

The seventy-year-old American president stands at a massive lectern here at the King Abdul Aziz International Conference Center. His words echo in the cavernous hall as he speaks slowly, enunciating carefully. Chandeliers hang from the ceiling. A line of flags decorates the stage behind, each from a different Muslim nation as well as the United States, as befits this "Arab Islamic American Summit." An audience numbering fifty Middle Eastern leaders reclines in large leather chairs as President Trump delivers a well-crafted message of peace. The president prefers to speak extemporaneously, but his remarks tonight are so important that he patiently sticks to the script, reading from a speech that required five drafts to perfect.*

"A better future is only possible if your nations drive out the terrorists and extremists. Drive. Them. Out."

Since taking office four months ago yesterday, Mr. Trump has repeatedly attacked "radical Islamic terrorism." He is advocating an

---

* Trump policy adviser Stephen Miller wrote the president's speech with the help of several White House aides. The identity of the speechwriters was a mystery for some time because the tone was such a gross departure from the president's normal orations.

"America First" foreign policy. Also, he has publicly stated that "defeating ISIS and other radical Islamic terror groups will be our highest priority." Since his inauguration the president has kept the focus on ISIS, mentioning the terrorists in more than two dozen speeches. He has also put into place a travel ban, denying Muslims and other citizens from seven countries visas to enter the United States because of security reasons.*

So, there is no doubt that America's allies in the Middle East are wary of both Trump's rhetoric and his tendency to view many Muslims as terrorists. They are aware that Mr. Trump has openly criticized his predecessor, Barack Obama, for his reluctance to use the words "radical Islamic terrorism." Mr. Trump sees that as weakness toward the jihad. The audience tonight also knows the president once stated, "I think Islam hates us." For these reasons, Mr. Trump is moderating his words now, even calling Islam "one of the world's greatest faiths."

Now the president lashes out at ISIS, taking care to describe the group as a threat to everyone in the audience.

"DRIVE THEM OUT of your places of worship.

"DRIVE THEM OUT of your communities.

"DRIVE THEM OUT of your holy land, and

"DRIVE THEM OUT OF THIS EARTH."

The president is tall, six foot two, with a strong stage presence. His blond daughter, Ivanka, sits on the dais behind him in a lavender business suit, hands crossed on her lap, listening intently. Her husband, Jared Kushner, a presidential adviser, is seated by her side.

President Trump continues. "For our part, America is committed to adjusting our strategies to meet evolving threats and new facts. . . . Will we be indifferent in the presence of evil? Will we protect our citizens from its violent ideology? Will we let its venom spread through our societies? Will we let it destroy the most holy sites on earth? If we do not confront this deadly terror, we know what the future will bring—more suffering and despair. But if we act—if we leave this magnificent room unified and determined to do what it

---

* Those seven countries are Iran, Iraq, Libya, Somalia, Sudan, Syria, and Yemen.

takes to destroy the terror that threatens the world—then there is no limit to the great future our citizens will have."

The president knows he must emphasize unity with the Muslim world. Saudi Arabia is the birthplace of Islam and home to two of its holiest sites—Mecca and Medina. Without the support of nations like Saudi Arabia, his battles with Abu Bakr al-Baghdadi and Qasem Soleimani will be more difficult to win. In fact, Mr. Trump hopes the Muslim leaders in the audience will actively join the fight. He calls ISIS "foot soldiers of evil" and reminds the crowd that "if we do not stand in uniform condemnation of this killing, then we not only will be judged by our people, not only will we be judged by history, but we will be judged by God."*

The president speaks for thirty-three minutes. Some in the audience are dressed in traditional Arab robes, while others are in business attire. Mr. Trump's tendency toward bombast is nowhere to be seen as he speaks in a voice so measured that some in the crowd even yawn.

"God bless your countries," he concludes. "And God bless the United States of America."

The applause is polite but not enthusiastic. However, some notice an unusual thing: the words "radical Islamic terror" have not been mentioned.

✦ ✦ ✦

Death is near.

It is 10:20 p.m. in the British Midlands, slightly more than twenty-four hours after President Trump's speech in Saudi Arabia. American pop singer Ariana Grande finishes her concert encore in front of an adoring crowd. Her Dangerous Woman Tour is a big hit, and the massive Manchester Arena is packed with an audience of 14,200—a very large portion of them young teenage girls.

Mothers and fathers crowd into the large arena foyer known as the City Room, awaiting the end of the show, when they will pick up their daughters to drive them home. The outer area is spacious and

---

* Donald Trump is a Presbyterian who occasionally attends services.

open, with high ceilings, very much like the arrivals hall at a large airport. This is the most popular exit in the building, with many concertgoers leaving through the glass doors and heading straight across the courtyard to the local railway station.

The foyer is at the opposite end of the arena from the stage. Those wishing to beat the crowds rush out first, even before Ms. Grande's final notes come to an end. Unknowingly, they pass a solitary man wearing black clothing and a hefty backpack. He has just come out of the toilet at the nearby train station, where he wired the bomb hidden within his pack, priming it for detonation. He leaves the stall just fifty-eight seconds before two British Transport Police officers conduct a security sweep of the lavatory.

But the mysterious man has not gone unnoticed. The solitary individual loitering in the lobby, making sure to sit in the blind spot of a security camera, has the appearance of being from North Africa or the Middle East. In fact, he is of Libyan ancestry. But no one questions the man "for fear of being branded a racist," in the words of one eighteen-year-old arena security guard.

One concert hall staff member even approaches two Manchester police patrolling the lobby about the mystery man, but the officers are more concerned with a drunk female patron. The cops, the staff member will recall, "didn't seem that interested" in the terror threat.

But there *is* concern. A local man named Neil Hatfield, whose four daughters are inside the show, is alarmed by the sight of the man in black protecting his large rucksack. "The bag," Hatfield will later tell reporters, "was massive and it was solid . . . I thought suicide bomber, straight away, with very little doubt in my mind. Honestly, my heart was racing as soon as I saw him."

But the Manchester police have left the foyer to direct traffic outside. Arena security guards are concerned with the crush of spectators who will fill the City Room just moments from now. Hatfield tries to get their attention, but watches helplessly as the man in black hoists the rucksack onto his shoulders and begins walking to the center of the room.

Another concerned father confronts the intruder. "What are you doing?" asks Christopher Wild, a Manchester local here to pick up his daughters.

"I'm waiting for somebody, mate," comes the response. "Have you got the time?"

Noting the lack of police in the foyer, Hatfield and Wild continue to vigorously warn security guards, but are ignored.

Inside the arena, the music comes to an end. The time is 10:30. A next wave of the crowd passes into the foyer as the roar of applause dies down. Concertgoers still riding the adrenaline high of the loud, fast-paced show flood through the arena doors, eager to be on their way. Tonight is Monday, and morning brings work and school.

Soon, the foyer is filled.

At 10:31, the assassin presses his thumb down on the detonator.

Rather than just explosives, twenty-two-year-old Salman Ramadan Abedi has filled the blue Karrimor backpack with sharp pieces of metal. Once the bomb blows, this shrapnel flies through the air, maiming and killing in a manner no less lethal than an artillery shell exploding on a battlefield. The blast radius is sixty-six feet, a swath encompassing a third of the foyer. In an instant, twenty-two people are killed and a staggering eight hundred wounded. Sixty ambulances will be needed to shuttle victims to every available hospital. The youngest casualty is an eight-year-old girl who lives for an hour after traumatic injuries to her legs lead to an enormous loss of blood. "Am I going to die?" she asks a paramedic as an ambulance takes her to the hospital.

Many of the wounded and killed are not much older.

Among the dead is the bomber himself. Soon, British intelligence shares the name of Ramadan Abedi with its US counterparts, standard operating procedure in the global war on terror. The Brits want the information kept secret, so as not to alert possible terrorist cohorts. Abedi is known to have a long history of association with terror groups, beginning at the age of fifteen, including al-Qaeda and ISIS. Despite this, he successfully applied for a $3,000 student loan funded by British taxpayers, using the money to build his bomb.

But within hours, someone leaks the confidential information to the media. The *New York Times* immediately publishes it, along with photos of the bombing site. When criticized for doing that, the *Times* is unrepentant, claiming First Amendment privilege.

In response, Manchester police immediately cease sharing any information. British prime minister Theresa May publicly scolds President Trump over the leak. This unwittingly gives ISIS an advantage. The killers well know that if Britain and America cannot share information, the potential for terrorists to slip through the cracks is enormous.

Speaking from a NATO summit in Belgium, President Trump deflects the leak fiasco and speaks only of the "evil losers" who committed the Manchester bombing.

ISIS is quick to claim responsibility.

✦ ✦ ✦

President Donald J. Trump is exhausted. It is Monday morning, one week after his speech in Saudi Arabia. Air Force One finally brought him back to America last night. He hits a button on the side of the Resolute desk in the Oval Office. Almost instantly, a glass of Diet Coke with ice is brought to him—one of at least a dozen he will drink today. Mr. Trump has just received his daily intelligence briefing, which includes the latest information on ISIS. Secretary of Defense James Mattis spoke at the United States Military Academy's graduation ceremonies over the weekend, reminding the newly minted second lieutenants that "we must never permit murderers to define our time or warp our sense of normal."

Mattis, speaking for the Trump administration, followed up on those comments with an appearance on CBS News's *Face the Nation*, stating that the US policy toward ISIS is no longer "attrition" but is now "annihilation."

Despite traveling for ten days, President Trump quickly returns to his normal routine after arriving home. He stays up until 3:00 a.m., watching news shows and following Twitter. He sleeps in his own bedroom. He currently lives alone in the White House on the building's upper floors, but his wife, Melania, and eleven-year-old son, Barron, are moving from New York City to Washington in two weeks. The president will continue sleeping alone, preferring they stay in separate rooms due to his fondness for late hours. When Mr. Trump is hungry, he picks up the phone and orders a burger from the White House kitchen—which is open twenty-four hours a day.

The president rises at about seven. He does not eat breakfast, nor does he drink coffee. By 10:00 a.m. he has gone downstairs from the residence to begin work in the Oval Office, where he receives his media and intelligence reports. At approximately 12:30, lunch is served. The president prefers shrimp salad and other comfort foods. He tends to eat very quickly. Then it's back to the office for meetings until 4:30. Afterward, Mr. Trump returns phone calls until at least 7:00 p.m. The president abstains from alcohol, so there is no "happy hour" in the Trump White House.

It is this way almost every day and night. Donald Trump does not change his schedule unless he is traveling or stepping away for a round of golf.

Along with the economy and illegal immigration, fighting terror is a top priority for Donald Trump. The battle is personal for him. Shortly after the 9/11 attack in New York City, he was criticized for stating that a Wall Street property he owned had become the tallest building in Manhattan when the World Trade Center was destroyed. But that unguarded remark was forgotten when he toured the rubble two days later. Looking visibly upset, private citizen Trump told a reporter, "This is a terrible thing for the world." Donald Trump personally knew people who were among the 2,606 killed in the World Trade Center collapse. Thus, emotion often drove his public statements about radical Islamic terrorism.

During his presidential campaign, Mr. Trump said there were "thousands" of Muslims celebrating the 9/11 attack. "I watched in Jersey City," he claimed, "thousands upon thousands were cheering." Subsequently, in a TV interview with Bill O'Reilly, the journalist challenged that statement.

"No videotape of thousands of people celebrating," O'Reilly told candidate Trump in a December 3, 2015, interview. "It doesn't exist. And we really looked everywhere. I mean, it's just not there."

"You don't know that there weren't, Bill," Trump shot back.

"I was here. I was reporting. And believe me, if there were thousands, it would have been reported," O'Reilly said.

"This article says that they were 'swarming.' Bill, this article says they were swarming all over the place. So, I don't know what that means, but it means a lot of people," Trump argued.*

"There were some people, not thousands," replied O'Reilly.

"You don't know that, Bill. Bill, you don't know that. Bill, you don't know that," Trump stated.

O'Reilly concluded the discussion: "As a man who wants the most powerful position in the world, you've got to kind of be careful in those speeches."

It is a lesson Donald Trump would take seriously while speaking in Saudi Arabia but would ignore in other venues.

Seven days after Trump takes office on January 20, 2017, he signs Executive Order 13769, which restricts citizens of Iran, Iraq, Libya, Somalia, Sudan, Syria, and Yemen from entering the United States for ninety days.† The order also cuts back acceptance of Muslim refugees seeking asylum. Immediately, the press accuses the president of being "anti-Muslim." He does not care. The new president is a man who bridles at criticism but does not change because of it. In his mind, the Muslim world is basically hostile to American interests. Mr. Trump is from the "if you're not with us, you're against us" school of diplomacy. Simply put, he is deeply suspicious of and sometimes hostile to the Muslim world.‡

✦ ✦ ✦

It is evening on June 4, 2017. The past two weeks have seen the Trump presidency almost completely focused on the war on terror: the speech in Riyadh, the Manchester bombing, the president's decision to taunt Middle Eastern terrorists by moving the American

---

* The article was a printout from the Breitbart News Network, a conservative commentary website.

† The executive order was based on security concerns in those nations.

‡ Bill O'Reilly chronicles Donald Trump's feelings toward Muslims in his book *The United States of Trump*.

embassy in Israel from Tel Aviv to Jerusalem, and now yet another vehicle ramming in London two days ago.

This time, three jihadis in a van ran over pedestrians on London Bridge, then crashed their vehicle on the south bank of the Thames; fleeing into a crowded marketplace, they begin stabbing innocent shoppers. Before London police shot them dead, the three followers of ISIS murdered eight people and injured forty-six others.

Now President Trump stands on the stage at Washington's Ford's Theatre. Another president, Abraham Lincoln, was murdered here in 1865, the victim of an act of terror. The box in which he was shot looks down on the stage as Mr. Trump begins to speak. He wears a tuxedo and stands behind a podium bearing the presidential seal, his wife, Melania, standing to his left. He has recently renewed his Twitter attacks against London mayor Sadiq Khan in the aftermath of the London Bridge attack, driving a deeper wedge between Britain and America.

But now Donald Trump not only makes it clear that he stands with Britain in this difficult time but publicly states that he is fed up. The time has come to declare all-out war on ISIS.

"America sends our thoughts and prayers and our deepest sympathies to the victims of this evil slaughter and we renew our resolve, stronger than ever before, to protect the United States and its allies from a vile enemy that has waged war on innocent life, and it's gone on too long," the president states.

"This bloodshed must end. This bloodshed *will* end."

But not immediately.

CHAPTER ELEVEN

OCTOBER 31, 2017
NEW YORK CITY
7:00 P.M.

Bizarre things are happening in Gotham.

Pounding drums and drag queens. Papier-mâché skeletons forty feet tall. Families dressed like Teletubbies. Marching bands. Stilts. Zombies, unicorns, handmaidens, Wonder Women.

It is Halloween in the Big Apple, where the annual tradition since 1974 is an outlandish parade. Fifty thousand costumed marchers now begin the festive walk up Sixth Avenue, some fueled by alcohol and the musical downbeat. Spectators line the broad thoroughfare, eager to witness the raucous spectacle.

But the parade was almost canceled, and many believe it should be. Just four hours ago and less than one mile away, New York City experienced its worst terror attack since 9/11. Today's disaster comes five months after another vehicle ramming—this one in Times Square—in which a lone criminal drove into a thick crowd of pedestrians.*

In addition, an ISIS-sponsored magazine called *Rumiyah* continues

---

* One person was killed and twenty wounded when US Navy veteran Richard Rojas drove his Honda Accord into the crowd. The attack was at first presumed to be the work of a terrorist organization, but Rojas later indicated he had ingested PCP beforehand and wanted to die by "suicide by cop." He did not get his wish. Rojas is pleading insanity to second-degree murder charges and is being held in a New York jail. He has yet to go to trial.

to encourage its followers to use trucks, when possible, to launch even more attacks. ISIS handlers around the world spend their days at keyboards communicating with would-be terrorists, methodically feeding a recruit's deranged desire to develop local networks or carry out attacks in their own countries. Terrorists who choose to become car killers are encouraged to subsequently leap from vehicles and stab people to death. Potential terrorists are also encouraged to carry ISIS leaflets, to show their fidelity.

In fact, ISIS media outlet the Centre Médiatique an-Nur ("The Light"), based in France, has been boasting that a killing spree will take place on Halloween—even going so far as to announce the pending murders on ISIS Twitter accounts. This attack could take place anywhere in the world, in keeping with the "kill where you are" philosophy the terrorist group encourages in its vast online following.

In the aftermath of this afternoon's attack, New York City police are carrying automatic weapons to protect the parade. Fifty thousand marchers is a "target-rich environment"—and the cops know it.

✦ ✦ ✦

At 2:06 this afternoon, as children are being let out of school to celebrate Halloween, an ISIS terrorist completes a pickup truck rental at a Home Depot store in Passaic, New Jersey. His name is Sayfullo Saipov, and he is twenty-nine years old, a legal resident of the United States, though born in Uzbekistan. Federal officials are aware of the young man's ties to terror groups, and even though several men of Uzbek heritage were recently arrested because of alleged ISIS involvement, Saipov was not among them. He lives in New Jersey and makes his living as an Uber driver.

Had Saipov purchased large amounts of fertilizer and diesel fuel—two combustible agents used in the 1995 Oklahoma City bombing that killed 168 people—it would have been cause for alarm. But renting a simple pickup truck concerns no one.

At 2:43 p.m., Saipov enters Manhattan by crossing the George Washington Bridge. Within twenty minutes, the terrorist arrives at Houston Street, in full view of the Hudson River.

Calmly, he veers onto a bike path parallel to the river. He then steps on the gas. For the next mile, the terrorist runs over joggers, cyclists, walkers, and anyone else out for a leisurely Tuesday-afternoon stroll. Eight people die, their last shocking moments defined by the sight of a truck driven by a man with a long black beard, intentionally coming right at them.

Four minutes later, where the bike path crosses the road at Chambers Street, the ISIS terrorist crashes into a school bus transporting children with special needs. He leaps from the pickup truck wielding a paintball gun and pellet gun, while screaming "Allahu Akbar."

No one is scared. The guns don't look real, and today is Halloween. Eyewitnesses believe they are seeing a man *pretending* to be a terrorist.

This delusion is short lived. The carnage on the bike path is obvious. Social-media posts quickly alert the world. New York City police officers respond, and Saipov is shot in the abdomen.

As of this writing, Sayfullo Saipov is still in prison, awaiting his day in court. *

✦ ✦ ✦

In the face of this brutal attack, New Yorkers are defiant. They have endured 9/11 and persevered. They will not let terror dictate their lives. So it is that the Village Halloween parade is *not* canceled. Though the party mood is more subdued than usual, the spectacle will proceed.

"Life has to go on," one parade participant, wearing a wedding dress, tells the press.

✦ ✦ ✦

Far away, Abu Bakr al-Baghdadi is very pleased by events in New York. Life has not been good for the ISIS leader, and he is badly in

---

* Saipov is being held at the Metropolitan Correctional Center in Manhattan. He has indicated willingness to agree to a plea bargain and to serve a life sentence in prison so long as the death penalty is not a consequence of his actions. Until July 2, 2021, when Attorney General Merrick Garland suspended all federal executions, federal prosecutors were insistent on seeking the death penalty for Saipov, leading to lengthy delays in his trial.

need of some victories. Just recently, it was reported that al-Baghdadi was killed in Syria by a Russian air strike, but in fact the brutal terrorist dodged yet another proverbial bullet. However, al-Baghdadi knows his caliphate is shrinking and that he himself is in grave danger. He is on the run not only from Western coalition forces but also from Muslim terrorists in Iran.

Iraqi government forces recently retook the ISIS stronghold of Mosul—though not before al-Baghdadi ordered the complete destruction of the Grand Mosque in that city, the scene of his long oratory in 2014. In addition, coalition forces are slowly recapturing other towns in northern Syria. It is there, in the area around Raqqa, that the remaining ISIS holdouts are dug in.

But while actual territory is being lost, the worldwide threat level brought about by al-Baghdadi's clever use of social media means that ISIS-inspired terror attacks continue to rise. Just today, a suicide bomber in Kabul, Afghanistan, murdered eight people in the name of ISIS.

The psychopathic al-Baghdadi feels only for himself. Since the missile attack targeting him a couple of years ago, he has ignored his personal appearance, gaining about fifty pounds and letting his beard grow unkempt. Al-Baghdadi is under tremendous pressure. He well understands the brutality he has ordered and the consequences of those actions if he is caught.

But Allah will surely protect his servant, or so al-Baghdadi believes.

A reckoning, however, is coming.

CHAPTER TWELVE

General Qasem Soleimani is enjoying vengeance.

He is in Syria, overseeing battlefield strategy, and this morning he writes to Iran's supreme leader, the ayatollah Seyyed Ali Khamenei, confirming a great triumph over ISIS. This is not just a strategic victory—it is payback for a humiliating strike into the heart of Tehran.

It is Monday, and the people of Iran start the morning with outstanding news of Iranian forces capturing a significant ISIS stronghold over the weekend. The citadel at Abu Kamal was the last significant town in Syria held by the Islamic State. Not surprisingly, photos of Soleimani commanding troops on the front lines were splashed across Iranian media. The general looks calm, even professorial, wearing a black jacket and a pair of olive drab binoculars as he surveys the action, surrounded by bodyguards in combat uniforms.

Tehran is jubilant about his most recent victory. November is perhaps the best time of year in the metropolitan vicinity, one of the most populous in the world at fourteen million residents. The Iranian capital is known for its traffic jams and air pollution so thick that respiratory problems are common. There is also a constant earthquake threat, due to Tehran's location atop the deepest seismic fault in the Middle East.

Until today, there was also another threat: the Islamic State.

✦ ✦ ✦

Five months ago, seven ISIS terrorists launched a surprise attack within the Iranian capital. Some of the fighters even infiltrated the Iranian Parliament. Others desecrated a lavish mausoleum containing the bodies of great Iranians like the Ayatollah Khomeini, the religious leader who overthrew the shah of Iran in 1979. Seventeen Iranians were killed and forty-three wounded—the first act of ISIS terror on Persian soil. The killings caused such a shock that the city of Paris, so hard hit by ISIS, showed sympathy for the Iranian victims by turning off the lights of the Eiffel Tower for a moment of mourning.

Now Qasem Soleimani is extracting revenge.

"Claiming to be defending Islam," the general writes about the Syrian victory, "over six thousand misled youths blew themselves up in suicide attacks with explosives-laden vehicles near squares, mosques, schools or even hospitals and public sites for Muslims."

Then, amazingly, Soleimani pivots. After placing the blame on ISIS for the conflict, he directs his energy at Iran's greatest enemy: the United States of America.

"All of these crimes were plotted and carried out by the leaders and organizations tied to the US, and this approach is still being pursued and implemented by the current US officials."*

Soleimani continues: "As a soldier commissioned by your Excellency in this battlefield, I declare the end of the dominion of this accursed and malignant tree with the conclusion of the liberation operations . . . and by pulling down the flag of this US-Zionist group and raising the Syrian flag and on behalf of all the commanders and unknown fighters.

"Victory comes only from God Almighty, the Wise.

---

* Soleimani pushed the outlandish theory that ISIS had the backing of Israeli and US governments.

"Your son and soldier

"Qasem Soleimani"

✦ ✦ ✦

The revenge Soleimani is celebrating has its origins on June 7, 2017—just another Wednesday in Tehran. The metro is filled with commuters, and the streets are tangled in the usual traffic. The rule of the Revolutionary Guard and Qasem Soleimani is repressive but has also produced a sense of security. The people of Tehran give no thought to groups like ISIS.

This is a mistake.

As the Iranian Parliament building opens for business, people waiting for paperwork to be processed sit in a small room near the main entrance. The time is 11:09 a.m., and the 290 members of the parliament are just beginning the daily session. Outside, the sun is shining.

Suddenly, four ISIS fighters wielding pistols and Kalashnikov automatic weapons burst into the waiting room, waving their guns and yelling in Farsi. People run and dive under chairs as the shooting begins. The terrorists have concealed their guns by wearing women's clothing. On the floors above, employees lock their office doors and barricade themselves inside. Members of parliament hear the gunfire but are confused by its meaning. At 12:56, one of the terrorists detonates a suicide vest.

The other ISIS fighters take hostages and wait. But not for long.

By midafternoon they are all dead. Iranian special forces stormed into the parliament building, saved the hostages, and shot down the three remaining ISIS assailants. It was a flawless rescue.

✦ ✦ ✦

One hour later, at a large cemetery south of Tehran, two more ISIS terrorists attack the large mausoleum holding the remains of the Ayatollah Khomeini and his family, as well as several other prominent Iranian leaders. A female suicide bomber blows herself up, even as security guards gun down a male terrorist brandishing an AK-47.

✦ ✦ ✦

ISIS immediately claims responsibility for the attacks. The Iranian Revolutionary Guard rounds up suspects. For Qasem Soleimani, it is clear that such an attack did not happen without planning. The terrorists must have been in place for months, surveilling their targets and obtaining weapons. Soleimani is determined to prevent such an incident from ever happening again.

Meanwhile, American president Donald J. Trump fans the flames of US-Iran conflict with his personal response to the attacks: "We grieve and pray for the innocent victims of the terrorist attacks in Iran, and for the Iranian people, who are going through such challenging times," Trump says.

"We underscore that states that sponsor terrorism risk falling victim to the evil they promote."

✦ ✦ ✦

It has been five months since ISIS attacked Tehran. And now the endgame is in motion.

Operation Fajr-3 (Dawn 3), as the assault on Abu Kamal is known, begins on October 23, 2017. Abu Kamal is a city of brown homes and flat roofs on the Euphrates River, located in eastern Syria, near the border with Iraq. Elements of the Syrian and Russian military, along with the radical Iranian-backed terrorist group Hezbollah, work together with the Revolutionary Guard as a belligerent attacking force. ISIS took control of the city after a three-month siege in 2014, and citizens have suffered grievously ever since, enduring the same beatings, rapes, and beheadings as those in other cities occupied by ISIS.

So far, more than a thousand members of Iran's Islamic Revolutionary Guard have been killed in this campaign. Yet the results please Soleimani a great deal. It was the general who sent Quds forces into Syria to prop up the faltering government of President Bashar al-Assad two years ago. Then, Soleimani accomplished a diplomatic coup—he convinced Russia to fight against Syrian rebel factions supported by the United States.

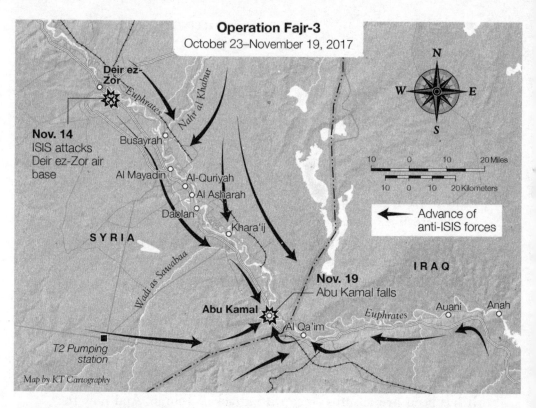

Operation Fajr-3
October 23–November 19, 2017

Deir ez-Zor
Euphrates
Nahr al Khabur

Nov. 14
ISIS attacks
Deir ez-Zor air
base

Busayrah

Al Mayadin

Al-Quriyah

Al Asharah

Dablan

Khara'ij

S Y R I A

Wadi as Sawabaa

Nov. 19
Abu Kamal falls

I R A Q

Abu Kamal

Al Qa'im

Euphrates

Auani

Anah

*T2 Pumping
station*

Map by KT Cartography

10   0   10   20 Miles

10   0   10   20 Kilometers

→ Advance of
anti-ISIS forces

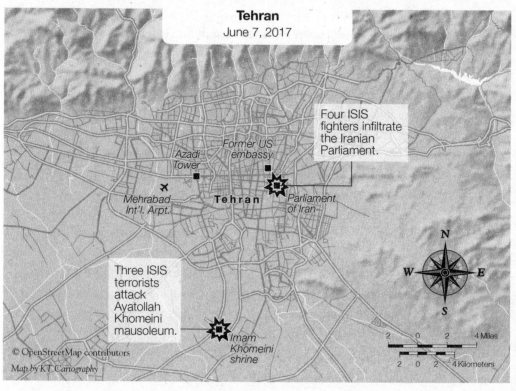

Tehran
June 7, 2017

Four ISIS
fighters infiltrate
the Iranian
Parliament.

*Azadi
Tower*

*Former US
embassy*

✕
*Mehrabad
Int'l. Arpt.*

T e h r a n

*Parliament
of Iran*

Three ISIS
terrorists
attack
Ayatollah
Khomeini
mausoleum.

*Imam
Khomeini
shrine*

© OpenStreetMap contributors

Map by KT Cartography

2   0   2   4 Miles

2   0   2   4 Kilometers

The fighting for Abu Kamal is slow in the early days of the battle. But it picks up after Soleimani arrives from Iran.

As is his style, the general arranges for his picture to be taken at the front. "The renowned Iranian Major General Qasem Soleimani has once again shown up on the Syrian battlefield," states an Arab news service. The article includes "leaked" photos of Soleimani surrounded by enthusiastic Syrian soldiers in camouflage uniforms. "This time to help the Syrian Arab Army (SAA) crush the last Islamic State Forces."

The mere presence of Soleimani bolsters the attack. Even as the pitched fighting goes back and forth, it is clear that his return to the battlefield is an inspiration. The stalled advance on Abu Kamal resumes anew.

Meanwhile, Abu Bakr al-Baghdadi knows he is losing the battle but accesses Western social media to place propaganda.

"Islamic State Leader Reported in Syrian Town," states the Reuters news service on November 10, completely missing the real story that is taking place.

The truth is, even though the terror group is on the defensive, ISIS remains a threat because it has heavy weapons and money—much of it accumulated by selling oil stolen from Iraq.*

However, Soleimani's coalition is far too much for the ISIS terrorists, who are just days away from capitulation. But before that happens, there is one final gruesome display.

✦ ✦ ✦

On November 14, four ISIS terrorists of Chechen descent breach the security perimeter at Syria's Deir ez-Zor air base. The facility is built in barren desert, with Russian fighter jets shielded from satellite cameras overhead by concealed hangars. It is from this location

---

* The black-market sale of ISIS oil begins with trucks leaving ISIS-held refineries in Iraq and Syria, then transporting their cargo into neighboring Turkey. Unrefined crude is bought at $25 per barrel and sold for twice that much. Russia has claimed that Turkey and Israel were key ISIS oil consumers. Those charges are unproven. Once crude oil was transported into Turkey, it was shipped on to Europe and China—indistinguishable from "legal" gas and oil products produced in nations such as Saudi Arabia.

that Russia launched a raid on an ISIS training base recently, killing two hundred men.

Speaking Russian with guards at the gate and dressed in Russian uniforms, the ISIS terrorists enter the facility and explode suicide vests. Fifty-eight Syrian Army soldiers are killed and several Russian aircraft destroyed. In a video shot before the attack, the four ISIS men are shown on camera praying and preparing for their deadly mission. They are fresh-faced teenagers, fair-haired and of European appearance, smiling into the camera, chatting amiably with their comrades.

The attackers die needlessly. The murders they commit do not affect the outcome of the battle for Abu Kamal; the city falls less than one week later. In the aftermath, al-Baghdadi has vanished—he is still alive and already plotting more murder.

✦ ✦ ✦

Seven thousand miles away, US Central Intelligence Agency director Mike Pompeo is assessing the situation. He is attending the Reagan National Defense Forum at the Reagan Library in Simi Valley, California. Pompeo has a long history with Qasem Soleimani, dating back to his own days as an army officer in the Gulf War.

"I was a soldier," he will say. "I'd seen how if one was focused and devoted resources and understood the mission, that you could accomplish an awful lot. And then, as a member of Congress, I just watched the entire Obama administration essentially treat this terror war event in the Middle East as if it was something that we feel *bad* that we're having to do this."

Pompeo's remarks in California are delivered on December 2, 2017. It has been two weeks since General Qasem Soleimani defeated ISIS in Syria. Since then, Director Pompeo has made it clear to the general "that we will hold him and Iran accountable for any attacks on American interests in Iraq by forces that are under their control."

Pompeo tells this to the Defense Forum, which responds with surprise. The admission is bold, a deliberate public attempt to take a stand against Iranian terror. It is well known that the CIA and Director

Pompeo now have the authorization to operate independently of the Department of Defense in the war on terror; the director is free to authorize a strike whenever he pleases. The pragmatic Pompeo could very well be of a mind to attack Iran if circumstances demand. He is a former soldier, having graduated first in his class from West Point. Pompeo is well aware of the covert tactics and strategy employed by Soleimani and is quietly sure the general has planned the murders of US troops. And for this reason, Mike Pompeo will not back down.

Pompeo even goes so far as to send Soleimani a letter, which is hand-delivered to him. In the letter, he states that the United States will push back aggressively against any terror committed by Iran.

Soleimani replies: "I will not accept your letter, nor will I read it."

But the message has been delivered—the United States is definitely at war with General Qasem Soleimani.

✦ ✦ ✦

And also with Abu Bakr al-Baghdadi.

The ISIS leader has disappeared, knowing that Soleimani is closing in. Al-Baghdadi has become so careful about being caught that he often holds strategy talks with his top aides inside a minivan, surrounded by a load of fresh vegetables to remain unseen. But in an act of defiance, al-Baghdadi is making plans to murder the Iranian general.

Sunni chasing Shia; Shia chasing Sunni.

One monster after another monster.

That is not an overstatement.

CHAPTER THIRTEEN

Donald Trump wants to get both monsters.

The president of the United States stands before Congress, about to give his first State of the Union address since taking office one year ago. He wears a dark-blue suit and royal-blue tie. A small American flag pin is affixed to his left lapel. Vice President Mike Pence and Speaker of the House Paul Ryan sit directly behind Mr. Trump. The room is full, a mixture of senators, representatives, Supreme Court justices, Joint Chiefs of Staff, and a host of invited guests. The weather outside is windy and the temperature below freezing, but it is warm and stuffy inside this massive legislative chamber.

"Mr. Speaker, Mr. Vice President, members of Congress, the First Lady of the United States, and my fellow Americans," the president begins. "Less than one year has passed since I first stood at this podium, in this majestic chamber, to speak on behalf of the American people—and to address their concerns, their hopes, and their dreams."

There is much for the president to talk about this evening—from the economy to ending a nuclear arms deal with Iran that the president considers unfairly weighted against America. But while the war on terror will not be mentioned until halfway through Mr. Trump's eighty-one-minute speech, the president's initial actions show his determination to end the ISIS threat.

One year ago, in Mr. Trump's first speech to a joint session of Congress, he called for the United States to "take decisive action to defeat ISIS." He noted that "ISIS has engaged in a systematic campaign of persecution and extermination in those territories it enters or controls. If ISIS is left in power, the threat that it poses will only grow. We know it has attempted to develop chemical weapons capability. It continues to radicalize our own citizens, and its attacks against our allies and partners continue to mount."

The president also vowed that the "development of a new plan to defeat ISIS will commence immediately."

In fact, it has already been implemented.

In a series of top secret actions, President Trump authorized the dropping of the largest nonnuclear bomb ever used—directly on an ISIS training camp.* Also, he has furtively sent US troops into Syria to confront the Islamic State.

The aggressive posture has worked.

By December 2017, the ISIS caliphate lost 95 percent of its territory, including its two biggest properties: Mosul, Iraq's second-largest city, and the northern Syrian city of Raqqa, its nominal capital.

However, the attacks on American targets keep coming.

On December 11, a twenty-seven-year-old Bangladeshi native who resided in the US as a citizen was inspired by ISIS to detonate a bomb on a New York subway train during morning rush hour. "Oh, Trump," the terrorist posted to Facebook while riding the A train into Manhattan, "you fail to protect your nation."

But the electrical worker's pipe bomb fails to fully detonate due to faulty wiring. Instead, he is burned after injuring a small group of

---

* On April 13, 2017, an MC-130 aircraft dropped a GBU-43/B Massive Ordnance Air Blast Bomb (MOAB)—also known as the "mother of all bombs"—on the Islamic State in Afghanistan's Nangarhar province. The purpose was the destruction of tunnels and caves used for training and weapons storage.

bystanders. The Bangladeshi native is quickly taken into custody and confesses that he had built the bomb to serve ISIS. Akayed Ullah would also later claim that he attempted the terror attack because "he was angry with Donald Trump."*

The attack takes place at 7:20 a.m. On the same day, the president demands a new policy to keep potential terrorists out of the United States, calling for an end to what is known as "chain migration." This policy grants a path to American citizenship to direct relatives of current citizens.

One week later, Donald Trump increases pressure on the terrorists by demanding that Congress renew Section 702 of the Foreign Intelligence Surveillance Amendments Act of 2008. That law makes it possible for the United States to collect text messages and emails from non–US citizens in foreign countries. The National Security Administration is allowed to do this without a warrant or legal pretext. Trump's extension is quickly passed.

"Terrorists who do things like place bombs in civilian hospitals are evil. When possible, we annihilate them. When necessary, we must be able to detain and question them. But we must be clear: Terrorists are not merely criminals. They are unlawful enemy combatants. And when captured overseas, they should be treated like the terrorists they are."

Trump's State of the Union remarks bring a loud ovation. Both sides of the aisle stand in applause, terror being a distinctly bipartisan issue.

The president continues.

"In the past, we have foolishly released hundreds of dangerous terrorists, only to meet them again on the battlefield—including the ISIS leader al-Baghdadi."

The president concludes: "I am also asking the Congress to ensure that, in the fight against ISIS and al-Qaeda, we continue to have all necessary power to detain terrorists—wherever we chase them down."

---

* Akayed Ullah was convicted on six counts of terrorism in November 2018. He is serving a life sentence in federal prison.

✦ ✦ ✦

But President Trump does not tell the world what is *really* happening. He wraps up his speech to polite applause and leaves the building knowing that death orders have already been issued against Abu Bakr al-Baghdadi and General Qasem Soleimani. In private, Trump is adamant that all terror threats be eliminated.

All. Terror. Threats.

✦ ✦ ✦

Donald Trump's strong posture against terror is not controversial to most Americans. But overseas there *is* alarm. The United States is now acting unilaterally—something that rarely happened under President Obama.

And in their desert habitats, both al-Baghdadi and Soleimani know it.

CHAPTER FOURTEEN

Ismael al-Ethawi does not know he is being watched.

The terrorist walks through the crowded bazaar wearing a checkered head covering and three-day facial stubble. He is fifty-five years old. The ISIS courier and top lieutenant to Abu Bakr al-Baghdadi moves easily past the vending stalls, in no particular hurry to conduct his shopping. He holds a PhD in Islamic studies from the University of Anbar in his hometown of Ramadi, Iraq, and is one of five men al-Baghdadi trusts. One of al-Ethawi's key roles is selecting leaders for the ISIS command-and-control structure, but he also delivers religious messages to various ISIS factions. Al-Ethawi is in charge of issuing a fatwa—religious punishment—for those accused of breaking with their faith. In short, Ismael al-Ethawi is personally responsible for stonings, beheadings, and murdering people by throwing them off rooftops.

The terrorist fled Iraq with his wife months ago, when US and Iraqi forces recaptured Mosul. The couple arrived in Turkey and live in this small town outside Istanbul. Al-Ethawi has taken on a new identity, using the name of his brother, but an informant now recognizes him from a photograph. Quickly, Turkish authorities place him under surveillance.

What happens next to Ismael al-Ethawi is still classified. What we do know is that he is arrested. The Turks keep him in custody for a time, extracting what information they can. The terrorist is then handed over to Iraqi authorities.

It is more than likely that al-Ethawi was taken to the Iraqi Intelligence and Counter Terrorism Office's prison in Qayyarah, forty miles south of Mosul, which has a very low release rate. This facility is notorious for torture. Interrogations start with being blindfolded and beaten, then grow more medieval. One method of extracting information is to handcuff wrists behind backs, then use a rope to slowly raise the arms to the ceiling, dislocating the shoulders.

As this is taking place, the suspect is whipped on his bare back and the soles of the feet with a metal cable. Iraqi interrogators call this the "bazooka." There is also the technique of burning a man's testicles with a hot steel ruler. Often, a combination of the two is utilized, with a man hung in the bazooka position and beaten while a one-liter bottle of water is tied to his penis with a thin string, cutting deep into the flesh.

It doesn't take long for Ismael al-Ethawi to "turn." In a word, he becomes an informant.

The ISIS terrorist begins telling the Iraqis what they want to know: how he and other ISIS leaders travel freely through Syria and Iraq, including the common method of hiding within a pile of vegetables inside a minivan. He reveals the locations of al-Baghdadi's many secret homes. Curiously, he says that the ISIS chief prefers to hide within a region of Syria controlled by a new rival terror organization called Hayat Tahrir al-Sham. That crew is led by a former ISIS leader turned enemy named Abu Mohammed al-Jolani. Al-Baghdadi's hideout is located in a mountainous and poor area, far from military patrols. His compound is honeycombed with escape tunnels. In fact, the ISIS leader is behaving in precisely the same manner as Osama bin Laden—sheltering in a walled compound just outside a busy town. The Iraqis soon pass the information along to the CIA, which immediately begins the process of spying on al-Baghdadi using drones and satellites.

The information provided by al-Ethawi leads to air strikes on hidden ISIS compounds and munitions factories in Syria. Thirty-six terrorists are killed. The fact that al-Ethawi is in custody is not known to ISIS—which thinks he is still operating freely. There is absolutely no suspicion that his confession led to the bombings.

"Ethawi gave valuable information which helped the Iraqi multi-security agencies team complete the missing pieces of the puzzle of Baghdadi's movements and places he used to hide," as one Iraqi security official describes the terrorist's confession.

One thing is for certain: al-Baghdadi never suspects his whereabouts have been compromised.

But Ismael al-Ethawi is not done providing information—and what he puts forth is horrible.

✦ ✦ ✦

Skulls, bones, blue jeans, ID cards, shoes made in India.

All that is left.

Ground-penetrating radar shows signs of a mass grave, but it takes Iraqi authorities nine months to finally begin digging. ISIS has murdered so many innocent citizens that there is a waiting list to excavate these atrocities. At one site, more than five hundred rotting corpses are discovered. Here, just outside Mosul, the fatalities number thirty-nine. All are Indian citizens, among the ten thousand laborers from the Punjab region who are risking their lives rebuilding Iraq. It was four years ago that these Indians were captured and murdered by the Islamic State.

This was no kidnapping. Families back home never received a ransom demand. The black-clad ISIS fighters who captured the men on June 11, 2014, were armed with assault rifles and had little interest in extracting money from the families of poor construction workers. The Indian government has provided medicine to ISIS, asking for proof of life in return—but none has been forthcoming.

Until today, there was no word of the laborers' fate. Relatives held out hope the captured Indians were being held prisoner. That fate would have been torturous, but even the thought of loved ones in an ISIS jail was better than imagining sons and husbands dead.

Now that hope is gone.

But one man escaped. His name is Harjit Masih. He was twenty when the ISIS attack took place, a wiry, pensive man with dark black hair. He escaped and made his way back to his home village of Kala Afghana, near India's border with Pakistan. His story is simple and brutal.

Forty workers are loaded into vehicles and driven into the desert. Ten trucks of ISIS terrorists stand ready as the Indian workers arrive near a small railway beneath a hill. It is almost sunset. The captives are of the Sikh religion. Many begin to cry and promise to convert to Islam if they are spared. They will not be.

The laborers are forced to kneel side by side. The staccato thunder of Kalashnikov rifles mows the group down—all but Masih. He is struck in the thigh and plays dead, buried beneath the body of a heavy older coworker whose weight almost smothers the young electrician. The firing lasts about two minutes. Only when the ISIS combatants leave does Harjit Masih escape.*

✦ ✦ ✦

Incredibly, the government of India refused to allow him to tell his story. Some leaders did not believe that ISIS executed so many men.

But they did. And there was no burial—no attempt to conceal evidence of the mass execution. Wild dogs and buzzards feasted. Four years of sand and shifting desert wind eventually covered the mutilated corpses. The excavation shows most bodies in a line, with a few facing in a different direction, as if they had tried to run. The hunt for the ISIS killers continues. But the trail is cold.

✦ ✦ ✦

His phone is the key.

One of the first items taken from Ismael al-Ethawi when he is captured is his cell phone. With the balding terrorist's help, the Iraqis unlock the device. Systematic interrogation follows, for the phone is a treasure trove of information—names, dates, locations of ISIS meetings and safe houses. Finally, al-Ethawi reveals the identities of the ISIS leaders whose names are encoded in the device.

The interrogators are stunned. They now have the names of some

---

* This mass execution is almost identical to German SS atrocities in World War II.

of the most infamous ISIS killers. Using an app known as Telegram, which is preferred in the terror world because of the ability to encode text messages, the interrogators begin a group chat. The American and Iraqi analysts begin assembling information. None of the terrorists on the chat know they are being played. One of those men is a person of incredible savagery.

"Ethawi gave us details on five men . . . who were meeting Baghdadi inside Syria and the different locations they used," an Iraqi official will reveal.

The trap will soon be set.

✦ ✦ ✦

The ordeal of Royal Jordanian Air Force pilot Muath al-Kasasbeh shocks the world. In 2014, he is shot down over Raqqa, Syria, and captured by ISIS. Stripped of his flight gear and forced to wear an orange prison jumpsuit, the twenty-six-year-old officer is placed inside a cage. There is no chance of escaping the five-by-five cell and its thick iron bars. Video cameras film al-Kasabeh as ISIS terrorist Saddam al-Jamal sets the cage on fire. The images soon flash around the world as the screaming aviator is burned alive. It is one of the most heinous ISIS murders on record.

In the perverse world of terrorism, Saddam al-Jamal quickly becomes a celebrity. He is thirty-six at the time, a former commander in a rebel Syrian army bent on bringing down the regime of Bashar al-Assad. In 2013, he made a video announcement that he was defecting to ISIS. Al-Jamal quickly became a favorite of Abu Bakr al-Baghdadi and was selected to rule as emir of the city of Abu Kamal. It is thought that he might one day succeed al-Baghdadi. Al-Jamal is also responsible for the murder of seven hundred Syrians in 2014, and is fond of executing children as their parents watch.*

On May 10, 2018, al-Jamal makes a mistake. He responds to a text from Ismael al-Ethawi. He does not know the text is a setup.

---

* In August 2014, ISIS defeated the Shaitat tribe, which had fought to defend their home territory in eastern Syria. Led by Saddam al-Jamal, the terrorists then beheaded, shot, and crucified seven hundred tribe members over a three-day period. The bodies were left unburied.

Three other top ISIS leaders also reply to al-Ethawi, who suggests they all meet across the border in Iraq, at a safe location.

Of course, it is the CIA and Iraqi National Intelligence Service that is extending the invitation. A trap is set. As American Special Forces wait, they see four motorcycles heading toward the designated meeting site.

As the cycles roll to a stop, the ISIS leaders are arrested.

They are taken into custody and never seen publicly again.

Even today, the fates of Ismael al-Ethawi and the four others are unknown. American and Iraqi officials are reluctant to disclose this information due to a need to keep intelligence networks that routinely share data from being revealed.[*]

✦ ✦ ✦

So it is that the ISIS leadership has been severely downgraded. But more than that, the proverbial noose is being tied tight. All that remains is to put one fat neck inside of it.

---

[*] Besides al-Ethawi, they are Saddam al-Jamal, Essam Abdel Qadeer al-Zawbai, Omar Shehab al-Karbouli, Mohammed Hussein Hadar al-Qadeer. Their fates are classified. However, it is known that in November 2018, Ismael al-Ethawi was sentenced to death by hanging in Iraq. May 2019 saw Saddam al-Jamal also sentenced to hang. It is unknown whether or not these sentences have been carried out. However, in the case of al-Jamal, it is widely believed he was turned over to Jordanian authorities, who then executed him for burning Muath al-Kasasbeh to death.

CHAPTER FIFTEEN

JULY 25, 2018
HAMADAN, IRAN
DAY

General Qasem Soleimani is also being hunted.

But unlike al-Baghdadi, he is not hiding.

The general has traveled three hours from his simple home in Tehran to deliver today's political address. "The Shadow Commander," as he is nicknamed, is normally averse to public speaking. His soft tenor voice does not lend itself to dramatics. Most everything about Soleimani is mysterious—and he prefers it that way. Movies have been written about his life and pop songs praise his name. Yet the most famous man in Iran is so private that he will not release the name of his wife to the public. The *Tehran Times* is not sure whether he has four children or five.* Some say he even has a black belt in karate. But Soleimani will neither confirm nor deny a single fact about his life.

Yet now is the time for Soleimani to come out of the shadows. The general and the ayatollahs who run Iran are involved in a heated

---

* In reality, Soleimani has three sons and two daughters. His oldest daughter, Nargis, was once a source of concern to the general, having moved to Malaysia and reportedly drifted from the Muslim lifestyle. His youngest daughter, Zeinab, married a Hezbollah guerrilla leader in 2020.

controversy with President Donald J. Trump. On May 8, Mr. Trump ended the Iranian nuclear treaty, despite global fears that Iran will accelerate its weapons program. The president has threatened war if it does.

Qasem Soleimani has been chosen to deliver Iran's response. His words must be forceful and specific.

A male-only crowd packs the auditorium at the Hamadan air base. They wear Western-style clothing and all but a few sit on the floor, legs crossed. Many cover their heads with an *araqchin*, the traditional Muslim skull cap. They are keen to hear the great general's response to the hated Americans—gaping as if they are in the presence of a great celebrity.

General Soleimani steps to the microphone. He wears a green uniform with a beige-and-black kaffiyeh draped over his epaulets. He refers to himself as "the smallest soldier," having long ago come to terms with his short stature. He often prays that he be allowed to martyr himself in the name of Islam and Iran. So, the general does not fear President Trump, nor the potential deadly outcome of the speech he is about to give—even though it *could* cost him his life.

The general begins calmly. "The US president, in response to statements by *our* president, made some idiotic comments on Twitter. It is beneath the dignity of the president of the great Islamic country of Iran to respond, so I will respond, as a soldier of our great nation."

✦ ✦ ✦

Qasem Soleimani invents his own legend of humble origins and commitment to toughness. And it begins with karate, all those years ago.

Soleimani wants the world to believe he was once obsessed with the sport.

Nineteen seventy-eight. The workday is over. Along with his cousin, Ahmad, he rides his secondhand bicycle through the streets of Kerman to the mosque. He knows religious education is important but would much prefer they head to the dojo, where the art of karate awaits. His small stature is a source of irritation to the young man, and he feels that these workouts elevate him in the eyes of others.

The young Qasem is the oldest son and second child of a fruit grower. But his father, Hassan, has taken out an agricultural loan from the government and gone heavily into debt. So, at age thirteen, Qasem leaves the family village in Qanat Molk, where the Soleimanis have lived for two centuries. He takes a job at a construction site to help his parents. He has little formal education and soon leaves that job for employment with a local water district, rising to the role of supervisor in a few short months. "At night, we couldn't fall asleep with the sadness of thinking that government agents were coming to arrest our fathers," he will write of his desperation to raise the 900 *toman*—about $100—needed to repay the family debt.

Once inside the Kerman mosque, the young man feels at home. He attends sermons preached by Seyyed Ali Hosseini Khamenei, a radical imam. Soleimani himself is becoming radicalized. The pull of religion and self-mastery learned in the dojo give him enormous inner strength.

Iran is now caught up in a religious revolution pitting the longtime monarchy, led by the shah, against the exiled Muslim cleric, Ayatollah Ruhollah Khomeini.* Qasem sympathizes with the ayatollah. His father's debts were brought on by the shah's monetary policies, plus the shah is supported by the despised United States of America. Qasem Soleimani admires the discipline of the Shia holy men and their patriotic desire to make Iran an unrivaled Middle Eastern power. In 1979, shortly after the shah flees into exile, Qasem chooses to become a soldier.

Life in the Revolutionary Guard suits the young man. He proves himself adept at command. His karate skills and muscular physical appearance are noticed. Soleimani is invited to an elite training camp for deep indoctrination into the new Iran's political, religious, and military policies. He excels, showing his toughness by refusing to take sick leave, even after being accidentally shot in the arm by a

---

* The ayatollah's life in exile began in 1964. He spent time in the Iraqi holy city of Najaf, followed by Turkey and Paris. Khomeini returned to Iran on February 1, 1979, in a chartered Air France jet.

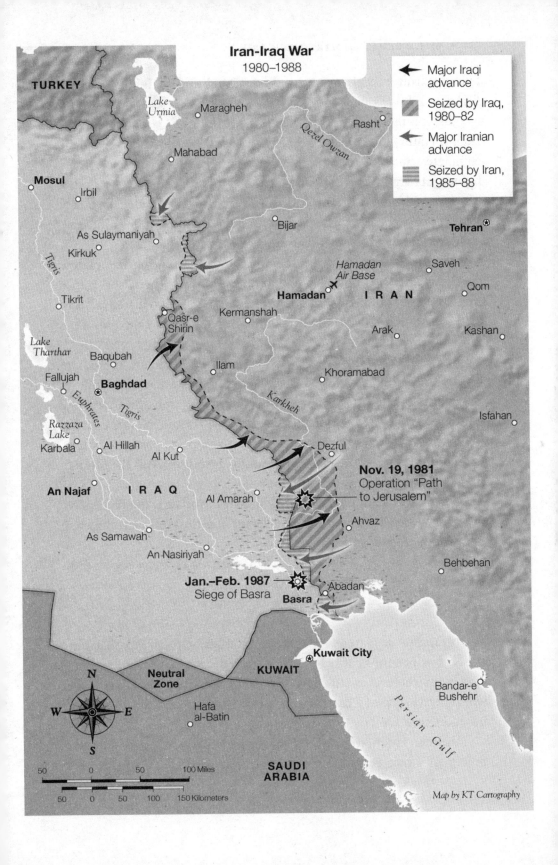

fellow recruit. His peers are awed at the sight of the injured Qasem firing an AK-47 one-handed.

But it is the war with Iraq that is the making of Qasem Soleimani. Iraqi dictator Saddam Hussein invades Iran shortly after Soleimani completes his elite training. The date is September 22, 1980. Iraqi fighter jets cross into Iranian airspace in a surprise attack. One day later, ground troops loyal to Saddam sweep over the border. The Iraqi army seems to be everywhere along the four-hundred-mile front, easily overwhelming the defending Iranians.

The roots of the war are religious: Iran's revolution has placed the Shia cleric Ayatollah Khomeini on the throne. There is a sizable Shiite population in Iraq. Saddam Hussein, a Sunni Muslim, claims he fears Khomeini will foment religious revolution in Iraq and overthrow his regime.

The United States is secretly aligned with Saddam, providing F-14 Tomcat aircraft and the latest technology in tanks and artillery. The fighting is reminiscent of World War I, with trench warfare and poison gas. Qasem is wounded several times but always returns to the front. The Iran-Iraq War instills two key principles into young Soleimani: Iraq must never again be a threat to Iran. And the United States must be destroyed at all costs.

Soleimani's karate training has shown him that a smaller opponent can overwhelm and defeat a larger foe through well-directed blows and strategic patience.

This is how Qasem Soleimani will eventually wage war against America.

✦ ✦ ✦

Thirty-eight years later, General Soleimani is on the warpath again.

"It has been over a year since Trump became US president, but that man's rhetoric is still that of a casino, of a bar. He talks to the world in the style of a bartender or a casino manager," Soleimani tells his audience. "One feels that a gambler is talking."

The men laugh, stunned to hear the general speaking so defiantly. Soleimani's face remains impassive, but it is clear he relishes this intended response. The general then speaks directly to the American president.

"Know this: not a night goes by without us thinking of you. Hereby, I am telling you, the gambling Mister Trump. Be aware that we're close to you where you can't even imagine. We are beside you. We are the nation of martyrdom. . . . Come, we are waiting for you. We are the man of this battlefield for you. You know that this war would mean the destruction of all you possess."

General Soleimani's words are incendiary, but his tone is measured.

"You shouldn't insult the Iranian nation," Soleimani tells Trump, speaking to the most powerful man in the world as if they are equals. "You shouldn't insult our president. You must be careful."

Every man in the hall understands the provocation. But the crowd does not seem to fear Soleimani himself—despite rumors about torture in the general's prisons. Those descriptions include reports of pepper-spraying genitals, waterboarding, and the "chicken kebab," in which a man's arms and legs are trussed behind his back as he's dangled above the ground on a skewerlike pole. Also, every Iranian knows that a reason can be found to arrest anyone.

Amazingly, one lone individual shouts from somewhere in the crowd, interrupting the general. The audience is tense as Soleimani pauses for a moment. His eyes seek out the violator. But he is aware of the cameras filming him and the optics of responding angrily. Instead, the general patiently wags a finger and gently scolds the man into silence. The waiting police stand down.

The audience once again gives Soleimani its complete attention. But should anyone in the crowd be arrested for disrespect, it will not be the general who oversees the inevitable prison torture. That duty will fall to Sohrab Soleimani, the general's younger brother, a brutal man whose very name *does* inspire fear.

✦ ✦ ✦

It is November 29, 1981, and the Soleimani brothers are enduring a rainy night fighting the Iraqis. This is Operation Path to Jerusalem, and company commander Soleimani is leading Iranian troops through minefields. Among the soldiers in his battalion are his brother and his cousin Ahmad.

The battle goes well at first, the Iraqi forces taken completely by surprise. Ahmad suffers a leg injury and is forced to remain behind as the Soleimani brothers push farther into Iraq. Sohrab is just seventeen. Qasem left home while his brother was still a young child. But now they are reunited in the Revolutionary Guard, Sohrab learning the rigors of warfare from Qasem. The brothers grow closer by fighting together.

Ayatollah Khomeini will one day call Path to Jerusalem a great victory. But for Qasem Soleimani, the battle will almost cost him his life. A shell strikes him hard in the torso, tearing open his chest, leading to a great loss of blood. Qasem is evacuated to one hospital and then another for emergency surgery. He survives, but just barely.

It is while he is convalescing that Qasem Soleimani has time to reflect on his career path. He commits his life to Iran and service as a soldier. Returning to the front lines as soon as he is able, Qasem pursues that calling with an even greater passion. He commands the 41st Tharallah Division, which fights in several major battles, among them the crucial siege of Basra through January and February 1987.

The war ends in deadlock, with more than one hundred thousand men killed on both sides. A cease-fire ends hostilities in 1988, but tension between the two nations remains high. An actual peace treaty is not signed for two more years.

In the mind of Qasem Soleimani, the war continues. Iraq must never threaten Iran again.

Soleimani's cousin Ahmad dies in battle in 1984. Qasem weeps at the loss but rejoices that Ahmad died a martyr, a death for a righteous cause being considered "soothing and pleasant." But Sohrab survives the war, never far from his brother's side.*

---

* "The Sacred Defense," as Iranians call the Iran-Iraq War, was fought from 1980–88. Photos of Qasem Soleimani during the conflict show a young man in fatigues with no sign of rank. Qasem was revered for his solo reconnaissance missions deep into Iraqi territory, from which he often brought back not just information but a stolen goat for his men to slaughter and roast. This renown led to his appointment as a brigade commander. Iranian radio nicknamed Soleimani "the Goat Thief," marking the first time he gained public notoriety for his military prowess.

The general's popularity and power rise greatly after the Iran-Iraq War. He becomes the subject of pop songs, with Iranian television documentaries about his life telling the story of how a boy born into an impoverished farm family, with little education, grew into one of the world's sharpest tactical masterminds. "To Middle Eastern Shiites," one CIA analyst writes, "he is James Bond, Erwin Rommel, and Lady Gaga rolled into one."

A former deputy Iraqi prime minister is more succinct in his description of Soleimani's broad appeal, which spills over the border into his own country: "All of the important people in Iraq go to see him. People are mesmerized by him—they see him like an angel."

An angel of death.

✦ ✦ ✦

The general's rise to power complete, he once again shows his deep loyalty to family: he hands power to his brother Sohrab by granting him control over the entire Iranian prison system.

Soon, Sohrab turns brutal, jailing innocent citizens, allowing guards to torture and beat the arrested, and holding men in prison for years without charges. All this is condoned by Qasem. Foreign journalists and tourists thought to be spies are at the top of the list for incarceration. Rumors leak out of the prisons about torture methods and other acts of brutality, like having prisoners run down a narrow hallway through a gauntlet of guards who beat them with clubs.

The situation becomes so bad that Sohrab is investigated by Amnesty International for human rights abuses. But in Iran that does not matter. As long as General Qasem Soleimani remains in power, so will Sohrab.

And so it is that the general's speech comes to a close at the Hamadan air base. By threatening the American president, he has greatly enhanced his reputation in the radical Muslim world.

But in Washington, DC, Qasem Soleimani's threatening message is received much differently: he has just signed his own death warrant.

✦ ✦ ✦

President Donald Trump stands in the White House Diplomatic Reception Room. This oval-shaped space on the ground floor is where a visiting head of state is normally received following arrival ceremonies on the South Lawn. But today's diplomacy is not of a welcoming kind. Knowing his actions might lead to conflict, Mr. Trump nonetheless announces he is taking harsh measures against Iran. He is going to blow up the so-called Iran nuclear deal.

"This is a horrible, one-sided deal that should never have been made," the president tells reporters. "It didn't bring calm. It didn't bring peace. It never will."

Under President Barack Obama, the United States and its European allies agreed to lift $110 billion in economic sanctions against Iran in exchange for a limitation of uranium enrichment by that country. But verification measures in the arrangement were weak.

Mr. Trump has long scorned the deal as a farce. It is well known that Qasem Soleimani and the Revolutionary Guard control Iran's nuclear facilities. The mullahs have continuously sought weapons of mass destruction. President Trump believes the Obama deal assists that ambition.

However, others say the end of the treaty is a precursor to war.

Minor hostilities have already begun. Under Soleimani's command, Iranian naval vessels consistently harass US merchant vessels and warships in the Persian Gulf. That action is a legitimate threat: Iran possesses the Seersucker antiship missile, which is capable of sinking an American destroyer.

Donald Trump doesn't want war with Iran. He just wants a new deal—a better deal, one that makes it impossible for the Iranians to build nuclear weapons. The United States soon reimposes tough economic sanctions meant to bring Iran back to the bargaining table. Israel and Saudi Arabia, two nations that would become immediate targets if Iran does develop a nuke, support Trump's action.

Predictably, Iran chafes, particularly when the US sanctions prevent it from selling Iranian oil to European countries.

In fact, Iranian president Hassan Rouhani issues a threat. "Don't play with the lion's tail. America should know that peace with Iran is the mother of all peace, and war with Iran is the mother of all wars."

President Trump's Twitter response to Rouhani is sent in capital letters: "NEVER, EVER THREATEN THE UNITED STATES AGAIN OR YOU WILL SUFFER CONSEQUENCES THE LIKES OF WHICH FEW THROUGHOUT HISTORY HAVE EVER SUFFERED BEFORE.

"WE ARE NO LONGER A COUNTRY THAT WILL STAND FOR YOUR DEMENTED WORDS OF VIOLENCE & DEATH. BE CAUTIOUS!"

✦ ✦ ✦

General Qasem Soleimani's hatred for America grows ever stronger. He is using the tension to gain even more power. Quietly, Soleimani is making plans to run for the Iranian presidency. He knows that he will have the support of Ayatollah Seyyed Ali Khamenei, who has become a friend. But no matter what happens in politics, Soleimani now has complete freedom to do whatever he pleases in the name of his nation.

Wasting no time, the general begins to accelerate a terror campaign against America and Israel.

In Washington and Jerusalem, the threat from Iran is becoming clear as intelligence reports pinpoint Soleimani as a "present danger." The US State Department declares the Quds Force a foreign terrorist organization.

"With this designation we are sending a clear signal to Iran's leaders, including Qasem Soleimani and his band of thugs," now–Secretary of State Mike Pompeo announces, "that the United States is bringing all pressure to bear to stop the regime's outlaw behavior."

President Donald Trump does not need any more convincing—to him, the situation has become personal.

Very personal.

CHAPTER SIXTEEN

APRIL 23, 2019
LOCATION UNKNOWN
DAY

Abu Bakr al-Baghdadi is showing his face.

And it looks like a bloody death mask.

"The war of Islam and its followers against the crusaders and their followers is a long one," he says to the camera. The terrorist leader is surfacing for the first time in five years. In an undated video released on the ISIS-run al-Furqan media network, al-Baghdadi admonishes his followers to fight on. The tips of his gray beard are dyed a bloody crimson. An AK-47 is at his side, locked and loaded. Heavyset, draped in robes and the type of beige, multipocketed vest worn by fishermen, the jihadist sits cross-legged atop ornate cushions, leaning back against a bare white wall. Al-Baghdadi is only forty-seven but looks a decade older. Three other men sit in the room, their faces concealed.*

For these specially chosen guests, the journey to enter this building and sit in the presence of their supreme leader began with the removal of wristwatches—ensuring that a hidden global positioning

---

* The men are essentially props. They are acolytes of al-Baghdadi but not major players in ISIS.

system (GPS) cannot be used. Cameras, cell phones, and any other electronics were also confiscated. A blindfold was then placed over their eyes. Each man was led into a van and driven for hours, never given a precise destination. Only upon arrival were the blindfolds removed. Then al-Baghdadi entered the room.

When the video session is complete, the three will remain sitting, supervised by armed guards. Abu Bakr al-Baghdadi will depart first. The jihadis will be forced to wait until the ISIS leader clears the area.

These are extreme measures, but Abu Bakr al-Baghdadi follows strict, paranoid guidelines every day. He well knows he is a hunted man. A single mistake could be the end of him.

This is a notable change from the smug al-Baghdadi who addressed hundreds from the pulpit of a Mosul mosque in 2014. Two years later, in 2016—at the height of his power—the terrorist sultan controlled a swath of land stretching from northern Syria to central Iraq, near Baghdad. Millions of people were under his rule, and tens of thousands of soldiers genuflected before him.

Now all that is all gone. ISIS is back where it once was: a guerrilla insurgency waging jihad, one of many such groups in the Middle East. Yet al-Baghdadi fights on.

It is known that one of the jihadist's sons, a teenager named Huthaifa al-Badri, was shot dead one month ago, while fighting for ISIS in Syria. But if that loss devastated al-Baghdadi, he does not show it now. The commander's animated voice betrays no hint of mourning.

American intelligence officials will soon discover the reason why: the video's release was delayed, to conceal the ISIS killer's whereabouts.

The filming actually took place five months ago.

The bounty on al-Baghdadi's head set by the American government is currently $25 million. His caliphate, as he admits in the video, is now just a brutal memory to the rest of the world. Raqqa, which acted as the ISIS capital city, is back under Syrian government control.

But al-Baghdadi makes it known that he is far from finished. ISIS cells are operating in Africa, the Middle East, and Southeast

Asia. To prove this, an edited clip shows an ISIS attack in Sri Lanka, where militants clad in suicide vests packed with nails killed 250 Christians on Easter Sunday 2019.

As the camera records, al-Baghdadi talks to his three "guests." He tells them he does not need the caliphate. He can strike anywhere in the world, at any time. The arrogant terrorist has avoided assassination for many years and believes he will never be found. He trusts no one and is comfortable with the elaborate security measures necessary to command his terrorist forces. Al-Baghdadi is confident that one day ISIS *will* triumph, and history will record him as a true world leader, no different than the Muslim clerics who run Iran. When that day comes, he will come out of hiding and be vindicated for all these years of hardship.

"Our battle today is a war of attrition to harm the enemy, and they should know that jihad will continue until doomsday," Abu Bakr al-Baghdadi says confidently, switching his gaze to the camera but not making eye contact with the lens.

Al-Baghdadi thinks waiting five months to release the video will be enough to cover his tracks. He is wrong. US coalition troops in Iraq and Syria are closing in.

And, after years of frustration, they finally know where the ISIS leader lives.

✦ ✦ ✦

Half a world away, in a secure facility at Ellsworth Air Force Base in South Dakota, American hunters track al-Baghdadi at thirty thousand feet over Syria. Two-person teams of air force drone pilots sit in air-conditioned cockpits that never leave the ground—video screens, joysticks, headsets, padded armchairs. These military people are flying remote-controlled unmanned aircraft over Syria from this remote location in the United States. They are young men and women in flight suits who were just children on 9/11. Though these pilots live at home, buy groceries at the base commissary, drive to work each day, and otherwise live a normal life, they go to war in a very high-tech way the instant they settle into their cockpit and speak into their communications devices.

Ellsworth is just one of the more than two dozen US military installations around the world that surveil ISIS with Predator and Reaper drones. Years ago, the base's primary arsenal was composed of B-52 Stratofortress bombers, always on standby to repel any global threat.

But today's generation of terrorists is not so easily found—or defeated—as conventional armies of yore. The brutal jihadist killers operate in a shadow world and must be observed by the most clandestine method possible. The deafening roar of a B-52 is replaced in the terror war by the almost total silence of a hovering drone. Known ISIS hideouts are watched from high in the sky without a hint that they are being observed. Recognizing that their nations must also prepare to fight terror attacks at home and abroad, coalition members France, Britain, Australia, and Spain are now training their own flight crews at a similar US base in Nevada, ready to join the fight.

The work is primarily tedious—but once in a while exciting. During a typical eight-hour shift, a drone pilot circles over a target continuously, studying the same vehicles and encampments over and over. The pilots can launch precision Hellfire rounds on order—killing killers who pose a threat. Some of the officers who have also flown combat missions in F-16 fighter jets say the stress level is about the same.

Most of the time, drone pilots simply wait. One jihadi usually leads them to another. ISIS leadership has learned that telephones, computers, and other electronic communications can reveal locations. Thus, jihadis prefer to speak with their fellow terrorists in person. So it is better to follow the ISIS thugs as they travel the back roads of Iraq and Syria. Drones tail them to every meeting, photographing the faces in attendance and recording the location.

This includes Abu Bakr al-Baghdadi.

The confessions of captured terrorist Ismael al-Ethawi and the four other top ISIS leaders have yielded several potential places where al-Baghdadi might be hiding. Drones fly above each of these locations for months, the faraway pilots scrutinizing every vehicle entering and exiting the potential lair.

Yet for all their scrutiny, the drone pilots have yet to catch even a momentary glimpse of al-Baghdadi. There is a good chance he might not even be in the compound.

What the American hunters do see is a facility surrounded by twelve-foot-tall dun-colored walls, fruit orchards, a dirt driveway snaking off the paved main highway, and two large buildings with flat roofs, flanked by what appears to be a red water tank. Strangely, there also appears to be an image looking very much like a tennis court outside, though if it is such a thing it goes unused, as the compound's occupants rarely venture outdoors.

The town of Barisha, in Syria, is in rugged, hilly country, popular with smugglers due to its location ten miles from the Turkish border. In another time, this was a land of prosperity. Farmers grew olives in large orchards and pressed them for the oil. Wine from the many local vineyards was widely renowned. Stone churches and homes showed this land as a place of prosperity. But that was during the Byzantine era, some 1500 years ago. The vineyards are now gone. The olive groves remain, though there is little interest in pressing the crop anymore. The Christian churches are rubble. The land around Barisha is sparsely populated, with some residents even living in caves.

The drones see all that, but they cannot see inside the buildings. Therefore, they do not know about deadly obstacles, hiding places, the number of women and children, the location of armed guards.

Despite that, a plan is slowly taking shape to attack al-Baghdadi's possible hideout. But, obviously, it is imperative to confirm he is actually there.

Two bits of luck will soon reveal the truth.

✦ ✦ ✦

For all his secrecy, Abu Bakr al-Baghdadi has a crucial weakness: family.

The terrorist is thought to have four wives and several children. Family members do not wear blindfolds or discard their cell phones when they rendezvous with the ISIS leader. Thus, those women suspected of attending to al-Baghdadi are easily traced. The CIA begins to focus on one woman in particular, who frequently travels outside the compound with a courier serving as her bodyguard.

Soon, intelligence agents from Iraq and Kurdish Turkey follow her. Days later, she is placed under arrest.*

This is the first stroke of luck.

The subsequent interrogation is like any other, starting with endless questioning, sleep deprivation, and a restricted diet. Torture is not used at first, and in the case of this unnamed wife, it is not known whether it becomes necessary. All of that is classified. But it is understood that both the wife and courier begin to talk.

The most important question the CIA interrogators want answered—does al-Baghdadi live in the hilltop Barisha compound?

Yes.

The wife's confession proves that almost everything Ismael al-Ethawi told interrogators is correct. The main entry doors are booby-trapped to explode when a hostile force attacks. A network of escape tunnels allows the ISIS leader multiple paths to freedom.

Drone surveillance of the fortress is immediately redoubled. Several unmanned aircraft fly simultaneously at different altitudes and send back a comprehensive picture of the compound. The comings and goings in the mountaintop area are intensely scrutinized, particularly the movement of cars and motorcycles.

Al-Ethawi's statement that al-Baghdadi conceals himself inside minivans carrying loads of vegetables becomes crucial, as such vehicles are regularly seen entering and leaving the compound. The United States requests the assistance of Iraqi and Kurdish intelligence, asking them to provide ground spies who can pinpoint al-Baghdadi's movements whenever he leaves.

Then comes the second piece of luck.

✦ ✦ ✦

The man is an Arab. His true identity will never be revealed, for if that ever happened he would be a dead man. He has decided to betray al-Baghdadi because a loved one has been killed by ISIS, and the Arab wants revenge.

---

* The best intelligence comes from Kurdish forces, a rebel group known as the Syrian Democratic Forces, and Iraqi surveillance. All interrogations of ISIS captives take place inside Iraq.

But just as important, he wants the $25 million reward for al-Baghdadi's capture or death.

The man contacts the CIA through the shadowy world of the global intelligence community. The would-be informant claims al-Baghdadi trusts him and holds him in the highest regard. The anonymous informer wishes to help capture the ISIS leader and is even willing to personally take part in the raid, leading US soldiers through the inside rooms and pointing out tunnel locations. To prove his knowledge, the Arab informs American intelligence that the compound has internet access, paid for in cash to the local service provider at a rate of $8 per month. Al-Baghdadi's personal username is "mhrab." His children play online video games.

But the CIA wants more. They think this may be a setup. So, the informant is asked to do something very unusual: provide a pair of al-Baghdadi's underwear.

He returns with an unwashed, white, baggy garment that extends from the waist to below the knee.

That, however, is *still* not enough for the CIA.

Federal agents demand a sample of al-Baghdadi's blood.

Amazingly, the informant comes back with a second stolen item, this time a used bandage.

Both items match DNA known to have come from Abu Bakr al-Baghdadi.*

So it is that, in summer of 2019, the CIA and the American military begin planning a mission to capture the ISIS leader. It will be the most significant raid on a terrorist since Osama bin Laden's demise eight years before. The comparison is apt—no jihadist since bin Laden has been as successful at remaining hidden while also being in command of his terrorist outfit.

---

* Al-Baghdadi's DNA was on file with intelligence agencies because he spent a short time in US custody in 2004, prior to the founding of ISIS. A strange ISIS rule forbade the wearing of Western-style underwear such as briefs or boxers, under penalty of death. ISIS underwear such as the long undergarment favored by al-Baghdadi was often brightly colored, a departure from the group's black outer robes.

✦ ✦ ✦

Mission planning is divided: Delta Force, Rangers, and Night Stalkers rehearse the combat aspect over and over, even as the intelligence community acquires as much detail as possible through informants, electronic eavesdropping, signal intelligence, and visual information from drones and satellites. It is the military action that will forever be given the spotlight, but intelligence analysis is no less necessary right now. Intelligence personnel follow a proven plan of attack known as "Find, Fix, Finish" to guide their investigations. Now, having found and fixed their sights on al-Baghdadi, they seek to finish him.*

Beginning in July, al-Baghdadi appears to take up permanent residence inside the compound. As training for the raid ramps up, it becomes clear that the house outside Barisha will almost surely be the site of the attack. But there are severe problems with this mission.

Al-Baghdadi has chosen his hiding place with a masterful tactical eye. There is currently no place on earth so devoted to the terrorist way of life as the land around Barisha. Terrorism has become so ingrained into the region's culture that many young males see this as their only future. Northern Syria is primarily controlled by an al-Qaeda cell made up of rogue ISIS fighters trying to reassemble for another war.

In addition, conventional troops of the of Syrian and Russian armies stake their own claim to the rugged terrain, living in large military bases and conducting patrols. Their presence is less of a problem in the early days of mission planning because one thousand US troops are also occupying northern Syria. But, just a few weeks before the al-Baghdadi mission is set to launch, President Trump

---

* Army Rangers are an elite group founded circa 1676 by an English colonist named Colonel Benjamin Church to serve as an irregular fighting force during the early Indian wars. The army's Delta Force was founded in 1977 as a small fighting unit tasked to deal specifically with the growing worldwide terror threat. Their maritime equivalent is the navy's Special Warfare Development Group, a group formerly known as SEAL Team 6. The aerial component—the 160th Special Operations Aviation Regiment, also known as the Night Stalkers—provided helicopters and air crews for both the bin Laden and al-Baghdadi raids.

makes a surprise decision to remove those American forces. Officially, there is not even one single American in the region surrounding Barisha.

This complicates everything. No longer can US forces approach on the ground.

And this presents another problem: Russian MiG fighter jets routinely patrol the airspace on behalf of Syria, eager to shoot down any threats appearing on radar. There is an unwritten agreement between the United States and Russia that drone flights will go unchallenged, but drones are not an invasion force. Thus, the likelihood of United States helicopters bristling with missiles and loaded with elite soldiers flying to the target undetected is nonexistent.

Delta Force would be quickly shot from the sky.

This leaves no doubt: the soldiers must launch from a location outside of Syria, using surprise to insert and exfiltrate by helicopter.

Just like with bin Laden.

✦ ✦ ✦

Time is running out.

Anbar province, in Iraq, has been chosen as ground zero for the raid. Gravel, rock, heat. Not a tree in sight. ISIS knows it well, having captured a town named, coincidentally, al-Baghdadi at the height of the caliphate. During that battle, ISIS laid siege to American and Iraqi troops who were based nearby. Constant mortar fire was leveled by the terrorists, but it caused little damage. The air base in Anbar is now considered safe enough that President Trump landed here last Christmas to greet troops and have his picture taken with SEAL Team 5.

Another plan takes shape. The warriors meet daily for physical training under the hot desert sun and a comprehensive study of their target based on drone and satellite footage. Everything about the raid is top secret, but the soldiers sense something big is about to happen. The operators taking part will not be Navy SEALs but Army Rangers and Delta Force.

This causes tension. There is an interservice rivalry among elite Special Forces. Many army officials believe that the SEALs involved

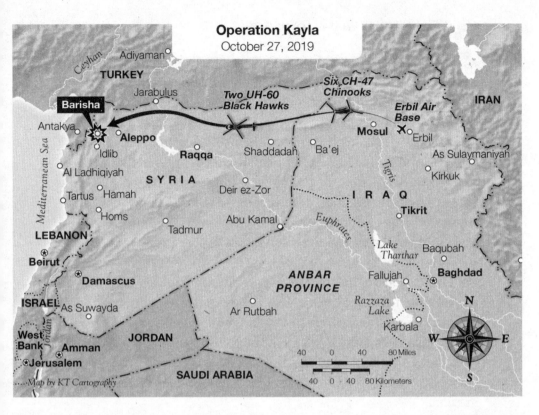

Operation Kayla
October 27, 2019

Adiyaman
Ceyhan
TURKEY
Jarabulus
Two UH-60 Black Hawks
Six CH-47 Chinooks
Erbil Air Base
IRAN
Barisha
Antakya
Aleppo
Idlib
Mosul
Erbil
Raqqa
Shaddadah
Ba'ej
As Sulaymaniyah
Al Ladhiqiyah
S Y R I A
Tigris
Kirkuk
Tartus
Hamah
Deir ez-Zor
Homs
Tadmur
Abu Kamal
I R A Q
Tikrit
Mediterranean Sea
Euphrates
Lake Tharthar
Baqubah
LEBANON
Beirut
ANBAR PROVINCE
Fallujah
Baghdad
Damascus
ISRAEL
As Suwayda
Ar Rutbah
Razzaza Lake
Karbala
West Bank
Amman
Jerusalem
Jordan
JORDAN
SAUDI ARABIA

40 0 40 80 Miles
40 0 40 80 Kilometers

N E S W

Map by KT Cartography

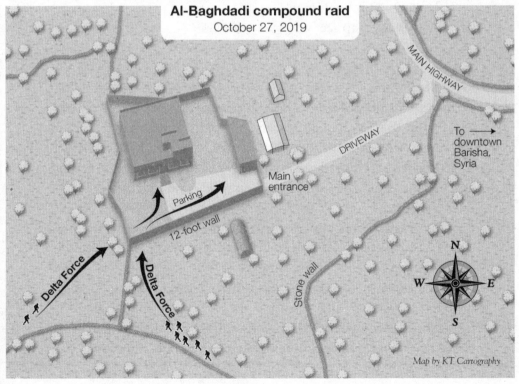

Al-Baghdadi compound raid
October 27, 2019

MAIN HIGHWAY
DRIVEWAY
To downtown Barisha, Syria
Main entrance
Parking
12-foot wall
Stone wall
Delta Force
Delta Force

N E S W

Map by KT Cartography

in the bin Laden raid eight years ago were eager to cash in on their experiences, enjoying a brief moment of fame by writing books and giving talks about the mission. Even fellow Navy SEALs and members of the US intelligence community feel the same. Delta Force vows there will be no such chatter about the hunt for al-Baghdadi.

Also, unlike the bin Laden operation, which limited manpower to a dozen SEALs on the ground, the hunt for al-Baghdadi will be a massive attack, utilizing dozens of Special Forces personnel, helicopters, a fleet of drones, and jet fighters providing air cover. And because the fighting will likely take place indoors, military dogs will also be utilized.

Fierce heat in the remote desert location makes each day of preparation a time of great rigor. The elaborate synchronization of so many aircraft and commandos grows more and more fine-tuned with every passing day. By September, as summer temperatures spike even higher, the teams are ready. Now all they need is the order to launch. The warriors gather to select a code name for their upcoming mission.

The decision is unanimous.

But, for now, top secret.

✦ ✦ ✦

Summer is gone.

And still no order to attack. It's been months. The Arab spy within the ISIS compound reports that al-Baghdadi is preparing to relocate north to a new house in the town of Jarabulus. Luckily, the ISIS leader hasn't moved yet, but the Special Forces teams are getting restless. He could run any day, meaning this one chance to get him will evaporate.

The frustration abates as the decision is made to train at a new site. It's not exactly authorization to go into battle, but it feels as though the teams are getting closer.

Men, aircraft, dogs, and munitions are moved to Erbil Air Base in Iraq for training. That facility is only a seventy-minute flight to al-Baghdadi's compound. Despite the threat of Russian fighter jets, aerial insertion is the only option. There is no other choice than this extremely risky plan of attack. The Black Hawk and CH-47 helicopters must fly at top speed through hostile Syrian airspace. They are specially equipped to refuel in the air. By hugging the ground, there is hope they can defeat Russian radar and remain unseen. This is the only way in—and the only way out. Technically, it is an act of war to enter a foreign country without permission.

The pilots are concerned about legalities. But they're even more worried about being blown out of the sky by a Russian Vympel R-73 missile.

As the aviators study flight maps, commandos rehearse the insertion again and again in complete secrecy. The Black Hawks will land *outside* the compound, the bin Laden raid memorably having shown that attempting to land *inside* can lead to a "vortex ring state" crash.

Upon touching down, the commandos will blow up the high walls rather than attempt entry through the booby-trapped front door. There will be women and children inside, and likely a small number of armed ISIS bodyguards.

The CIA informant will also be inside. Throughout the planning, he has visited with al-Baghdadi a number of times and is trusted enough that he is not blindfolded when led into the compound. He has already provided key details about the interior layout. When the attack comes, he will make himself known and guide the soldiers through the building, maybe taking them directly to al-Baghdadi. Should the mission be a success, the Arab and his family will be secretly relocated to some other part of the world, there to spend the $25 million bounty.

Meanwhile, Abu Bakr al-Baghdadi waits, apparently thinking he is completely safe.

✦ ✦ ✦

Go time.

President Trump grants permission to attack. Pilots and soldiers immediately assemble and load into helicopters. Now it's for real. Finally, they will have their date with Abu Bakr al-Baghdadi.

Then, crushing disappointment: the order is soon rescinded, no reason given. Deflated, the teams return to their air-conditioned quarters. Little do they know that high-level negotiations are currently taking place among Washington, Moscow, and the Syrian government. It appears these talks will allow the attack to proceed without any interference from Russian aircraft. But there is a communication breakdown, thus the last-minute decision to scrub.*

One week later, the order comes again.

However, more complications arise, and the teams are again told to stand down. There is grumbling and a frustrating sense that this mission might *never* happen. Some of the men remember the attempt to rescue Kayla Mueller five years ago, when US forces arrived just one day after she had been moved to a new location. No one wants that to happen with al-Baghdadi.

And then, on October 26, the green light. The elite commandos and pilots slip into the helicopters, rotors power up, and the dangerous seventy-minute ride over Syria begins. The time is just before midnight. Eight helicopters filled with sixty-five commando warriors lift into the night.

Operation Kayla Mueller, as the warriors have named the mission, is about to become real.

---

* The complex negotiations required several adversarial factions to work together with the United States: Russia, Turkey, Syria, Iraq, Kurds.

CHAPTER SEVENTEEN

ISIS fires first.

This is a mistake.

The Night Stalkers drop low for the final approach. Black fuselages. Sunday morning, rustler's moon beaming pale light, headlights from a lone olive-green minivan on the two-lane road below. The Black Hawks and Chinooks have taken small-arms fire on their dash across Syria, but nothing like the precision volleys from automatic weapons now aimed their way from the terrain surrounding al-Baghdadi's suspected compound. Bullets ping off each armored helicopter as muzzle flashes give away the location of ISIS shooters. The soldiers inside are annoyed but unhurt.

The Americans respond. Forward-firing machine guns mounted on each Black Hawk are fully integrated with the aircraft's digital flight controls, automatically calculating range and ballistics. This all happens in less than a second. The Night Stalker pilots blast the ISIS defenders with .50-caliber Gatling guns and Hydra-70 rockets.

Targets neutralized.

◆ ◆ ◆

It is estimated that a dozen or more ISIS fighters outside the compound are killed from the air. But the exact number remains classified.

Every effort is being made to avoid civilian casualties. The two pilots are in the unenviable position of making split-second life-or-death decisions. So it is with the minivan: al-Baghdadi was seen leaving the compound yesterday with his family in such a vehicle. But tonight, although the pilots cannot know this, the ISIS leader has chosen to stay home. Instead, the minivan's three occupants are within four hundred meters of the targeted compound. The vehicle is blasted off the road in an instant.

Later, the men in the van will say they are not ISIS, just innocent civilians out for a late-Saturday-night joyride, drinking coffee and eating pumpkin seeds. Two of them, cousins, will eventually die of shrapnel wounds. A third man will live, but one of his hands is severed by a Hydra.

Both Black Hawks quickly descend outside the compound. The early morning sky is now alight from the flaming vehicle. A ten-man Delta Force team jumps to the ground, then spreads out—eight men in one group, just two in the other. The soldiers walk toward the dwelling with weapons already in firing mode. From Iraq, mission control speaks into their earpieces, reporting that drone footage shows no sign of guards.

The night is active. The air is full of six Chinook helicopters carrying reinforcements, a phalanx of drones, and a number of supersonic fighter jets keeping watch in the upper atmosphere.

Delta Force arrives at the wall, then attaches explosives to the side at a spot precisely four feet off the ground. Each man steps away and turns his back to shield himself from the blast. The surgical detonation explodes as planned. A loud boom and percussive shock wave ensue. Rubble flies into the compound. A second hole is quickly blasted in another section. The team does not wait for the smoke to clear, advancing forward quickly.

The Delta Force team are identically clad: black helmet, night vision goggles, body armor, M4 assault rifle, and a Glock 9mm pistol on the hip. Each soldier carries a knife of his own choosing. In addition, they are armed with fragmentation hand grenades as well as extra clips of ammunition.

The second Black Hawk lands, dropping off another team and Conan, a Belgian Malinois military dog named after the late-night television host. He is a four-year veteran with fifty missions to his credit. As with the bin Laden raid, the dog will be used to pursue any fleeing terrorist and to intimidate Muslims, who are generally afraid of dogs.

Now the Delta teams prepare to enter the buildings thought to house al-Baghdadi and his family.

The reckoning is here.

✦ ✦ ✦

Approximately ten minutes after landing, a Delta Force soldier calls out in Arabic, requesting that al-Baghdadi surrender. Moments pass, but the team is not in a hurry. They know air and ground is totally controlled by US forces. What they don't know is where the ISIS leader is located.

Suddenly, eleven children under the age of twelve and two women step into the courtyard. They are immediately searched for weapons, especially suicide vests, then led into a waiting helicopter—but not before they reveal that al-Baghdadi is not alone in the compound. There are other children, four more women, and at least four ISIS fighters.*

Once the thirteen children and women are off the premises, Delta Force soldiers move smoothly across the hard dirt between the houses. As drones watch overhead, the voice of their far-off mission commander confirms that no one has escaped from either building.

The final assault is ready.

✦ ✦ ✦

Six thousand miles away, in the White House Situation Room, President Donald Trump watches the mission unfold in real time on large

---

* The names of the thirteen people who surrendered at the onset of the raid are still confidential, but they are thought to be the wives and children of the ISIS terrorists protecting al-Baghdadi. None of them accompanied US soldiers back to the base at the end of the raid; instead, they were released to local Syrian officials.

President Donald J. Trump is joined by Vice President Mike Pence; National Security Advisor Robert O'Brien, left; Secretary of Defense Mark Esper and Chairman of the Joint Chiefs of Staff US Army General Mark A. Milley; and Brig. Gen. Marcus Evans, Deputy Director for Special Operations on the Joint Staff, at right, in the Situation Room of the White House monitoring developments as US Special Operations Forces close in on notorious ISIS leader Abu Bakr al-Baghdadi's compound in Syria with a mission to kill or capture the terrorist.

monitors. Also in the room are Vice President Mike Pence, National Security Adviser Robert O'Brien, Secretary of Defense Mark Esper, and General Mark Milley, chairman of the Joint Chiefs of Staff. A tangle of secure phone lines covers the large rectangular conference table.

Earlier today, after authorizing the mission, the president played golf with Rob Manfred, the commissioner of baseball. Tonight is Game 4 of the World Series, and Mr. Trump took great pains not to deviate from his long-prepared schedule. Everything must look normal.

By 5:00 p.m. Washington time, just as the first helicopters are leaving for the al-Baghdadi compound, the president has changed into a dark-blue suit and light-blue tie to watch the raid. This is a signature moment in the war on terror. The Trump administration has taken a hard line on ISIS, but Abu Bakr al-Baghdadi has remained at large for the three years Mr. Trump has been in office, confounding all efforts to take him into custody. The mood in the Situation Room is tense, all present hoping that the terrorist does not find a way to escape one more time.

✦ ✦ ✦

Meantime, things are moving fast inside the hideout.

Delta Force has swarmed both houses. The buildings are not large, and the informant has already disclosed the layout—right down to the location of the bathrooms and bedrooms.

The Arab himself is inside al-Baghdadi's residence. Shouting and screaming in English and Arabic, he makes himself known to the soldiers. His photograph has been shown to Delta Force, who immediately confirm his identity. With the Arab's guidance, US troops go from room to room in rapid fashion.

The women are captured first. Four were sleeping but were awakened by the explosions. Quickly, they rose and dressed themselves in long black robes and head coverings. Soldiers burst into their room and, in Arabic, order the women to put their hands in the air. This is to make it impossible for them to ignite suicide vests.

The women refuse.

And they *are* wearing suicide vests!

Among these women are two of al-Baghdadi's wives.

A stand-off ensues. Delta Force prefers to arrest the women, not kill them.

Mission details remain classified, and what happens next still has not been revealed. But the authors of this book can confirm at least one of the women reaches down to trigger the explosives strapped to her body.

There is no hesitation. All four are shot in the head and die instantly. To shoot them in the torso would have detonated the vests.

In another part of the compound, two ISIS fighters, men, are also shot dead trying to detonate explosives. Delta Force is too quick for them, and the terrorists are eliminated.

The death toll is now six.

But where is Abu Bakr al-Baghdadi?

Conan the dog is brought forward to find him. Working with the Arab, the Americans discover the compound escape tunnels deep below the buildings. There, another ISIS terrorist surrenders. Now it's just al-Baghdadi at large.

The ISIS leader is desperately trying to flee underground. Conan chases him down a tunnel. Delta Force suspects that the ISIS leader may be wearing a suicide vest, so the soldiers keep their distance. What they don't know is that the cowardly al-Baghdadi has two small children with him. In the distance, voices of the frightened kids echo down the enclosure. And then comes a defiant taunt in Arabic, stating that the great Abu Bakr al-Baghdadi will never be taken alive. The man who is hiding behind his children is somehow portraying himself as special.

The tunnel is primitive, with many exposed electrical fixtures. As Conan goes farther into the shaft, barking to alert the soldiers of his progress, the dog brushes up against a live wire. Badly shocked and gravely wounded, Conan is rushed back to a helicopter for medical assistance.*

Al-Baghdadi continues to taunt the Americans, hoping to draw them into a death trap. But Delta Force is above all disciplined, and the warriors refuse to be lured. By this time, the Arab has pinpointed the tunnel's exit for the American troops, and soldiers have blocked any escape. The tunnel is now a dead end. An American calls out to al-Baghdadi in Arabic, demanding he release the children.

At first, nothing happens.

Unbeknownst to Delta Force, the coward Abu Bakr al-Baghdadi has now pulled his two young children to his side. Neither is over the age of ten. The terrorist grips them tightly, feeling the fear in their

---

* Conan survives the injury and is present at a White House ceremony one month later to celebrate the successful mission. Early media reports suggested Conan was female, but the Belgian company that performed his initial training later confirmed the dog is male. The seven-year-old Conan answers to commands in German, not English. He is still on active duty as of this writing.

Syria: Reported ISIS-Leader Al-Baghdadi Compound

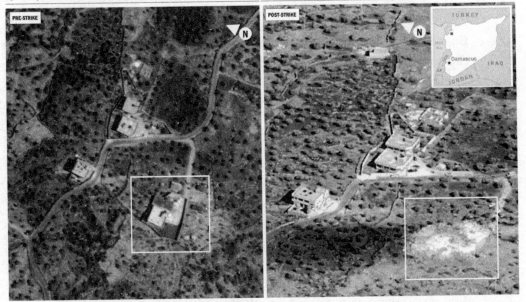

A side-by-side comparison of the compound before and after the raid that led to the death of Islamic State leader Abu Bakr al-Baghdadi, October 26, 2019. There was no collateral damage to adjacent structures.

young bodies. Al-Baghdadi finds the detonator switch attached to his suicide vest, then presses down hard with his right thumb.[*]

The explosion kills the villain and his children instantly. The tunnel collapses, crushing the corpses. All three bodies are severed into pieces, arms, legs, and torsos poking from the rubble. Al-Baghdadi's head remains intact, which will allow quick facial recognition of the body. But not until his identity is proven through DNA testing can Delta Force be completely sure they got their man.

The killer Abu Bakr al-Baghdadi goes out in a despicable way—murdering his own offspring. The names, ages, and genders of the children remain classified to this day.

Delta Force works quickly, lifting rocks and mortar in the narrow space to extricate the bodies in order to confirm the terrorist's death.

---

[*] The last moments of al-Baghdadi and his children were put together by forensic experts. The terrorist was right-handed.

✦ ✦ ✦

Back in Washington, DC, the president and his advisers cannot see the real-time fate of al-Baghdadi; drones can only show open space. The Situation Room is very quiet. Mr. Trump believes the mission has been a success, and his speechwriters are already preparing remarks. But no one is celebrating. The faces of the president and his top officials are grim as they await the special code word confirming al-Baghdadi's death.

The minutes tick past. No one leaves the room. On the video screens, images of dozens of US troops can be seen entering the two buildings to scavenge for intelligence: cell phones, laptops, flash drives, and whatever documents they come across. No bit of information is too trivial.

The Army Rangers and Delta Force are in no hurry to complete their task, taking as much time as they need to find every last bit of data on the scene. Each man wears a body camera, but images from inside the building are not transmitted on the live feed.*

Upon leaving, soldiers can be seen carrying not just the information cache but also body bags to the helicopters. Al-Baghdadi, his wives, and his children will be buried at sea within the next twenty-four hours—the bin Laden ritual repeated again.

✦ ✦ ✦

Also at the compound are special medical technicians, who are in the process of verifying DNA from al-Baghdadi's torn up body. The techs flew to the area with samples of the ISIS leader's DNA in hand. The body is in pieces, each of which is carried from the tunnel for testing and burial. The jubilation over the ISIS leader's death is tempered by the reality that this could have been a body double.

It takes fifteen minutes for scientific confirmation to come

---

* American Special Forces once wore helmet cameras but switched to body cameras. Helmet cameras transmitted video in real time, while body cams record images for downloading *after* the mission is complete. The reason for the switch was the confusing second-guessing from high-level officials, watching from a remote location, that often took place while a mission was underway.

through. Finally, they have their proof: Abu Bakr al-Baghdadi is in hell.

✦ ✦ ✦

It is 2:15 a.m. in Barisha—7:15 p.m. in Washington. The long-awaited code word is transmitted: "Jackpot."

"Got him. One hundred percent confidence."

One hour later, as the eight helicopters containing the soldiers depart the compound for the seventy-minute flight back to Iraq, the night is quiet—though only for a short time. In order that this area not become an ISIS shrine, it must no longer exist. F-15 Strike Eagle fighter jets and Reaper drones fire on the site, leveling everything. This is no simple rocket attack but rather a pulverizing combination of Hellfire and stand-off missiles, as well as laser-guided bombs.

Nothing is left of the evil hiding place.*

✦ ✦ ✦

In Washington, DC, President Donald Trump once again turns to Twitter to communicate with the world. "Something very big has just happened," he tweets at 9:23 p.m.

A press conference will be coming soon, he promises.

Intense and elated, Mr. Trump ignores the speech his writers are working on. He prefers to tell the story in his own words.

Which he will do. But on his own timetable.

---

* No American casualties resulted from the raid. An estimated forty-five to sixty men took part. All the combatants and pilots received commendations, but secretly, as publicizing their identities would put them at risk.

CHAPTER EIGHTEEN

OCTOBER 27, 2019
WASHINGTON, DC
MORNING

The president of the United States is feeling a surge of satisfaction. "Last night, the United States brought the world's terrorist leader to justice." Speaking in the White House Diplomatic Reception Room, Donald Trump wears a dark suit and red tie. His voice is somber. Reporters and television cameras fill the spacious oval room. This morning's address has been delayed thirty minutes so the president can put final touches on his speech.

"Abu Bakr al-Baghdadi is dead."

This accomplishment is sorely needed good news for the Trump administration. The president is on the verge of being impeached for allegedly soliciting foreign assistance from Ukraine in his reelection bid. Trump's relationship with Russian leader Vladimir Putin is the subject of another controversy. And Turkish president Recep Erdoğan boldly ordered President Trump to remove American troops from northern Syria earlier this month—a demand with which the usually defiant US president complied.

So just as the Osama bin Laden commando operation boosted the Obama administration, President Trump hopes that the al-Baghdadi raid will do the same for him. He chose not to break the news last night, knowing many Americans would be distracted on a Saturday. Instead, he has chosen Sunday morning, a time when the nation tunes in for morning network news shows as well as football pregame programs.

Donald Trump also hopes to downplay his predecessor's bin Laden accomplishment, stating that al-Baghdadi was a much bigger threat. Knowing the power of visual imagery, the president has ordered that a photo be released of himself and his top officials taken in the Situation Room shortly after the raid.

For Donald Trump, the death of al-Baghdadi is a personal triumph. He has long loathed all the jihadists. He still remembers 9/11 vividly.

"The United States has been searching for Baghdadi for many years. Capturing or killing Baghdadi has been the top national security priority of my administration. US Special Operations Forces executed a dangerous and daring nighttime raid in northwestern Syria and accomplished their mission in grand style," the president says.

"The US personnel were incredible. I got to watch much of it. No personnel were lost in the operation, while a large number of Baghdadi's fighters and companions were killed with him. He died after running into a dead-end tunnel, whimpering and crying and screaming all the way."

Mr. Trump speaks for ten minutes, his voice rising as his contempt for al-Baghdadi grows more theatrical.

"Last night was a great night for the United States and for the world. A brutal killer, one who has caused so much hardship and death, has violently been eliminated—he will never again harm another innocent man, woman, or child. He died like a dog. He died like a coward. The world is now a much safer place."

With that, the scripted speech is over. When President Obama announced the bin Laden killing, he gave a simple address to the nation, then turned around and departed.

But Donald Trump owns the airwaves right now. America is watching. This opportunity cannot be ignored. So, the president begins taking questions.

✦ ✦ ✦

As commander in chief, a role Donald Trump relishes, he has the authority to frame the antiterror action in Syria any way he wants.

"From the first day I came to office—and now we're getting close to three years—I would say, 'Where's al-Baghdadi? I want al-Baghdadi.' And we would kill terrorist leaders, but they were names I never heard of. They were names that weren't recognizable and they weren't the big names. Some good ones, some important ones, but they weren't the big names. I kept saying, 'Where's al-Baghdadi?' And a couple of weeks ago, they were able to scope him out . . .

"And that's why he died like a dog, he died like a coward. He was whimpering, screaming, and crying. And, frankly, I think it's something that should be brought out so that his followers and all of these young kids that want to leave various countries, including the United States, they should see how he died. He didn't die a hero. He died a coward—crying, whimpering, screaming, and bringing three kids with him to die a certain death. And he knew the tunnel had no end. I mean, it was a—it was a closed-end—they call it a closed-end tunnel. Not a good place to be."

The number of children killed and the type of tunnel are inaccurate. But the president's message is clear. He believes al-Baghdadi is a more important target than Osama bin Laden. So he continues to put forth that narrative.

"Was he being chased?" a reporter asks, referring to al-Baghdadi.

"These people, they were moving—they were chasing, yeah. They were chasing. But again, because of the suicide vest, you can't get too close," answers the president.

"Again, one of the reasons with the wives is if they have a suicide vest, you know, you have to be very, very careful. These vests are brutal. Brutal. And they go for a long distance."

The reporter follows up: "Have you spoken or will you speak to the families, like the Foley family?"

"I'm calling the families now. It will be a pleasure to do that. The Foley family, who I know. We'll be calling Kayla's family. What—what he did to her was incredible. It's a well-known story, and I'm not going to say it, but you know that. He kept her in captivity for a long period of time. He kept her in his captivity, his personal captivity. She was a beautiful woman, beautiful young woman. Helped people. She was there to help people. And he saw her and he thought she was beautiful, and he brought her into captivity for a long period of time and then he killed her. He was an animal."

✦ ✦ ✦

With the hate-Trump American media dominant, the speech as well as the Q&A is almost instantly denigrated.

"The episode became another pointed illustration of the perils of the president's confrontational style of governing and the bitter partisanship into which the US has descended," notes the British Broadcasting Corporation. "It stood in contrast to Barack Obama's solemn evening announcement of Osama Bin Laden's death, although that should not be surprising at this point. Mr. Trump has said that his conduct is 'modern-day presidential'—and his blunt, frequently casual language is part of that package."

Dozens of newspapers compare the two speeches, many preferring Obama's low-key approach to Trump's taunting. The *New York Times* takes a different angle, speaking to high-level officials who fear President Trump's rhetoric will have a long-term negative effect on the terror war. The newspaper quotes Juliette Kayyem, a former assistant secretary of homeland security under President Obama: "In other words, the impact of his gloating is more harmful to us . . . and takes a winning moment that our allies needed and our enemies should fear and turns it into a question of credibility."

Lost in the partisan coverage of al-Baghdadi's demise is an objective look at geopolitics with ISIS weakened. Also missing: an analysis of the methodical effectiveness of the American military and intelligence apparatus.

Neither President Obama nor *his* predecessor, President George W. Bush, issues a statement about the death of Abu Bakr al-Baghdadi. It is widely known that both men despise Donald Trump.

✦ ✦ ✦

The global response to Abu Bakr al-Baghdadi's death, however, is overwhelmingly positive. British defense secretary Ben Wallace notes that "the world will not miss al-Baghdadi."

French president Emmanuel Macron notes that the fight must continue: "Al-Baghdadi's death is a hard blow against Islamic State. But it is just a stage. With our partners in the international coalition, the fight continues to finally defeat this terrorist organization. It is our priority in the Middle East."

Even Russia applauds the death of the ISIS leader.

In Arizona, Kayla Mueller's parents finally know that their daughter's killer has been brought to justice. "I'm glad that evil person is gone," Mueller's father says on NBC's *Today* show. "If you were a parent, and this man did what he did to Kayla to your child, and then they got him, how would you feel?"

"That was just an amazing gift for Kayla," her mother adds. "I know Kayla; Kayla would say this was for all of us. This is for all the hostages."

But in Iran, General Qasem Soleimani is not impressed. The general directs his secretary of information to tweet: "Not a big deal. You just killed your creature," implying that the United States is the reason ISIS exists in the first place.

As for the terrorist organization itself, it refuses to even acknowledge that al-Baghdadi is dead. However, two months after the raid, the West African branch of ISIS—a group of thugs and rapists known as Boko Haram—kills eleven Christian hostages, claiming their executions are revenge for the death of Abu Bakr al-Baghdadi.

✦ ✦ ✦

President Trump basks in the public praise but seethes over some media criticism. Game 5 of the World Series is being played in Nationals Park, a stadium not far from the White House. In his youth, the president was a decent ballplayer and once even pondered making the game his profession. He now sits in a luxury box with his wife, Melania, and several Republican dignitaries. Red, white, and blue bunting lines the railings. The spectators largely wear red and white, the colors of the Washington team.

A stadium camera pans over the crowd, settling on the face of Mr. Trump. Even at a ball game, he wears a coat and tie.

Many in the stadium applaud enthusiastically at the sight of the president. Patriotism is in the air tonight, and the killing of al-Baghdadi elicits chants of "USA! USA!"

Then come some boos.

During their terms in office, Jimmy Carter, Ronald Reagan, Richard Nixon, and both Bushes were booed while attending baseball games. Such is the fickle nature of the American populace.

A chant soon arises from the crowd, loud enough to be heard clearly over the buzz of a packed stadium. These are words referring to Donald Trump's ongoing impeachment issues, a taunt that he originated against political rival Hillary Clinton during the 2016 presidential race: "Lock him up."

A short while later, the president and his wife leave the stadium before the game is over.

✦ ✦ ✦

The takedown of al-Baghdadi generally helps the Trump administration. But it is not a complete victory. The bitter partisanship that has consumed America soon blocks out the ISIS raid. The Democratic Party is invested in playing down all accomplishments of Donald Trump's, but the truth is that ISIS has been severely degraded and is no longer the top terror threat against America. That description now belongs to Iran and its ferocious military leader, General Qasem Soleimani. President Trump knows this, and because of Soleimani's public insults, America's leader has another score to settle.

And the endgame is now underway.

CHAPTER NINETEEN

US intelligence presses its advantage against ISIS. But there is someone looking over the shoulder of the Americans.

Six thousand miles from Washington, on the night of World Series Game 5, the next potential leader of ISIS rides inside an empty gasoline tanker truck. He is mourning the death of al-Baghdadi, but there is nothing that can be done. The Islamic State must carry on.

The wheels of transition are already in motion. In accordance with the Koran, a group known as the Majlis-ash-Shura—or simply the Shura Council—will soon gather in a secret location to vote for a new ISIS leader. These men are advisers to the caliph. The size of the group varies, but right now the council numbers almost thirty. They consider themselves deeply religious but also hyperpolitical, with many former members of the Baath Party, dedicated to unifying the Middle East into a single Islamic state. And like al-Baghdadi, a number of these men were held in US custody at a prison known as Camp Bucca during the American invasion of Iraq.

The man riding in the tanker is confident he will be chosen to lead the militant group.

Abu Hassan al-Muhajir has been the official ISIS spokesman for the last five years. He has risen through the ranks, devoting his life to the cause. Al-Baghdadi was a friend and mentor to him, and it is from the departed terrorist that al-Muhajir learned how to rule. Above all, al-Baghdadi was adept at demanding loyalty from the many factions within the Islamic State. Al-Mujahir must do the same.

Like the deceased al-Baghdadi, the spokesman is never seen in public. Very little is known about him, not even his age. His name is adopted, meaning "the immigrant," leading some to believe he was born in Saudi Arabia—which is, in fact, true. He never allows his photograph to be taken, nor has he appeared in an ISIS video. He is scornful of the internet theories saying he was born in Texas and studied at a music conservatory in Italy.

What *is* known about al-Muhajir is that he is a hard-core terrorist. As the mouthpiece for ISIS, he released audio statements celebrating heinous torture and murder. When President Trump visited Al-Asad Air Base in Iraq last Christmas, but left quickly due to security issues, it was al-Muhajir who mocked the president's hasty departure.

"How strange for a victor who can't even announce publicly an official visit to a country he claims to be bringing peace and stability to. He could only come like a frightened and cowardly thief," al-Mujahir said.

In his latest speech on an ISIS website, delivered after fifty Muslims were murdered by a white supremacist in a New Zealand mosque, al-Mujahir closed with a warning about the use of electronic devices. If ISIS's practice of killing is to continue, the group must avoid surveillance.

But the truth is, the internet is vital to the ISIS jihad. More than forty thousand young men and women from at least ninety nations have traveled to Syria and Iraq to join the Islamic State. Many are Middle Eastern, but a large number arrived from Europe, Australia, Russia, and the United States. Almost all come from politically stable nations with low unemployment and a high level of economic development, so it is not poverty that is driving ISIS recruitment. It is simply a powerful desire to wage war in the name of religion.*

The average candidate is a twenty-six-year-old male who has been inspired by violent ISIS social media posts on Facebook, Twitter, Telegram, and YouTube. Recruiting websites often show videos of the three hundred beheadings that have taken place since ISIS assumed control of Iraq and Syria, as well as documentaries about life inside the Islamic State.

But while this manipulation of the worldwide Muslim population requires a high level of technological savvy, ISIS leaders like Abu Hassan al-Muhajir never know when some intelligence analyst will track their cell phones. So caution is the word.

✦ ✦ ✦

The rolling claustrophobic cylinder smells of benzene and is completely dark. To avoid suspicion, hatches and valves are all closed tight, leaving just small ventilation holes to let in fresh air. The paved road is smooth but al-Muhajir can feel every bump, for there is no padding and no place to sit. He must simply lean against the metal walls. But the potential ISIS leader is not complaining. Better discomfort than extinction.

✦ ✦ ✦

There are very few men within ISIS leadership who share al-Muhajir's Saudi Arabian heritage. So he is quite familiar with the Arab who guided US Special Forces to Abu Bakr al-Baghdadi's compound. They know each other by name. But the spokesman does *not* know that his colleague has betrayed the jihad. And he is completely unaware that this betrayal has led to him being monitored on this lonely highway tonight.

The road passes the ancient city of Aleppo, a three-hour drive from where al-Baghdadi died yesterday. The phony gas truck follows a small pickup down a two-lane desert road. Night is coming. Headlights on.

Al-Muhajir can only see the blackened interior of the space that

---

* Researchers from Lebanon-based Quantum Communications identified the common reasons an individual chooses to join ISIS as a recruit: status, identity, thrills, redemption, revenge, ideology, justice, and death.

will soon become his tomb. He is being watched by Americans at an air base thousands of miles from northern Syria. A young pilot is receiving confirmation of his target and the verbal command "Cleared hot"—the official go-ahead to launch Hellfires.

A Hellfire missile does not miss. It features a millimeter wave-radar system that delivers the weapon on target with such complete precision that pilots use the term "fire and forget" to describe the Hellfire's path of destruction.

So Abu Hassan al-Muhajir is already a dead man, though he does not know it.

✦ ✦ ✦

General Qasem Soleimani is also taking a very personal interest in ISIS developments.

It is not just because the supreme leader of Iran, Ali Khamenei, has issued a *takfir*—a declaration of apostasy—against the Islamic State. Soleimani sees ISIS as a tactical threat because it is a Sunni organization; thus, a threat to Iran. "The so-called Islamic State is neither Islamic nor a state," is the belief of the Iranian government.

Those practicing Iran's Shia version of Islam are considered infidels by ISIS, which routinely murders them and levels Shia mosques. As the size of its caliphate grows, ISIS comes to control land stretching all the way to the Iranian border. When the Pakistani Taliban swear loyalty to al-Baghdadi, Iran is put in the difficult position of having yet another group of Sunni extremists nearby.

Qasem Soleimani sees the big picture. The growth of the Islamic State puts it at odds with the general's ambition to control the entire Middle East. By establishing dominion over Iraq, Syria, Lebanon, and Yemen, the general will be following in the footsteps of Darius the Great, ruler of Persia in the sixth century BC.* But to eliminate the Islamic State, the general needs a powerful ally.

---

* Darius the Great of Persia ruled the Achaemenid Empire from 522 to 486 BC. He developed the "Royal Road," a corridor across the Middle East to encourage communications and move personnel safely from what is now Iran all the way to the Mediterranean. Before Soleimani, the last time Iran had a powerful presence on that sea was 330 BC.

In July 2015, Soleimani decides it is time to speak with Moscow. He knows that Russia has almost no military presence in the Middle East.

Syria is the ideal location for Iran and Russia to collaborate. Syrian president Bashar al-Assad, an ally of both Iran and Russia, is fighting a civil war that could remove him from power. Should he be toppled, there is every possibility that a new government backed by the United States will take control. This possibility, combined with the ISIS caliphate, would render Iran and Russia powerless in the Middle East.

So, Soleimani directs Iranian leadership to solicit help from Vladimir Putin.

The Russian leader replies: "Send Qasem Soleimani."

The general has been banned from international travel by the United Nations since 2007, but that does not stop him. Soleimani flies to Moscow, where he is escorted to Putin's office in the Kremlin's north wing. The room is rectangular, with light-red curtains, matching armchairs, and inlaid oak panels on the walls. Two enormous chandeliers hang from the ceiling. The front of Putin's dark-brown hardwood desk actually slides out to form a working surface. By placing a chair on either side, Putin conducts intense face-to-face discussions with world leaders. It is on this surface that Qasem Soleimani, fresh off his four-hour flight from Tehran, unfurls a map of Syria. He looks down on the five-foot six Russian leader from across the desk. Putin is a former KGB spy for the Soviet Union. A brutal and cold man, he is one of the most feared leaders in the world.

But Soleimani is not afraid.

After pointing out the battle sites between rebels and Syrian troops now threatening Assad, Soleimani states adamantly that the dictator must remain in power—and that Iran and Russia must work together to make it happen.

Russia and Iran both depend upon the Assad regime. Russia has a vital strategic naval base in the Syrian port of Tartus. This is Putin's only warm-water base on the Mediterranean, making it crucial to the Russian Navy.

Iran uses Syria as a land bridge to transport men and arms to Hezbollah guerrillas in Lebanon. These terrorists, like Soleimani himself, are dedicated to the destruction of Israel.

Quickly, Soleimani and Putin make a deal. Russian aircraft will control the skies over Syria, preventing rebel armies from overthrowing Assad. Soleimani's Quds Force, with the assistance of Hezbollah rebels, will control the action on the ground.

The alliance with Russia has other benefits for Iran: it gains access to the Russian S-300 air defense system—and to Putin himself. When Moscow deepens its diplomatic friendship with Iranian enemies like Saudi Arabia and other Sunni states, it is Soleimani who visits Moscow to express concern.

Now sixty-two, Soleimani has never held greater power, but time is running out for him to fulfill his lifelong goal of destroying the Israeli state and imposing complete Shia dominance of the Middle East.

Thus, the general has prepared his final solution.

✦ ✦ ✦

The Hellfire missile strikes the truck at 995 miles per hour. The explosion is intensified by the gasoline residue still inside the container. Abu Hassan al-Muhajir dies instantly. The subsequent fire and the convection effect of the small enclosure ensures that he is cooked beyond recognition. Once again, DNA must confirm the identity of a dead ISIS leader.

CIA medical personnel are on the way.

✦ ✦ ✦

President Donald Trump is elated.

"Just confirmed that Abu Bakr al-Baghdadi's number one replacement has been terminated by American troops. Most likely would have taken the top spot—now he is also dead!" tweets the president.

In Iran, Qasem Soleimani is also jubilant. But he remains on guard, knowing that ISIS is weakened but not defeated. And even if that were the case, Sunni terror organizations like al-Qaeda, which are hostile to Iran, would rush in to fill the void. So the general watches every interaction, supervises the interrogations of ISIS captives, and is poised to take immediate action against all perceived dangers.

But, little does General Soleimani know, there is a deadly threat hovering over him.

CHAPTER TWENTY

OCTOBER 30, 2019
BAGHDAD, IRAQ
DUSK

The image of Qasem Soleimani is being spit upon.

Baghdad is ablaze. There have been three weeks of protests against Iran. Now, angry Iraqis wave their country's flag, chanting anti-Iranian slogans in the streets. The air smells of smoke and tear gas, and echoes with chants of the furious.

With the collapse of ISIS in Iraq, Soleimani and his Quds Force have aggressively moved in and are trying to control the country. Iran has invaded Iraq without the world noticing. Many Sunni Muslims object—and Iranian flags are being set on fire by the mob. The greatest ire is directed at portraits of General Soleimani, whom the Sunni loathe.

But behind closed doors at a secret location here in the capital, Soleimani himself works with Iraqi officials to stop the protests. The general has come to "offer advice," though his real motivation is to assert Iranian power over Sunni Iraq. "We know how to deal with protests in Iran," Soleimani tells the Iraqi officials. Indeed, since the demonstrations began, Quds militia fighters embedded within Iraqi military units have killed hundreds of suspected dissenters. The death toll now stands at 450.

Soleimani blames America for the violence, but it is Iran stoking unrest throughout the Middle East by actively enriching uranium in anticipation of producing a nuclear weapon. Israel, fearful of such a reality, is on alert. One month ago, three Israeli spies were arrested in Soleimani's hometown of Kerman, caught while trying to dig a tunnel beneath the local mosque. The plan was to fill the hole with explosives and assassinate the general by detonating the arsenal as he attended a Shia mourning ceremony.

Qasem Soleimani is confident that his Quds Force is more than capable of thwarting any future assassination attempt. His deep network of spies is everywhere in the Middle East.

And though he conducts his strategy in secret, the general has chosen to become a more prominent public figure by running for the Iranian presidency. The election is set to take place in June 2021. As he seeks to calm the chaos in Baghdad, Soleimani is increasing his social media profile, portraying himself as a peacemaker.

Soleimani is anything but that. He is a murderer and drug lord, raking in millions of dollars to fund terror organizations that are actively killing American soldiers in Iraq and Afghanistan.

"I swear on the grave of Khomeini I haven't authorized a bullet against the US," the general says.

Perhaps not a bullet—but something far worse.

✦ ✦ ✦

In Washington, Arkansas senator Tom Cotton is speaking before the Senate Armed Services Committee. The Republican is an army veteran who served as an infantry officer in Iraq and Afghanistan. The subject is Qasem Soleimani.

"I know the total number of soldiers, sailors, airmen, and marines that were killed by Iranian activities, and the number has been recently quoted as about five hundred. We weren't always able to attribute the casualties we had to Iranian activity, although many times we suspected it was Iranian activity even though we didn't necessarily have the forensics to support that."

In fact, the number of Americans actually killed by Soleimani is far higher. Estimates suggest that as many as 4,500 soldiers have lost their lives or were maimed by devices supplied by the general's Quds Force.

Soleimani's hatred for Americans means that he does not deal in basic explosives. Instead, he favors a brutal bomb known as an EFP—explosively formed penetrator—which is a leading cause of battlefield amputations suffered by American soldiers.

Roughly the size of a coffee can, each device curves a thin sheet of copper into an extremely deadly projectile upon detonation, traveling at six times the speed of sound—2,000 meters per second—as opposed to just 900 meters for a .50-caliber machine-gun round. This "shape charge" is powerful enough to punch a hole in the thick armor of a tank.

The devices are usually concealed inside a fake brick or rock. A passive infrared lens embedded within senses movement and triggers the explosion. The result is a supersonic teardrop of metal that severs limbs and extremities instantly.

General Qasem Soleimani not only provides the EFPs to militias in Afghanistan and Iraq but also helps them procure the training, factories, supply facilities, and even instructional videos necessary to employ the deadly weapon.

And though Soleimani is correct when he says he has never personally fired a weapon at American soldiers, he has most assuredly murdered and maimed thousands of them.

✦ ✦ ✦

In Washington, DC, Saudi Arabian ambassador Adel al-Jubeir is a vehement critic of Soleimani. "Iran is the chief sponsor of terrorism in the world. Iran has total disregard for international law and fundamental principles of international relations, such as good neighborliness and noninterference in the affairs of others. Iran has committed acts that no other country would do," al-Jubeir states in an interview with the PBS news show *Frontline*.

Qasem Soleimani takes notice of al-Jubeir's words and decides to kill him.

The plot to murder the Saudi ambassador will take place in Washington, DC. The killer tasked with the mission is Colonel Gholam

Shakuri, a Quds Force commander. The plan is code-named Chevrolet. Shakuri and his accomplice, a fifty-six-year-old naturalized American citizen of Iranian birth named Manssor Arbabsiar, will place bombs in a Washington restaurant frequented by the Saudi ambassador.*

Some United States senators and congresspeople are also likely to be at the popular bistro. But Soleimani does not care. "They want that guy done, if a hundred go with him, f**k 'em," Arbabsiar says in a call monitored by the Drug Enforcement Agency.

The assassination is thwarted. Soleimani's plot is discovered by undercover agents of the FBI and DEA. Manssor Arbabsiar is arrested, convicted of attempted murder, and sentenced to twenty-five years in a federal penitentiary.

His partner, Quds commander Shakuri, is more fortunate. He is charged in absentia by the United States for his crimes because he has coordinated the plot from Iran, where the FBI cannot detain him.

✦ ✦ ✦

The suitcases are heavy, weighing more than eighty pounds each.

The bags are lined up in a neat row at Tehran's Imam Khomeini International Airport. Uniformed Quds officials stand guard over the luggage. Mahmoud al-Zahar, a founding member of the Palestinian terror group Hamas, has come to Iran seeking financial assistance for his nefarious activities. His nine-man delegation met with Qasem Soleimani yesterday to request funding.

Transferring money to a terrorist organization through normal banking channels is impossible. But there are other ways. General Soleimani has provided Hamas with thirty suitcases—each containing more than US$1 million in cash.

There are so many pieces of luggage that the Hamas agents cannot carry them all. The terrorists travel home with $22 million they will use to purchase weapons in order to wage war against Israel.

---

* The name of the chic restaurant is Café Milano. The Saudi ambassador dined there at least two times a week.

"Soleimani had agreed to more money, but there were only nine of us, and we couldn't carry more than that," al-Zahar will lament.*

Soleimani will later increase Iranian aid to Hamas by sending Russian-made Kornet missiles to Gaza—"missiles that can destroy targets in the heart of Tel Aviv, Haifa, and other cities of the Zionist regime," al-Zahar will state.

Among the many attacks by Hamas using the laser-guided missiles, there is one especially heinous. An Israeli yellow school bus is destroyed. When paramedics rush to help the children, Hamas launches mortar rounds on the rescuers.

One student, sixteen-year-old Daniel Viflic, is killed when shrapnel pierces his brain.

Chalk up another victim for Qasem Soleimani.

✦ ✦ ✦

The hanging will take place slowly. The accused is a drug dealer, a crime calling for the death penalty in Iran. Hundreds of people are executed each year for selling or just simply possessing heroin, opium, and methamphetamines. Iran takes a very hard line against narcotics, and these public executions are meant to discourage such depravity. And yet these laws do not apply to Qasem Soleimani and the drug deals that fund his operations.

A crowd gathers at the hanging site in Tehran. A construction crane sits in the public square, its boom raised high in the sky. A cable extends from the raised arm, dangling down to the ground. At the end is a noose. The accused is led forward, hands tied behind his back. The death loop is cinched tightly around his neck. Slowly, so as to make the hanging more excruciating, the crane operator raises the cable, pulling the condemned upward.

Unlike a "drop" hanging, which breaks the neck immediately, this preferred Iranian method takes several minutes to completely deprive a man's lungs of oxygen.

Afterward, the accused is left dangling thirty feet in the air. Sometimes, when several men are hung at the same time, a small

---

* The Hamas leader told this to Iran's Tasnim News Agency.

fleet of cranes is required, and the executed swing in the wind together. Very often, the brutality is televised. The men are not taken down until families pay for the noose and the rental of the construction machinery that facilitates the killings.

But not *every* drug dealer suffers the death penalty.

Certainly not Qasem Soleimani.

His elite Quds Force controls the Iranian drug trade, netting millions of dollars in profits each year. Revolutionary Guard ships and planes transport narcotics to Albania, Bulgaria, and Romania. From there they are transported into western Europe and around the world. Soleimani runs the operation with the blessing of his good friend the supreme leader of Iran, Ayatollah Khamenei.

One Revolutionary Guard member will explain to the *Times* of London: "We were told that the drugs will destroy the sons and daughters of the West, and that we must kill them. Their lives are worth less because they are not Muslims."

The Quds drug cartel has a global reach, ensuring that Soleimani will always have access to the money he needs to fuel his terror ambitions. His actions are meant to destabilize the Middle East. Soleimani controls Hezbollah, Hamas, Houthi rebels in Yemen, and the al-Ashtar Brigades in Bahrain. He provides GPS-guided missiles, small arms, and training in guerrilla warfare and terror to all those groups. Soleimani also funds cyberattacks, weapons, aircraft, and ships. Starting in May 2019, he provided drones as well. This allows the general to observe and attack US forces in neighboring Iraq, as well as harass American vessels in the Persian Gulf. The United States Navy has already downed two Iranian drones that strayed too close its ships.*

Iran has been a terror haven for a long time. Beginning in 1979, agents of the regime illegally seized the US embassy in Tehran, holding more than sixty Americans hostage during the 444 days of the crisis. Hezbollah twice bombed the American embassy in Lebanon— once in 1983 and again in 1984. Another Iranian-supported attack

---

* In Syria alone, Soleimani funds the following militias: Harakat Hezbollah al-Nujaba, Kataib Hezbollah, Fatemiyoun Brigade, 313 Brigade, Quwat al-Ridha, Liwa al-Baqir, and assorted other local defense forces.

in 1983 killed 241 American military personnel when a truck bomb exploded their barracks.

In 1996, the Iranian regime directed another bombing of American military housing in Saudi Arabia, murdering 19 Americans in cold blood. Iranian proxies provided training to operatives who were later involved in al-Qaeda's bombing of the American embassies in Kenya and Tanzania, killing 224 people, and wounding more than 4,000 others. The regime continues to harbor high-level terrorists in the wake of the 9/11 attacks, including Osama bin Laden's son. In Iraq and Afghanistan, groups supported by Iran have killed hundreds of American military personnel.

And under General Soleimani, Iran's ability to attack Americans continues to increase.

The Quds Force possesses the largest and most diverse ballistic-missile program in the Middle East—more powerful than even that of Israel. By 2022, Soleimani plans to have missiles capable of striking western Europe. In 2025, a next generation of weapons will have the capacity to attack the United States.

The general also has a close connection with Osama bin Laden, having sheltered Hamza, the thirty-year-old son of the 9/11 mastermind. Despite President Trump's claim that the young bin Laden was killed in a counterterrorism operation in Afghanistan earlier in 2019, there is evidence he is still alive in the Iranian capital.

The terror world has many tentacles, but most lead back to Qasem Soleimani.

✦ ✦ ✦

The general feels untouchable, so exalted in his country that the Ayatollah Khamenei recently bestowed upon him Iran's most prestigious medal, the Order of Zulfaqar. He is the first man to receive the award since the Iranian Revolution, forty years ago.

These are indeed heady times for the Quds Force and its leader. Iran is on the verge of controlling Iraq, it is aiding the killing of US soldiers in Iraq and Afghanistan, and Soleimani himself is incredibly wealthy.

But all the money in the world will not save him.

✦ ✦ ✦

It is another hot day in Tampa, Florida. Leadership of the US Army Central Command, meeting in private, is compiling a list of reasons to take action against Qasem Soleimani.

As far back as 2007, the United States has targeted Soleimani. In that year, a team led by General Stanley McChrystal observes a convoy carrying the Iranian general as it travels through northern Iraq. The general is watching from a drone satellite transmission and could fire upon the vehicles in an instant. But McChrystal hesitates to give the kill order, allowing Soleimani to slip away.[*]

Shortly afterward, Israel targets a vehicle containing Soleimani and a Hezbollah leader. Once again, the United States is reluctant to pull the trigger.

But twelve years later, there is a new commander in chief and a new set of rules for the American military hunting terrorists.

Now, targets of opportunity have expiration dates.

And one is fast approaching for General Qasem Soleimani.

---

[*] General McChrystal wanted to gain more information about the convoy before it was vaporized, but the vehicles split up in the darkness and escaped.

CHAPTER TWENTY-ONE

DECEMBER 27, 2019
KIRKUK, IRAQ
7:20 P.M.

Death strikes without warning. Rockets are in the air.

It is evening here at Camp K-1, just after dinner. Sandbags line the perimeter for protection against terror attacks. Without warning, the first explosion hits. Men dive for cover as shrapnel flies. The sun went down two hours ago, making the brilliant light of the detonations visible from miles away.

The rockets are deadly Iranian antitank weapons, most likely fired from several miles distant. The launchers are welded to cargo-truck beds, allowing the terrorists to change locations immediately after firing.

Camp K-1 is shared by American and Iraqi troops, but the five-foot-long Katyusha rockets focus only on the American side. More than thirty rounds land, wounding four US service members and two Iraqi security personnel and killing Nawres Hamid, a civilian contractor working as a linguist for the Americans.

Hamid is thirty-three, a married father of two from Sacramento, California, and known for his gentleness. He is originally from Iraq but has since become a naturalized US citizen. The translator is a

Muslim, and his body is immediately flown home for burial in accordance with the tenets of his religion.

Quickly, Secretary of State Mike Pompeo speaks out against the attack. More than fourteen thousand American troops have been assigned to Iraq in response to the growing ISIS and Iranian threats. There have been eleven rocket incidents targeting coalition bases since November, but no one has been killed until tonight. This brazen attack is an act of war.

The secretary of state is blunt: "We must use this opportunity to remind Iran's leaders that any attacks by them, or their proxies of any identity, that harm Americans, our allies, or our interests will be answered with a decisive US response."

✦ ✦ ✦

Three thousand miles south of Iraq, in Mogadishu, Somalia, there is more Iranian mayhem. General Qasem Soleimani has funded al-Qaeda terror squads since the death of bin Laden ten years ago. Now, one day after the rocket attack in Kirkuk, Iranian-backed terrorists keep a close eye on a security checkpoint in the busy hub of the chaotic city.

A truck filled with explosives parks in front of a tax-collection center. Truck bombings have long been a favorite Iranian killing method. It is Saturday morning, the first day of the workweek in predominantly Muslim Mogadishu. Streets are filled with workers. Students walk quickly, late for class.

The truck bomb explodes.

Windows shatter. A percussive blast rolls outward from the place of detonation, shattering the eardrums of those nearby. In an instant, more than 90 people are dead and more than 125 wounded. Their bodies litter the sidewalks. Almost all are university students. Black plumes of smoke blot out the blue morning sky. Nearby vehicles are burning skeletons.*

---

* The attack was intended to kill Turkish soldiers and construction workers sent into Somalia to train the nation's military and build roads. Of the dead, only two were of Turkish descent. The al-Shabab extremist group, linked to Iran through al-Qaeda, is responsible. It previously conducted a murderous rampage in a Kenyan shopping mall in 2013, and then attacked a Nairobi luxury hotel in 2019.

After seeing the carnage, Secretary Pompeo tells the world it is time for "a decisive US response."

✦ ✦ ✦

American fighter jets go hunting the next morning.

The time is 11:00 a.m. United States Air Force F-15E Strike Eagles fly in formation over Iraq and Syria. Far below is the Euphrates River Valley, where mankind has waged war for thousands of years. The American pilots are vectoring toward Iranian ammunition depots and command posts that have been used by General Soleimani to launch attacks on US forces. Five targets, three in Iraq and two in Syria, have been preselected. The sites are guarded by Hezbollah terrorists loyal to Iran. Each American aircraft has precision-guided bombs affixed to a hard point beneath the wings. Overflight in Syria means potential conflict with Russian MiG fighters, but that is a risk the American military is now willing to take. The F-15 pilots are focused on their mission, ready to deal with the Russians if needed.

President Donald Trump has named his war against terror the "maximum pressure" campaign. So far, the United States has refrained from directly attacking Iran. Trump's focus has been on eradicating ISIS. But tension between the mullahs and the United States has escalated since America pulled out of the nuke deal.

The fighter pilots do not hesitate as they reach their targets, releasing their bombs and then turning back toward home base in Iraq. They see each bomb detonate, sending thick black clouds pluming into the air. Secondary explosions follow as ammunition dumps are blown up. The American attack comes without warning; there is no time for the terrorists to flee. Twenty-five militants will die, and another fifty-five are injured.*

Back in Somalia, American forces of the United States Africa Command also strike. This time, another wave of US jets kill the militants responsible for the Mogadishu truck bombing. The air strikes, conducted in conjunction with the Somali government, kill four

---

* These figures were announced by Iraqi security forces and the Hezbollah militia. Among the dead was Abu Ali Khazali, an Iran-allied militia leader.

militia members at two separate sites. The lethal actions against the terrorists send a clear warning.

Iran immediately pledges revenge. "Our response will be very tough on the American forces in Iraq," says senior commander Jamal Jaafar Ibrahimi, leader of a paramilitary group loyal to Qasem Soleimani.

Russia calls the American action "unacceptable" and "counterproductive."

Israeli prime minister Benjamin Netanyahu immediately phones Secretary Pompeo to congratulate him.

Pompeo himself issues a statement—knowing Soleimani will hear his words almost immediately. "What we did is take a decisive response that makes clear what President Trump has said for months and months and months. Which is that we will not stand for the Islamic Republic of Iran to take actions that put American men and women in jeopardy."

President Trump stays silent, allowing the military action to speak for itself.

✦ ✦ ✦

Baghdad is ablaze.

New Year's Eve. Vandalism and arson are rampant. After three months, protests continue in the Iraqi capital and show no signs of abating; if anything, the tension has escalated. Thousands of Sunni Muslims are taking to the streets to condemn the Iranian military. But now they are also engaged in a war of words with Shia counterprotesters funded by Iran.

A third group joins the confrontation. Mourners dressed in militia uniforms are just leaving the funeral for Hezbollah militiamen killed in the US bombing two days ago. They march down Kindi Street, near what is known as the Green Zone. This heavily fortified sanctuary is home to the American embassy. Iraqi security forces guard a checkpoint marking the entrance to the zone—but step aside as the angry mob marches closer.

Shouting "Death to America" and "Death to Israel," the mob throws rocks at the American embassy, then breaks windows and spray-paints graffiti over the entry building. The outer walls of the embassy are breached. Waving pro-Iranian flags, the protesters force their way inside storage facilities and ransack files.

Fire soon breaks out in the Green Zone. US ambassador Matthew Tueller is out of the country on personal travel, but the agitators do not know this. The terrorists have been instructed to take control of the embassy and parade captured staffers before the world.

Soon, more militia fighters join the fracas. US marines stand atop the main embassy building, their guns trained on the pro-Iran crowd below them.*

In Washington, a furious President Trump takes to Twitter. "Iran killed an American contractor, wounding many. We strongly responded, and always will. Now Iran is orchestrating an attack on the US embassy in Iraq.

"They will be held fully responsible."

✦ ✦ ✦

Back in Baghdad, the militia protesters settle in for a long siege. Tents are pitched throughout the Green Zone as the angry mob forms a perimeter around the Americans trapped inside the embassy. One thousand militia members spend the night. By morning, images of the mob are flashed around the world, allowing American intelligence to identify several of the men inciting the violence as cohorts of General Soleimani.

The Iraqi government makes no attempt to dislodge the attackers, even though the terrorists are a direct threat to American embassy personnel. This is in contrast to the way the Iraqis treat dissenters threatening them; tear gas and live ammunition are routinely used. After a nighttime rest, the mob once again launches a siege.

To the staff inside the embassy, the attack is clearly premeditated. "They were going around with large poles and knocking down the [security] cameras to limit our views on the outside of what was going on," one American security official will later note.

"They were disciplined and had an agenda," another CIA agent inside the embassy will add, noting that the mob threw Molotov

---

* The marines did not fire, out of fear of causing an international incident.

cocktails inside the grounds in an attempt to detonate the fuel depot. As American employees worked to battle the blazes, they were pelted by rocks.

The biggest fear in the minds of embassy employees fighting back the attackers is, "Benghazi." In 2012, protesters attacked the American consulate in Libya, causing the deaths of several Americans.

"Benghazi definitely . . . crossed everyone's mind," one American official said.*

Finally, the marines have had enough. They fire tear gas into the crowd, and two AH-64 Apache helicopter gunships zoom low in a show of force. Word circulates among the terrorists that America is sending several hundred soldiers to protect the embassy.

Twenty-four hours after their arrival, the Shia mob marches away. "We rubbed America's nose in the dirt," one protester gloats to the press.

✦ ✦ ✦

It is now January 1, 2020, as the embassy siege comes to an end. The death of Nawres Hamid occurred just five days ago. Every day since has seen the threat level between Iran and the United States rise.

"The game has changed," states Secretary of Defense Mark Esper, adding that American forces will shortly begin launching preemptive strikes against Iran.

Nevertheless, General Soleimani feels he has an advantage. He decides to oversee a new wave of Iranian attacks on American troops. Soleimani quietly makes plans to travel from Damascus to Baghdad—hoping to provoke war between his country and America.

The general boards a Syrian airliner for a flight to Baghdad International Airport. His name is not on the official passenger manifest, and the plane has been delayed several hours to accommodate his schedule.

The time is shortly after ten on the night of January 2.

The man with two hours to live is walking into a trap.

---

*The Benghazi attacks took place on September 11–12, 2012. Terrorists overwhelmed the American diplomatic compound, killing Ambassador J. Christopher Stevens and three other diplomatic personnel.

CHAPTER TWENTY-TWO

JANUARY 3, 2019
BAGHDAD, IRAQ
12:32 A.M.

Cham Wings Flight 6Q501 touches down at Baghdad International Airport.

The Airbus A320, one of just four aircraft comprising the Syrian airline's entire fleet, is three hours late. Officially, the cause is bad weather. But the real reason is the five men who boarded just before departure, taking seats in the forward cabin for the one-hour flight from the Syrian capital.

General Qasem Soleimani sits in the front row, as always. He wears dark slacks and a shirt buttoned to the throat, but no tie. The rest of his entourage dresses the same. The only real difference is the prominent silver ring with a stone of red carnelian worn by the general.*

Among those making the trip are loyal longtime bodyguards Hadi Taremi and Vahid Zamanian. Both are Quds Force members. The general is also accompanied by two top Iranian officials: Major General Hossein Pourjafari, Soleimani's right-hand man

---

* Red carnelian is believed by some Muslims to bestow blessings on its wearer.

and founder of the Quds spy agency, and Colonel Shahroud Mozafarri Nia, a Quds intelligence officer specializing in Syria and Lebanon.

Soleimani trusts each man completely.

The white aircraft with the dark lettering along the fuselage taxis to the large, modern terminal in Baghdad. As the plane pulls up to the gate, passengers in the rear remain seated, not making a move to leave the craft until Qasem Soleimani and his entourage exit the front doors.

The men do not walk the Jetway into the terminal. Nor do they wait in line at customs. Instead, Soleimani's team exits down a long stairwell to the tarmac. They are met by a longtime ally, Abu Mahdi al-Muhandis, the gray-haired founder of the Kataib Hezbollah militia. The terrorist guides Soleimani's party to two SUVs parked near the aircraft.

The vehicles then drive away, exiting though a cargo gate. In all, the two cars hold ten men.

General Soleimani believes he is completely secure.

But, in fact, he and his men are being followed from twenty thousand feet in the air.

✦ ✦ ✦

CIA director Gina Haspel has been monitoring Soleimani's travels all day. She knows that he flies commercial, often buying tickets on several different airlines before selecting one just before takeoff. She has informants in the Damascus Airport watching the general, hoping to make a positive identification and confirm which airline he is flying.

The director knows Soleimani is not flying to Iraq this evening to conduct a peace mission. Instead, the general is meeting with his militia allies to plan more attacks against US troops. Soleimani's goal is ridding the Middle East of all American forces.

Ms. Haspel agrees that now is the time to deal with General Soleimani.

But that decision has already been made. President Trump signed off on lethal action shortly after the embassy in Baghdad was attacked five days ago.*

For years, American intelligence has compiled a list of the world's top terror targets. Soleimani has long been among the most wanted but has avoided assassination through covert movements and stealth.

But now the general's current location and intention to harm Americans are known beyond any doubt. Informants confirm Soleimani's presence on Flight 6Q501. Deeper-level informants within the Quds Force have relayed the general's movements in Syria and Lebanon over the past three days. There is even word that Soleimani is being betrayed by a close friend—similar to the Arab who informed on Abu Bakr al-Baghdadi.

✦ ✦ ✦

The drones have been circling for almost four hours.†

The actual number of unmanned aerial vehicles now over Baghdad International Airport will remain classified, but there are at least two MQ-9 Reaper drones training their high-definition cameras on the vehicles carrying Soleimani and his men.

Preparations for this moment began long before the general boarded the flight from Damascus. Armed with informant information, personnel at Al-Asad Air Base, in northern Iraq, and Al-Udeid Air Base, in the Arabian Peninsula nation of Qatar, began readying the Reapers for flight late this afternoon.

Each MQ-9 is thirty-six feet long, with a wingspan of twenty meters. Maximum takeoff weight is five tons, with much of that fuel and weapons. A propeller at the rear of the Reaper provides power.

Technicians enter the hangars housing the drones and run a series of tests on the cameras, which are capable of clearly photographing the name on a golf ball from three miles in the sky.

---

* Senator Lindsey Graham was notified of the attack while visiting President Trump in Florida one day after the embassy siege. Eric Trump, the president's son, tweeted on December 31, stating that the United States was "'bout to open a big ol' can of whoopass." That tweet was quickly deleted.

† Each Reaper drone costs $32 million.

A small truck then tows the drones onto a runway, accompanied by two US Air Force personnel who walk alongside and conduct last-minute visual safety checks.

Thousands of miles away, remote pilots at Creech Air Force Base in Nevada fire up the engines. The drones emit the sound of a small Cessna aircraft. The pilots then push the throttles forward. Each drone labors down the runway and lifts into the air. Aloft, the Reapers soar toward Baghdad at two hundred knots. The drone launched from Iraq requires just thirty minutes to get into position; the UAV from Qatar will take five hours.

Soon, bad news: Soleimani's flight is delayed. The operational range of the fully armed drones is fourteen hours, and the aircraft from Qatar may have to return to base if the holdup continues too long.

But then the flight crew and the CIA team tracking Soleimani's movements catch a break. The flight to Baghdad finally departs Damascus at 10:30 p.m.

The Reaper based in Qatar will have plenty of time to do its job.

✦ ✦ ✦

At Creech Air Force Base, thirty-five miles outside Las Vegas, two-person teams of air force pilots from the 432nd Air Expeditionary Wing monitor each Reaper. The drones remain in position over Baghdad. Video screens in front of each pilot show a clear image of two vehicles driving the perimeter road. Having been on target for several hours now, the air crews know the layout of the airport. They well understand that once the SUVs depart and head east toward the Tigris River and the heart of Baghdad, they will blend in with many other cars.

But for now, the targets are the only vehicles on the road.

It is not known whether the remote pilots are briefed on the identities of the men they will soon kill. But the officers are certainly aware these SUVs are a threat to America's national security.

✦ ✦ ✦

General Soleimani sits in the backseat of one Toyota vehicle, next to Abu Mahdi al-Muhandis. Two Hezbollah terrorists drive. Soleimani has ordered the four men from his entourage to ride in the other vehicle so that he and al-Muhandis can discuss strategy privately.

The airport is dark. No planes are landing so late at night, and, despite the presence of runway lights, there is little activity other than that of the two cars on the perimeter road. Baghdad, and the secret location where Soleimani will spend the night, is five miles distant. The drive into the city will take them past the Green Zone and the American embassy, the scene of Soleimani's most recent triumph.

The general has had a long day; it is well past his preferred early bedtime of nine o'clock. But a strategy discussion is a good use of his time.

Sleep will come soon enough.

✦ ✦ ✦

The soft propeller thrum of the drones at twenty thousand feet is imperceptible to anyone on the ground. And unlike jet aircraft, the Reaper does not leave a distinguishing white contrail in the sky. It is also the middle of the night in Iraq, which means no chance that a sunbeam reflecting off the drone will give away its position.

Back in Nevada, there is talk among the pilots about the vehicles they are tracking.

Not that it matters. In a few minutes, there will be no vehicles.

The order comes at 2:55 p.m. Las Vegas time.

✦ ✦ ✦

It is 12:55 a.m. in Baghdad.

Qasem Soleimani is excited about the future. He is not a man given to regrets, preferring to always look forward. At sixty-two, despite his prostate issues and back pain related to his many wounds from the Iran-Iraq War, he exudes a healthy demeanor. His mind works feverishly, always thinking of ways to benefit Iran. His children are grown, he has unlimited access to drug money, and his power will only increase when he wins the Iranian presidency.

Also, it is good to be sitting in the backseat with his friend, Abu Mahdi al-Muhandis. "The Engineer," as the sixty-five-year-old Hezbollah leader is nicknamed, has been waging terror war even longer than Soleimani. The Iraqi was a longtime foe of Saddam Hussein and has served the Quds Force as a special military adviser.

As they discuss the next wave of violence to be inflicted upon the United States, Soleimani and al-Muhandis most likely speak in the casual shorthand of two friends in complete agreement.

The driver and bodyguard sitting in the front seats know better than to speak—or listen. So the only sound in the SUV is that of Qasem Soleimani and the Engineer having a conversation.

Until it is not.

A Hellfire missile travels supersonically, so the loud sound of its rocket propellant directing the deadly weapon toward its target is a few seconds behind its actual flight path.

And at almost a thousand miles an hour, it takes a very short period of time for a Hellfire to approach a target when fired by a drone four miles up in the sky.

In addition, the drone cameras are so precise that the pilots back at Creech Air Force Base can see which vehicle Soleimani is riding in. They actually watched him get in—knowing he will never get out.

✦ ✦ ✦

The last sound the general hears on earth is the split-second roar of a Hellfire rocket.

Two missiles slam into his car.

A third missile, then a fourth, obliterate the vehicle carrying his security team. Drone photos of the destruction show two flaming mounds of metal. Everyone inside is burned beyond recognition.

But one thing does remain of Qasem Soleimani. Even as his body is ripped to shreds by the direct hit from back-to-back Hellfires, commingling his parts with those of his confederates, the hand of the general is seen clearly. His silver and red ring, remaining on his finger, now lies with the severed hand on the shoulder of the road—illuminated by the flaming hulks of the two destroyed cars.

The rest of Qasem Soleimani is just mist.*

---

* The ten men killed were medically analyzed by Iraqi security forces before being handed over to families for burial. The remains of Qasem Soleimani were identified by his ring, but those of Abu Mahdi al-Muhandis were never located.

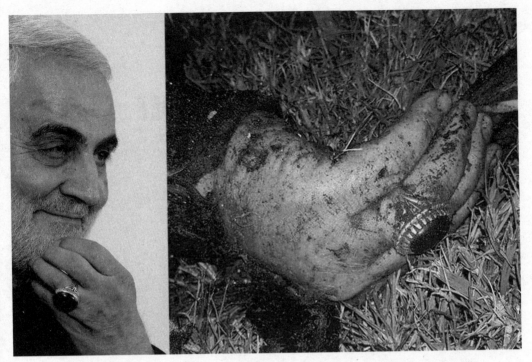

The hand and ring of Major General Haj Qassem Soleimani, the commander of the Quds Force, an elite unit of Iranian Islamic Revolutionary Guards Corps (IRGC) killed when two US helicopters attacked two convoys carrying the Quds Force.

✦ ✦ ✦

Iran is stunned. Sputtering to respond, the mullahs dither. *They* could be next. Although the Iranian protest is predictable, it is muted.

But not so with other demonstrations of disgust. All around the world, anger is being directed at the United States of America.

Even though a mass killer has himself been killed—President Trump and the United States are soon portrayed as the *real* villains.

CHAPTER TWENTY-THREE

The long knives are out.

Rachel Maddow of the MSNBC cable news network wears all black as she looks into the camera. Her guest, wearing a lavender suit, is former Obama national security adviser Susan Rice. Ms. Rice's scheduled appearance to promote a new book coincides with the killing of General Soleimani. The two women appear on a split screen, with Maddow on the left. "The US had previously assessed that it would be more dangerous to kill Qasem Soleimani, the head of the Quds Force in Iran, than to allow him to live," Maddow begins. "There's a lot of discussion about that reporting now that this air strike has happened. . . . Is there any reason to think that calculation somehow changed?"

"Judging from what I know, and from what we're likely to see, I think there's real reason to believe that in all likelihood the benefits will be outweighed by the risks," Susan Rice responds.*

---

* MSNBC is a division of NBC News. It presents information solely from a leftist perspective. The guest, Susan Rice, misled the world about the 2012 terror attack in Benghazi, Libya. Ms. Rice is presently Joe Biden's top domestic adviser.

✦ ✦ ✦

On another cable channel, CNN news anchor Becky Anderson joins the list of those criticizing the decision to strike Soleimani. She is British, one of the network's international personalities. Her comments about the late general's assassination go out around the world.

"Earlier, we heard US president Trump justify the operation, saying he acted before Soleimani could carry out more attacks against Americans. Have a listen," she begins. A video clip rolls, showing Donald Trump announcing the successful assassination from the White House.

"Last night, at my direction, the United States military executed a flawless strike that terminated the terrorist ringleader responsible for gravely wounding and murdering thousands and thousands of people and hundreds and hundreds, at least, of Americans. He was planning a very major attack. And we got him."

The segment then shifts, showing images of an Iranian mob. News anchor Anderson narrates the voice-over: "These images showing you the outrage being felt in Tehran as well, where we heard chants of 'Death to America' and saw flags being burned. Iran is promising that it will strike back."

Now the images on the screen change once again, showing a small, bespectacled individual. This is Majid Takht Ravanchi, Iran's ambassador to the United Nations:

"There will be harsh revenge," the diplomat vows. "Iran will act based on its own choosing. And the time, the place will be decided later on.

"They should expect anything as a result of this aggression."*

✦ ✦ ✦

In Qom, one of Iran's holiest cities, the red flag of revenge is being raised.

---

* CNN's international and domestic presentations took a sharp turn leftward once Donald Trump was elected president. While he was in office, CNN gained viewers. However, since Mr. Trump departed, the network has lost more than half its audience.

As the sun ascends on this winter morning, a bloodred standard is being hoisted above the towering dome of Jamkaran Mosque. The words "those who want to avenge the blood of Hussein" are written in large white lettering on the flag.* This mosque is a central location in the Shia religion. The flag on display during the morning call to prayer is normally blue. But as news of Qasem Soleimani's execution becomes widely known throughout Iran, the color of revenge is chosen instead.

On Twitter, the hashtag #WorldWar3 is already trending.

✦ ✦ ✦

One hundred miles north, in Tehran, the streets are filled with chanting mourners dressed in black. The Ayatollah Khamenei is declaring that "severe revenge" awaits the United States as three days of national grief begin. Soleimani will be buried in his hometown tomorrow, and the ayatollah will lead the service. Iran is already moving its ballistic missiles in secret, preparing to possibly strike US positions.

✦ ✦ ✦

In Washington, US Senator Lindsey Graham issues a statement confirming his support for the Soleimani assassination—saying he had been briefed about the operation by President Trump in Florida. "We killed the most powerful man in Iran short of the Ayatollah," Graham tweets. "This was not an act of revenge for what he has done in the past. This was a preemptive, defensive strike planned to take out the organizer of attacks yet to come."

Some Democrats, however, disagree, stating that President Trump did not have the authority to execute Soleimani.

"[Trump] has the ability to prevent an imminent attack against the United States without coming to Congress," Democratic senator Chris Murphy of Connecticut stated in an interview with National Public Radio. "I think we need to see if that, in fact, is true. He does

---

* The words refer to Hussein, the grandson of the prophet Muhammad. He was decapitated in 680 BC during the Second Islamic Civil War. Many considered his death unjust and responded with brutal attacks on those responsible. Today, the red flag is a call for violent action.

not have any other standing authorization to take out a strike against a country that we have not declared war against."

Former vice president Joe Biden, a Democrat now campaigning for the presidency, is also critical of the operation. "While Soleimani deserved to be brought to justice for his crimes against American troops, and thousands of innocents throughout the region, the assassination is like throwing dynamite on a tinderbox."*

✦ ✦ ✦

The world takes sides.

Israel and Saudi Arabia support the assassination. Russia condemns it. The United Nations claims the attack is in violation of its charter, stating that there is no proof Soleimani was planning an attack against Americans. Iraq claims the US action is a blow to its sovereignty.

And with every passing day, the world awaits the Iranian response.

Turbulence continues. Peace rallies are held around the world. Holding signs demanding that the United States pull its troops from the Middle East, protesters fill Times Square in New York City and stand outside the White House. In all, eighty American cities are the scene of nonviolent protests, and there are others around the globe: London, Berlin, Moscow, Prague, Istanbul.

In Baghdad, protesters are unified for the first time in three months, demanding the United States exit their country.

On the other side, the website for the United States's Selective Service System crashes—overwhelmed by young men wishing to know how they might be affected by a potential military draft. Just as in the days after 9/11, when patriotic fervor fueled enlistments, the possibility of war with Iran has stimulated interest in the American armed forces.

---

* Joe Biden's record on terrorism is mixed. He originally supported the war in Iraq, ordered by President Bush to eliminate weapons of mass destruction allegedly held by Saddam Hussein. However, Mr. Biden opposed the action that killed Osama bin Laden but later reversed his position. Today, as president, his posture against Islamic terror is largely undefined.

✦ ✦ ✦

On January 4, 2020, President Trump holds a press conference at his Mar-a-Lago resort in Florida to defend the attack. "We took action to stop a war. We did not take action to start a war," President Donald Trump tells reporters. "If Americans anywhere are threatened, we have all these targets already fully identified, and I am ready and prepared to take whatever action is necessary, and that in particular refers to Iran."

In fact, the United States is already gearing up for conflict. Troops are heading to the Middle East. American warships in the region are on high alert. President Trump set a redline of "no US casualties" and has warned Tehran not to cross it. He is promising to defend American personnel and interests from Iranian proxies who have already killed Nawres Hamid, the US contractor in Iraq. He defends at length the decision to kill Qasem Soleimani, insisting the action was necessary to save American lives.

As criticism of Trump and America grows, the president becomes more bellicose. "Let this serve as a WARNING that if Iran strikes any Americans, or American assets, we have. . . . . . . targeted 52 Iranian sites (representing the 52 American hostages taken by Iran many years ago), some at a very high level & important to Iran & the Iranian culture, and those targets, and Iran itself, WILL BE HIT VERY FAST AND VERY HARD," Trump tweets.

Later, Donald Trump ups the rhetoric even more. "They attacked us & we hit back. If they attack again, which I would strongly advise them not to do, we will hit them harder than they have ever been hit before!"

✦ ✦ ✦

All the saber-rattling causes the left-wing American media to up the attacks against Donald Trump. The situation quickly becomes political, not one of national security, with CNN leading the dissent.

"The US has provided few details about those specific threats posed by Soleimani and failed to clearly outline the legal underpinnings," reports the global network.

"The administration has failed to connect the dots in a way that provides a clear picture of an imminent threat, and that argument has been obscured by inconsistent messaging from US officials.

"One thing that has become relatively clear is that the operation to take out Soleimani did not hinge on some kind of golden opportunity to target the Quds Force commander, unlike the missions that killed Osama bin Laden and ISIS leader Abu Bakr al-Baghdadi."*

National Security Adviser Robert O'Brien quickly defends the president.

"Soleimani was in the Middle East, in Iraq, and traveling around the Middle East. He had just come from Damascus, where he was planning attacks on American soldiers, airmen, marines, sailors, and against our diplomats," O'Brien states.

The national security adviser speaks the truth. CIA documents show that captured intelligence pinpointed a number of attacks being planned by Soleimani. But for the media, unfriendly to President Trump, opinion overrode fact.

✦ ✦ ✦

In Tehran, tens of thousands of mourners gather for the funeral of Qasem Soleimani. The words of a weeping Ayatollah Khamenei, praying over the general's wooden coffin, are broadcast by loudspeakers. An Iranian flag drapes the casket. Then, in a surprise appearance, Soleimani's twenty-seven-year-old daughter Zeinab is given the chance to speak. She is dressed in black, her head covered by a scarf but her face visible. Zeinab is due to marry Riza Safi al-Din, a Hezbollah leader thought to be the terror organization's second-in-command, this June. Their nuptials portend an even tighter relationship between the Lebanese terror group and Iran.

As the funeral grows in intensity, Zeinab Soleimani continues. "The families of American soldiers in West Asia," she tells the crowd in a loud, angry tone, "will be waiting for the news of the deaths of their children."

---

* Those statements were made by CNN's Zachary Cohen. He covers the Pentagon as a reporter. His comments, however, are obviously editorial in nature.

Zeinab's threat is passionate but confusing. Her speech rambles. But the crowd does not care. The general's daughter inspires them, whipping the mob into a frenzy; loud chants of "Death to the USA" are heard.

✦ ✦ ✦

Hours after Soleimani's body is put into the ground, Iran launches "Operation Martyr Soleimani." Ballistic missiles target a US air base in Iraq. The attack begins an hour and a half past midnight, roughly the same time Soleimani was assassinated five days ago. Iranian Fateh-313 and QAAM short-range missiles, the length of a telephone pole, suddenly rain down on American forces. Cries of "Incoming!" send troops racing for the safety of underground bunkers—all the while reeling from the enormous blast waves as Iranian armament explodes less than thirty yards away.

The projectiles are deadly, carrying high-explosive warheads weighing almost one ton. They are designed to fragment into a thousand pieces of shrapnel upon striking a target. In the twenty-year history of America's war on terror, these are the most powerful weapons ever fired at US forces. The Al-Asad Air Base in northern Iraq is soon a scene of fire and destruction—craters thirty feet wide, incinerated vehicles, and the taste of "ammonia-flavored moon dust," in the words of one soldier, referring to explosive residue wafting through the night air.

But when the shelling stops and the all-clear finally sounds, Iran is frustrated. No United States troops are killed by the incoming rounds.*

"All is well," President Trump tweets shortly after the attack.

✦ ✦ ✦

The atmosphere in Iran is tense. Nervous soldiers of the Revolutionary Guard—the same troops led and funded by Qasem Soleimani—

---

* Although there were no American fatalities, more than a hundred US troops suffered brain injuries and post-traumatic stress disorder due to the percussive effects of missiles landing close to their positions. Twenty-nine soldiers were concussed so badly that they received the Purple Heart, an honor only given to soldiers wounded in battle.

believe the United States will soon return fire with cruise missiles. But they are mistaken. No missiles are launched by the Trump administration. However, the Iranian military is so jumpy that it reacts impulsively to a strange image on its radar. Incompetent commanders believe it is a cruise missile over Iran. In reality, it is a Ukrainian passenger jet.

The 737 is blasted from the sky—killing all 176 passengers and crew on board. The vast majority of passengers are traveling on Iranian passports. Ukraine International Airlines Flight 752 is traveling to Kyiv, the capital of that nation. The action occurs three minutes after the jet took off from Tehran. The cockpit is hit first, but flight recorders show the pilots do not die immediately, struggling for three minutes to get control of the aircraft. They fail. No one on board survives.

One day later, before international investigators comb through the rubble, Iranian bulldozers level the crash scene. The flight data boxes are recovered, but to this day, Iran refuses to share the recordings of Flight 752's final moments. The mullahs initially claim that a fire in one of the aircraft's engines caused the destruction. "It was nothing compared with the main event," Iranian television boasts, referring to the missile attack on Americans.

But soon the clerics admit that "human error" spurred the launching of two Tor-M1 surface-to-air missiles which ended the lives of the passengers and crew.

In essence, General Soleimani has claimed his last victims.

CHAPTER TWENTY-FOUR

President Trump is not through with the mullahs.

Less than two weeks after the assassination of General Solei-mani, the world is now distracted by new events in Iran. Thousands are defying the Iranian government and taking to the streets of Teh-ran to protest the downing of Flight 752. Iranian public anger, which was once directed at Donald Trump, is now focused on the false story that the Ukrainian aircraft crashed due to mechanical error. The people well understand they have been deceived.

And even though the claim has since been changed by the mul-lahs, there is continuing anger. Protesters are now being arrested. Television journalists reporting on the dissent are fired. Elected members of the Iranian Parliament—or, the Majiles, officially known as the Islamic Consultative Assembly—who support the protesters are banned by the mullahs from running again.

There are also rumors that demonstrators are being shot dead.

Inside the White House, President Trump senses weakness. He takes to Twitter: "To the leaders of Iran—DO NOT KILL YOUR PROTESTERS. Thousands have already been killed or imprisoned by you, and the World is watching. More importantly, the USA is watching. Turn your internet back on and let reporters roam free! Stop the killing of your great Iranian people!"

The president is still annoyed about the criticism of the Soleimani attack. So he is looking to turn the tables. He is also searching for other terror targets.

This is a departure from Donald Trump's usual philosophy in the Middle East. He does not actively support American troops being based on the ground in places like Afghanistan and Iraq. He thinks those countries should fight their own battles. He does not want to spend the money or manpower defending places he believes are not vital to American interests.

Nevertheless, the fight against terrorism has become very personal for Mr. Trump. His assessment of his predecessor, Barack Obama, is that he showed weakness, thereby encouraging terror acts all over the world. Also, President Trump is influenced by Israeli prime minister Benjamin Netanyahu, who has provided intelligence information indicating that Islamic terrorism is on the rise.

And so it is that President Trump has decided to become extremely aggressive in the elimination of known terrorists. And a man named Qasim al-Rimi, a leader of al-Qaeda in the Arabian Peninsula, is at the top of his list. Al-Rimi's group is not only active in the Middle East, it is responsible for an attempted bombing of a commercial airliner in the United States on Christmas Day 2009.* More infamously, it was AQAP terrorists who stormed into the Paris offices of *Charlie Hebdo* and slaughtered its employees.

In addition, President Trump has a personal motive for wanting al-Rimi dead. Just three days after being sworn in as president in 2017, Mr. Trump authorized a mission into Yemen that resulted in the death of a Navy SEAL. And while the Trump administration

---

* Northwest Airlines Flight 253 from Amsterdam to Detroit on Christmas Day 2009 was the subject of a failed attempt to detonate a bomb placed inside a terrorist's underwear. Umar Farouk Abdulmutallab, twenty-three, a Nigerian member of al-Qaeda, set fire to the plastic explosives in his pants but alert fellow passengers wrestled him to the ground and put out the flame before the bomb could detonate. The terrorist was sentenced to four life terms in prison and is currently incarcerated in a high security "supermax" facility in Florence, Colorado.

publicly proclaimed the raid a success, the president still sees that foray as a blemish on his terror record.

Chief Petty Officer William "Ryan" Owens of SEAL Team 6 died in that 2017 raid. Three years are an eternity, and the mission is all but forgotten. But Donald Trump has not lost the memory.

However, he needs an immediate provocation to go after Qasim al-Rimi.

He gets one sixteen days after the assassination of Qasem Soleimani.

✦ ✦ ✦

The moon is nearly invisible. It is the night of January 29, 2017. The V-22 Osprey tilt-rotor aircraft goes "feet dry" as it crosses from the Indian Ocean into Yemeni airspace. Ten minutes later, a joint team of Navy SEALs and United Arab Emirates commandos touches down five miles outside the village of al-Ghayil, a reputed terrorist stronghold. Tonight's mission is a "sensitive site exploration" (SSE) to search for electronics and other sources of information that pinpoint al-Qaeda forces in Yemen. This data will then be used to launch a quick series of strikes on the terrorists. The SEALs have been in the Middle East for months, undertaking "kill or capture" operations. A successful strike receives no media coverage and remains top secret.

Tonight will *not* be a successful operation.

This mission deep into Yemen was in fact planned years ago. Though the terror threat in Yemen is very real, officials in the Obama administration considered the plan too high risk. The president well remembered a raid he authorized in 2014 to free an American who had been held hostage in Yemen for fifteen months. Forty US Army Special Forces operators took part in the action, believing thirty-three-year-old American photographer Luke Somers was in "imminent danger," in the words of President Obama. The raid was not a covert operation and included drone strikes, strafing runs by American jets, and the assistance of Yemeni government ground troops. Despite this great show of force, things went wrong. The resulting firefight saw the terrorists kill Somers and fellow hostage Pierre

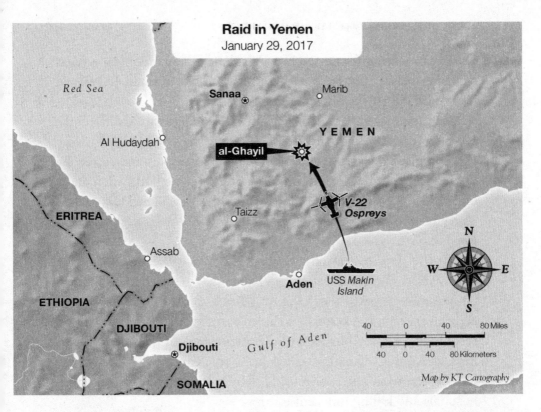

Raid in Yemen
January 29, 2017

Red Sea

Sanaa

Marib

al-Ghayil

Y E M E N

Al Hudaydah

V-22 Ospreys

ERITREA

Taizz

Assab

Aden

USS *Makin Island*

ETHIOPIA

DJIBOUTI

Djibouti

Gulf of Aden

SOMALIA

N
W E
S

40 0 40 80 Miles

40 0 40 80 Kilometers

Map by KT Cartography

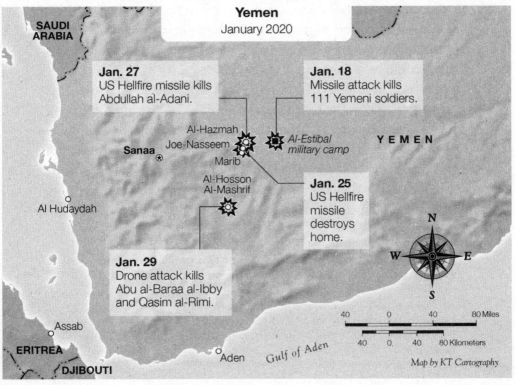

Yemen
January 2020

SAUDI ARABIA

Jan. 27
US Hellfire missile kills Abdullah al-Adani.

Jan. 18
Missile attack kills 111 Yemeni soldiers.

Al-Hazmah
Joe-Nasseem

Al-Estibal military camp

Y E M E N

Sanaa

Marib

Al-Hosson
Al-Mashrif

Jan. 25
US Hellfire missile destroys home.

Al Hudaydah

Jan. 29
Drone attack kills Abu al-Baraa al-Ibby and Qasim al-Rimi.

N
W E
S

Assab

ERITREA

Aden

Gulf of Aden

DJIBOUTI

40 0 40 80 Miles

40 0 40 80 Kilometers

Map by KT Cartography

Korkie, a South African teacher. President Obama received a great deal of criticism after the raid's failure. With this in mind, he refused to sign off on another attack in Yemen.*

But new secretary of defense James Mattis sees things differently. He believes the plan against al-Qaeda has the potential for a very substantial payoff. The desert location has been monitored closely by drones and satellites for months and appears to be lightly defended. Over dinner at the White House just four days ago, Secretary Mattis aggressively lobbied President Trump to formally authorize the mission.†

At the very least, Mattis believes the raid will capture sensitive information. But there's also the chance that al-Qaeda leaders may be on-site—in particular, Qasim al-Rimi. Born in Yemen thirty-eight years ago, the terrorist's career dates to the 1990s, when he served with Osama bin Laden in Afghanistan. An average-looking man, al-Rimi is a fanatic and has been on a list of the world's most wanted terror suspects since 2011. He is responsible for bombing hospitals and killing innocent tourists.

Secretary Mattis reminds President Trump that this sensitive site exploration offers him a chance to differentiate himself from his predecessor by taking a bold risk. The general believes the raid on al-Ghayil could be a "game changer."

The next morning, Mr. Trump signs what is known as the "execute order"—EXORD—giving the go-ahead. Within hours, Navy SEALs and counterparts from the UAE are flown to the amphibious ship USS *Makin Island*. The ship will serve as a Quick Reaction Force site if the raid runs into trouble, launching aircraft and helicopters to assist the Special Forces personnel inside Yemen. More

---

* Somers was alive when American Special Forces finally neutralized the terrorists. He was flown to the USS *Makin Island*, where he died in surgery. Korkie was killed during the firefight.

† Also present were Vice President Pence, National Security Adviser Michael Flynn, Chairman of the Joint Chiefs of Staff General Joseph Dunford, CIA director Mike Pompeo, presidential strategist Steve Bannon, and Mr. Trump's son-in-law, Jared Kushner.

than two thousand marines are on board, prepared to go into battle as a backup force.

On the night of January 29, 2017, the teams are flown from the *Makin Island* by V-22 Ospreys and dropped at a position five miles from the known terrorist location. The flight is a short fifteen minutes. Al-Ghayil is a series of stone homes and buildings atop a rugged mountaintop. The land is windswept and treeless, a barren desert fortress.

As the commandos walk quietly uphill toward the village in almost complete darkness, drones pick up intense movement from inside some houses. Night vision cameras record images of al-Qaeda fighters taking up positions. Despite every attempt at stealth, the terrorists *know* the SEALs are coming.

The raid has been compromised.

To this day, it is not known how al-Qaeda received this information. Yet despite the new risk, the commandos press on, determined to complete the mission. Their opponents are not disorganized fighters—each of the terrorists has spent months learning military tactics at training camps in Afghanistan and Iran. They have prepared their positions well in advance. They take cover in homes, a medical clinic, even a mosque. The ground is mined.

And the terrorist soldiers are not just men; even the wives of the al-Qaeda fighters are armed and dangerous. As the three dozen elite troops approach al-Ghayil, heavy fire breaks out. The SEALs and their UAE counterparts are pinned down. They cannot know the size of the force arrayed against them. The fighters have no choice but to call for help.

Out in the Indian Ocean, the alert sounds aboard the USS *Makin Island*. The Quick Reaction Force is launched. American fighter aircraft and helicopter gunships race to the battlefield and pour down fire on al-Qaeda positions. The village of al-Ghayil is leveled, and fourteen al-Qaeda fighters are killed.

But the mission is not a success. Despite efforts to prevent the loss of civilian lives, sixteen children are killed—ten of them under the age of thirteen. SEAL Team 6 collects no electronics or other documents. An Osprey is sent to extract those SEALs teams. The damaged aircraft is intentionally destroyed so that its onboard technology does not fall into terrorist hands.

Several American troops are wounded. Chief Petty Officer William Ryan Owens, a Navy SEAL and married father of three, is killed when a bullet strikes him in the torso just inches above his protective body armor.*

And despite all the effort, there is absolutely no sign of Qasim al-Rimi.

Back in Washington, White House Press Secretary Sean Spicer quickly calls the mission a "very successful raid." But Arizona senator John McCain publicly disagrees.

"When you lose a $75 million airplane and, more importantly, an American . . . life is lost and [there are] wounded, I don't believe that you can call it a success," says McCain, the powerful chairman of the Senate Armed Services Committee.

President Trump appears on the television show *Fox and Friends* soon afterward to offer his side of the story.

"Well, this was a mission that was started before I got here. This was something that was, you know, they wanted to do."

The botched terror raid in President Trump's first week in office results in enormous criticism. Mr. Trump never forgets that he was thwarted by fighters loyal to Qasim al-Rimi. A bounty of $10 million is quickly placed on al-Rimi's head.

The terrorist is not impressed. A week after the failed raid, al-Rimi openly taunts President Trump in an eleven-minute al-Qaeda video.

"The new fool of the White House received a painful slap across his face," the terrorist crows.

✦ ✦ ✦

It is almost three years later, January 18, 2020. The Muslim call to prayer echoes over the al-Estibal military camp in the village of

---

* William Ryan Owens was a longtime Navy SEAL operator. His father, Bill Owens, a former Green Beret, turned down a meeting with President Trump when his son's body was returned to America and demanded an investigation into what he called a "stupid mission."

Marib, Yemen. It is almost dark as soldiers in uniform file in and kneel on their prayer mats. Their nation is engaged in a war with the Houthi rebels, a Shia terrorist movement sponsored by Iran. Qasim al-Rimi is not part of the Houthi organization but helps it in order to secure a remote hiding place for his organization.

Al-Rimi knows he is being hunted. In 2019, his group publicly supported a terror attack inside the United States when a gunman opened fire on pilots in training at Naval Air Station Pensacola, in Florida. Three servicemen were killed, two sheriff's deputies wounded. Al-Rimi calls the al-Qaeda killer "a courageous knight."

✦ ✦ ✦

As the government troops continue their prayer service, a missile slams into the mosque. Instantly, 111 Yemeni soldiers die. In this moment, the world of terrorism changes. As the mosque implodes from the explosion, confusion about the source of the attack follows. There was no suicide bomber exploding a vest. No one drove a car into the building. And there was no sound of artillery or a mortar round. The only possible explanation is that someone launched a drone strike.

America is immediately suspected. But that makes no sense. Under President Trump, the United States has reduced its presence in Yemen. In 2017, his first year in office, 131 air strikes were launched by American jets in Yemen. In 2018, there were just 36; in 2019, only 6. Secretly, Donald Trump has upped the ante in the war on terror. But striking Yemeni soldiers is not on his list because they are actually fighting Islamic terrorists.

As for the destruction of the mosque in Marib, no one takes responsibility. The mystery deepens. But soon, US and Israeli intelligence see the fingerprints of Iran. On June 20, 2019, the Iranians shot down an American Global Hawk drone over the Strait of Hormuz using surface-to-air missiles. In addition, they are the only country in the region to have drone capability. The White House is quickly informed that Iran now has the weaponry to strike American troops in the Middle East at any time.

Also, in the hands of a terrorist like Qasim al-Rimi, an unmanned aerial drone could be flown almost anywhere to commit an act of terror. It is clear al-Rimi is a very dangerous person. Thus, Secretary of State Mike Pompeo issues a statement shortly after the mosque attack, stating that such mayhem "produces instability that terrorist groups and other malignant actors can exploit for their own purposes."

So with Iran and al-Qaeda working together in Yemen, President Trump has a decision to make. It comes quickly.

✦ ✦ ✦

The date is January 25, just one week after the Marib mosque attack. The time is 11:00 a.m. At a house in the Joe-Nasseem area of Marib, the Saturday morning is uneventful—that is, until a Hellfire missile fired by an American drone destroys the home and kills its occupant. To this day, his name and status within al-Qaeda is unknown.

Two days later, in the Al-Hazmah area, another Hellfire destroys another house. This one leaves behind the charred body of an individual named Abdullah Al-Adani. Three hours after the attack, an al-Qaeda crew comes to remove the body for identification.*

But once again, Qasim al-Rimi survives. The terrorist then goes quiet, correctly believing the drone strikes are aimed at him. Al-Rimi's continuing ability to evade death is considered remarkable by his trackers.

Until things change.

On January 29, in the village of Al-Hosson Al-Mashrif, a car bearing two men rolls through a Houthi roadblock, heading for a small house. The men depart the vehicle. They step inside. Within an instant, an explosion shatters the midday calm. Both men die instantly, casualties of two drone rockets.

One of the men is Abu Al-Baraa Al-Ibby, a senior al-Qaeda official.

The other man is Qasim al-Rimi.

President Trump does not announce the assassination. In fact, it is several days before confirmation of the mission is made public. It is

---

* Abdullah Al-Adani was a nom de guerre for a lower-level al-Qaeda official. It is thought he may have been waiting for al-Rimi's arrival at the time of his death.

left to the State Department to make the official statement: "At the direction of President Trump, the US conducted a counterterrorism operation in Yemen that successfully eliminated Qasim al-Rimi, a founder and the leader of al-Qa'ida in the Arabian Peninsula and a deputy to al-Qa'ida leader Ayman al-Zawahiri." *

✦ ✦ ✦

Abu Bakr al-Baghdadi is gone.
  Qasem Soleimani is gone.
  Qasim al-Rimi is gone.
  But the war on terror remains.
  However, it is now shifting to a new battlefield.

---

* The seventy-year-old al-Zawahiri succeeded Osama bin Laden as worldwide leader of al-Qaeda in 2011. The Egyptian physician is widely considered the planner of the 9/11 attacks and is now in hiding, with a $25 million US bounty on his head. He is currently the most wanted terrorist in the world.

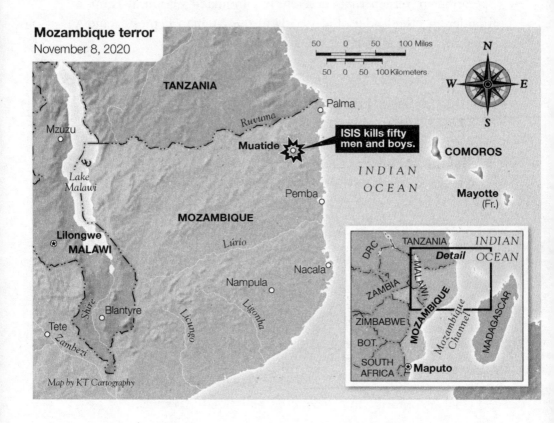

Mozambique terror
November 8, 2020

TANZANIA

Palma

Mzuzu

Ruvuma

Muatide

ISIS kills fifty men and boys.

INDIAN OCEAN

COMOROS

Mayotte (Fr.)

Lake Malawi

Pemba

MOZAMBIQUE

Lúrio

Lilongwe
MALAWI

Nacala

Nampula

Ligonha

Shire

Blantyre

Licungo

Tete

Zambezi

Map by KT Cartography

50   0   50   100 Miles

50   0   50   100 Kilometers

N
W   E
S

DRC   TANZANIA   INDIAN OCEAN

Detail

ZAMBIA   MALAWI

ZIMBABWE   **MOZAMBIQUE**

BOT.   *Mozambique Channel*   MADAGASCAR

SOUTH AFRICA   **Maputo**

CHAPTER TWENTY-FIVE

NOVEMBER 8, 2020
MUATIDE, MOZAMBIQUE
DAY

The victims can see the end of their lives.

Three thousand miles south of the Middle East, Islamic State terror reigns. Today is Sunday. Smoke fills the air from the many local homes burned by ISIS terrorists over the last three days. Young African men who have sworn loyalty to the Islamic State herd local villagers onto the town's small football pitch. The terrorists carry machetes and wear automatic weapons slung around their necks. The playing surface is red dirt instead of grass. Dead bodies litter midfield—all murdered by ISIS killers who are now yelling "Allahu Akbar" and firing shots into the air.

The "infidels" being herded are boys and men who have refused to join the Islamic State. Many ran into the woods outside of town when the terrorists began raiding Muatide three days ago. But the killers have been thorough, searching the forests and rounding up victims one by one. Some men are shot immediately, left to die in the trees along the Lúrio River. Their wives and daughters have been allowed to live—forced to serve as sex slaves.

The men now kneeling on the dirt soccer field can see for

themselves the barbaric fate that awaits them. For the dead bodies of their friends are not in one piece: heads are missing, arms and legs hacked off. Torsos have been chopped into small pieces—carrion birds are now feasting on the entrails.

The "infidels" have a choice to make: they can join ISIS and live, or they will suffer a slow beheading with a dull machete—one which might require several blows to do the job. However, should these men choose to join ISIS, they must prove their loyalty through a simple initiation rite: accept the machete and perform the beheading and dismemberment of a fellow villager.

It seems useless to resist. ISIS now controls a growing African caliphate. Their extremist Muslim faith is modeled upon that of fighters in the Middle East. Even tourists caught in their sweep through southern Africa are beheaded.

By the time the terrorists depart Muatide tomorrow, fifty local men and boys will be hacked to pieces. Local women will emerge from hiding and sort through the corpses, collecting the body parts of loved ones for burial.

But the Islamic State will never be far away. Abu Bakr al-Baghdadi has been dead a year, but his followers are worse than ever. The world may be watching the Middle East, but *Africa* is now the new home of terror.

✦ ✦ ✦

Savage death is nothing new to the people of Africa, where the terror group known as Boko Haram is a deadly menace. Once loyal to al-Qaeda, BH terrorists defected after the death of Osama bin Laden. The militants now swear allegiance to ISIS and are committing atrocities in a number of countries.*

In 2014, two thousand miles northwest of Mozambique, Boko Haram begins the most murderous year in terrorist history. The date

---

* Correspondence between Boko Haram and Osama bin Laden was among the documents removed from the al-Qaeda leader's compound after his assassination. The switch over to ISIS took place in March 2015, with Boko Haram leader Abubakar Shekau sending a videotape to Abu Bakr al-Baghdadi swearing his loyalty to the Islamic State. ISIS quickly responded, claiming West Africa as part of their caliphate.

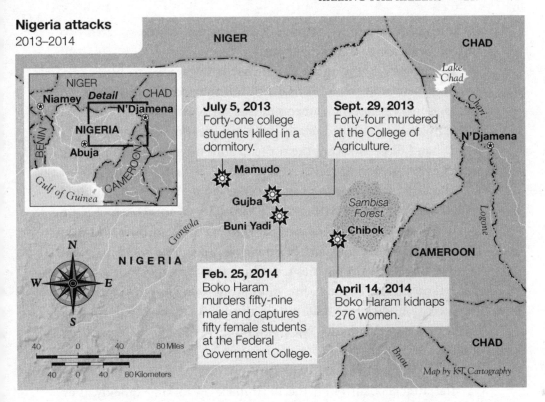

Nigeria attacks
2013–2014

NIGER

CHAD

Lake Chad

Chari

Detail: NIGER, Niamey, N'Djamena, CHAD, NIGERIA, Abuja, BENIN, CAMEROON, Gulf of Guinea

July 5, 2013
Forty-one college students killed in a dormitory.

Sept. 29, 2013
Forty-four murdered at the College of Agriculture.

N'Djamena

Mamudo

Gujba

Gongola

Buni Yadi

Sambisa Forest

Chibok

Logone

NIGERIA

CAMEROON

Feb. 25, 2014
Boko Haram murders fifty-nine male and captures fifty female students at the Federal Government College.

April 14, 2014
Boko Haram kidnaps 276 women.

CHAD

Bnou

Map by K.T. Cartography

40 0 40 80 Miles

40 0 40 80 Kilometers

is February 25. It is 2:00 a.m. in the town of Buni Yadi, Nigeria. Students at the Federal Government College are asleep in single-story yellow buildings with black roofs. All are between the ages of eleven and eighteen. No one stirs as the terrorists emerge from their hideout in the thick Sambisa Forest and take up positions.

Boko Haram is dedicated to its own version of Islamic purity and seeks to eradicate other faiths as well as rival Muslim sects. Its terrorists now creep out of the darkness and surround the college. There are twenty-four buildings in all. Some attackers dress in Middle Eastern fashion, wearing flowing robes and keffiyeh head coverings. Others wear battlefield camouflage, with extra ammunition strapped to their chests. Their weapon of choice is usually the AK-47 rifle, although tonight they prefer flame.

The name "Boko Haram" means "Western education is sinful." The group believes that reading any book other than the Koran is a violation of sharia law. Its goal is to create an Islamic state in Nigeria.

Its adherents have killed thousands and displaced an estimated two million Africans to make that a reality.

No atrocity is too much. Terrorists strap bombs to little girls, sending them into public markets to kill themselves and others. In fact, a US congressional subcommittee on terrorism will note: "In 2014, Boko Haram killed nearly 7,000 people—murdered is a better word than killed—making them the deadliest terrorist group in the world, even surpassing ISIS."

The brutal Islamists have attacked more than two hundred schools all throughout Africa. These "soft targets" are chosen because Boko Haram believes they spread Western philosophy—and also because schools are unguarded. Six months ago, in a shocking mass murder, Boko Haram fanatics crept into the dormitories of an agricultural college and opened fire, murdering forty sleeping students.

Two months before that, in July, the group attacked a dormitory in the town of Mamudo, Nigeria, killing forty-one young college students with grenades and machine guns.*

But tonight will be far worse in Buni Yadi.

The attackers surround the dormitories. Working quickly, they throw grenades into the rooms and set fire to those buildings housing male students. Phone lines have already been cut, so there is no chance Nigerian government soldiers can be summoned. As flames consume the dorms, students throw open doors and windows and try to make a run for it.

Most are cut down. Several terrorists fire at once, ensuring that each victim has multiple gunshot wounds. Throats are then slit.

Boko Haram is in no hurry. As the night sky is lit by fire, terrorists watch the dormitories burn. Dozens of dead male students lie in the dirt parking lot, puddles of blood forming around them. Others die in their beds, many burned to ashes. By sunrise, all twenty-four buildings comprising the college will be destroyed.

Fifty-nine male students are murdered. Approximately fifty female students are captured. Executions are reserved for the boys. Radical

---

* American and European news consumers rarely see video of Boko Haram's atrocities because it is too dangerous for photographers to track the group.

Islam is a patriarchal society that values masculine authority and the subjugation of women. So instead of being killed, the girls are ordered to return to their villages to marry. Should the young ladies fail to do that, Boko Haram reminds them of the brutality that will happen.

Two months later, on the night of April 14, 2014, the terrorists keep their promise.

✦ ✦ ✦

The world will simply call them "our girls."

Boko Haram prefers to call them sex slaves.

Another night, another school. Boko Haram fighters surround the government girls' secondary school in the northern Nigerian town of Chibok. The raid takes place under a bright half moon instead of total darkness. The girls are Christians, which could result in grave consequences if they are taken captive.

This is not a surprise attack. The phone lines are not cut. Nigerians from miles away have been calling the school all evening, warning that caravans of heavily armed Boko Haram fighters are filling the roads, most likely headed for the girls. Due to the terror threat, schools throughout the region have been closed. But now is the time for final examinations. The secondary school has been shut for weeks but reopened so that students can take their tests. All the girls are between sixteen and eighteen and in their last year of secondary education. Boko Haram knows this and sees the chance to score a decisive victory.

The government of Nigeria has adopted a tactic of arresting family members of Boko Haram leadership in an attempt to bring the band to heel. "Since you are now holding our women, just wait and see what will happen to your own women," terror leader Abubakar Shekau has announced.

The threat on the girls' school is payback. However, a small force of Nigerian soldiers is waiting for the Boko Haram vehicles. Both sides are weaponized, armed with grenade launchers and automatic machine guns. Confusingly, the terrorists are wearing stolen government military uniforms tonight, making it difficult to distinguish between the two sides.

The battle rages for five hours. But the Nigerian government refuses to send reinforcements. The terrorists eventually overrun the soldiers and descend upon the school, shouting "Allahu Akbar" and "We are Boko Haram."

The frightened girls are rounded up. A terrorist leader makes an announcement: "If you want to die, sit down here. We will kill you. If you don't want to die, you will enter the trucks."

Sobbing, 276 young women choose to live. They board the trucks, allowing themselves to be taken prisoner. There are so many girls that some are forced to walk for several miles until other trucks can be brought in to carry them.

A fortunate fifty-three girls seize an opportunity to slip away— they will testify to the abductions.

Quickly, there is international pressure to find "our girls." The United States and Britain take the extraordinary step of flying manned aerial patrols over the thick jungle along the border of Chad and Nigeria where the girls are thought to have been taken.

The Nigerian government seeks to defuse the worldwide outrage by claiming all the female students are safe and on their way home.

This is a lie.

No act of terror committed by Boko Haram before or since the kidnapping has brought the terror organization as much publicity. Despite the best efforts of satellite and drone technology, the girls simply vanish.

On May 5, three weeks after the raid, Boko Haram leader Abubakar Shekau makes a chilling video announcement. "Allah instructed me to sell them," the middle-aged terrorist proclaims. He is a thickset man with a long beard. Shekau is rarely seen without his camouflaged uniform and automatic weapon. He continues: "I will carry out his instructions."

The abducted girls are forced to convert to Islam, then sold as brides. The price is just $4 for a member of Boko Haram. For the men of nearby Chad and Cameroon, who cross the border, the price is $12.

For a time, Shekau is among the most famous terror leaders in the world, achieving the sort of notoriety once enjoyed by Abu Bakr al-Baghdadi. But soon Boko Haram splinters as a result of intramural fighting. The faction that wins the civil war is called the Islamic State West African Province, or ISWAP.*

✦ ✦ ✦

With little control over vast expanse of jungle, most African governments cannot defeat Boko Haram on their own. But because of the untapped mineral wealth of Africa, the world's superpowers are now getting involved. Armies of the United States, China, and Russia are on the ground, monitoring the terrorist situation. American Special Operations Forces comprised of US Navy SEALs, US Army Green Berets, and US Marine Corps Raiders operate covertly in twenty-two African nations.†

The American presence in Africa is largely kept secret, but these warriors serve at the invitation of African governments. The US mission is to "advise, assist, and accompany"—AAA—African soldiers to combat the Islamic State and Boko Haram, which are now operating together.‡

These shadow campaigns are not without peril. It is exceedingly dangerous to operate in territory not under government control. That's what happens in 2017, when Navy SEAL Kyle Milliken, a thirty-eight-year-old senior chief petty officer, is killed while on an AAA mission in Somalia, shot dead by the militant Islamist group al-Shabab.

The fact is that US Special Forces are now being directed to the most dangerous places on earth.

Like Niger.

---

* Abubakar Shekau did not survive the terrorist civil war. On May 19, 2021, he exploded his suicide vest as he was being surrounded by ISWAP fighters in a jungle encampment.

† Algeria, Botswana, Burkina Faso, Cameroon, Cape Verde, Chad, Côte d'Ivoire, Djibouti, Egypt, Ethiopia, Ghana, Kenya, Libya, Madagascar, Mali, Mauritania, Niger, Nigeria, Senegal, Somalia, Tanzania, and Tunisia.

‡ Despite the high level of terror activity in Africa, the number of American soldiers is much greater in other parts of the world. There are six thousand US troops in all of Africa, as compared to forty thousand in Japan, thirty-five thousand in Germany, and twenty-five thousand in South Korea.

✦ ✦ ✦

Tourists do not vacation in Niger.

The landlocked nation is twice the size of Texas but offers no big cities and very few conveniences. Niger (pronounced NEE-zhair) is considered the poorest country in the world by the United Nations. Few of its citizens can read or write. French is the national language, but the people more often speak in tribal dialects. The terrain is arid and sprawling, suitable for subsistence farming but offering no prospect of industry to the population of sixteen million.*

Most notably, the former French colony has been independent for sixty years but is unable to establish a democratic system of government and is now under military rule.

But "rule" is an arbitrary term. Niger is a lawless haven for smugglers and terrorists. No one is in charge. Guns rule.

✦ ✦ ✦

The date is October 4, 2017. Eleven members of the US 3rd Special Forces Group known as Team 3212 stop in the village of Tongo Tongo, in western Niger. These Green Berets are still new to the area, joining the eight hundred Americans on the hunt for Islamic terrorists.

Niger is infested with militant factions: ISIS controls land to the north, al-Qaeda owns territory to the west, and Boko Haram has a powerful presence to the south and southeast. This is one of the most hostile regions on the planet, with forty-six terror attacks in the last twenty months.

Special Forces Team 3212 is exhausted, having stayed up almost all night. They travel in three vehicles, a Toyota Land Cruiser and two four-wheel-drive pickup trucks. Two machine guns are mounted in the pickups; they are called "technicals." Also on patrol with the Americans is a thirty-man group of soldiers from the Nigerien army

---

* The United Nations' Human Development Index ranks nations on the basis of life expectancy, education, literacy, and per capita income. Niger finished 189th out of the 189 countries surveyed in 2018 and 2019.

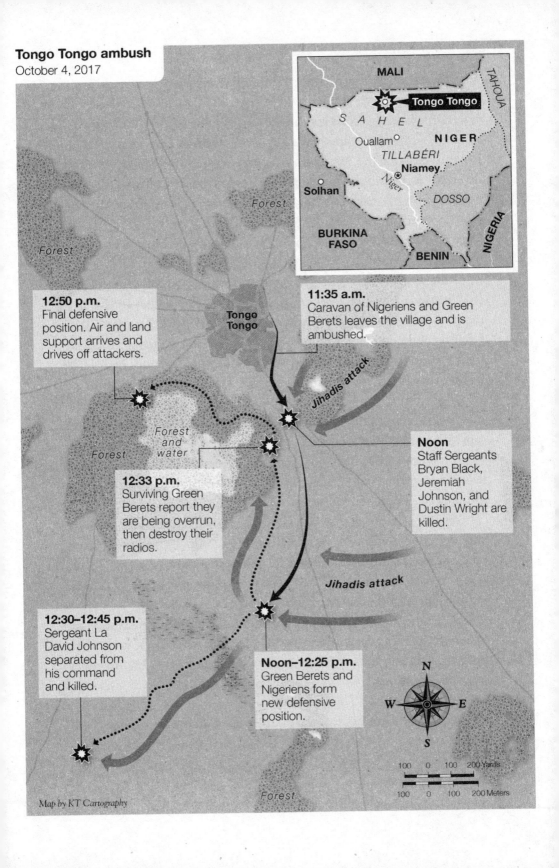

Tongo Tongo ambush
October 4, 2017

MALI
Tongo Tongo
TAHOUA
S A H E L
NIGER
Ouallam
TILLABÉRI
Niamey
Niger
Solhan
DOSSO
BURKINA FASO
NIGERIA
BENIN

12:50 p.m.
Final defensive position. Air and land support arrives and drives off attackers.

Tongo Tongo

11:35 a.m.
Caravan of Nigeriens and Green Berets leaves the village and is ambushed.

Jihadis attack

Noon
Staff Sergeants Bryan Black, Jeremiah Johnson, and Dustin Wright are killed.

Forest and water

12:33 p.m.
Surviving Green Berets report they are being overrun, then destroy their radios.

Forest

Jihadis attack

12:30–12:45 p.m.
Sergeant La David Johnson separated from his command and killed.

Noon–12:25 p.m.
Green Berets and Nigeriens form new defensive position.

N
W   E
S

100 0 100 200 Yards
100 0 100 200 Meters

Forest

Forest

Forest

Map by KT Cartography

who travel in five large trucks—one of which was provided by the Central Intelligence Agency.

At first, the mission is routine, starting out as a daylong journey to meet local tribal leaders in a show of goodwill. But when that job is complete and the team is on its way back to base, it is suddenly diverted. A raid on the hideout of a known Islamic State commander is in motion. A team of American commandos is being flown several hundred miles by helicopter to lead the attack. The French air force will provide cover. Team 3212 is charged with backing up the operation.

American intelligence has intercepted a phone call from a local ISIS leader named Doundoun Cheffou. He is a suspect in the kidnapping of American aid worker Jeffery Woodke in October 2016. Cheffou is known for raiding into Niger with his group, then retreating back across the border into Mali, where he hides in a dense forest. This is an opportunity to arrest Cheffou and maybe bring Woodke home.*

The Green Berets are told that Cheffou is a "TST"—time-sensitive target. Speed is vital.

But the weather does not cooperate. Dusty winds cancel the helicopter insertion before the commando strike team ever leaves the ground. The French air support is also scrubbed.

Yet the mission is not canceled. The lightly armed Green Beret and Nigerien force will conduct the search alone. The Americans take a short nap, sleeping until 2:00 a.m., then approaching the ISIS camp in darkness. Team 3212 enters the location cautiously, checking for jihadis hiding in the forest and rocks.

The camp is abandoned. Just a camouflage uniform, spent shell casings, leftover rations of tea and sugar, and a motorcycle are found. Ominously, the tracks of other motorcycles can be seen leading away from the location.

But no jihadis.

Just as well. Though trained to execute an attack on a terror com-

---

* Woodke, fifty-nine, is still in captivity as of this writing. The government of Niger believes he is alive.

pound, the Green Berets and their Nigerien counterparts are not equipped to confront a large terrorist presence. Most of the Americans carry M4 carbines, while the Nigeriens are armed with medium machine guns. The vehicles are not bulletproof, and the teams are not armed with heavy weapons such as mortars. The original mission was supposed to be so low-key that only one American soldier thought to bring along a grenade launcher. It is clear that the ISIS fighters who once lived in the camp are much better armed.

With a sense of relief after seeing no targets, the team begins the journey back to base, one hundred miles away.

✦ ✦ ✦

The stop in Tongo Tongo, a hamlet on the borderlands of Niger and Mali, is meant to be brief. The plan is to eat breakfast, refill hydration bladders from the village well, meet with local leaders, and then return to base near the town of Quallam. When the local chief says some of the village children are sick, the Green Berets offer medicine. The Nigerien soldiers are relaxed, taking their time to eat. They have previously visited Tongo Tongo nineteen times, never once having an issue with the local population. This calms the weary Americans, still learning the ways of Niger.

The time is 10:30 a.m.

But unbeknownst to the Americans, Islamic State fighters have been tipped off about their location. Terrorists wielding automatic weapons race toward Tongo Tongo to set up an ambush. They travel in a caravan of more than a dozen "technical" vehicles and twenty motorcycles, speaking openly of decapitating any Americans they find. There are about fifty of the jihadis, a strong force. They stop one hundred yards outside of town and take up positions in the woods lining both sides of the road.

Inside Tongo Tongo, the Americans grow suspicious. Their meeting with the local chieftains was meant to last thirty minutes but has now lasted almost an hour. In fact, the chief's cell phone contains the phone number for Doundoun Cheffou, and the two men are in touch—but the Green Berets don't know that. They do see young men from the village driving out of town on their motorcycles for no apparent reason.

The Americans sense a setup and quickly end the meeting. Along with the Nigerien soldiers, they enter their vehicles and drive out of town in a single-file line. Home base is ninety miles away.

The time is 11:35 a.m.

The Green Berets are cautious. The Sahel desert, in the Tillabéri region of Niger, is almost without vegetation, but the land just outside Tongo Tongo marks the beginning of a wide forest of scrub and small trees. The road is dirt, the terrain thickly wooded. The Americans keep eyes left, where the trees are thickest, watching for signs of terrorist movement.

They don't have to wait long. After thirty seconds of driving, the convoy takes fire. The ambush comes from the left, as predicted. A deafening volley of automatic-weapons fire strikes the convoy. Rocket-propelled grenades fill the air. The soldiers exit their vehicles and return fire.

The team's commander, Captain Mike Perozeni, is hit and wounded. Radio operator Sergeant First Class Brent Bartels is also struck by gunfire—but not before sending a message to base that the Green Berets are under fire.

The battle rages. ISIS fighters can be seen trying to surround the American force. The Green Berets and their allies return to their vehicles to make a run for it. The fight is now twenty-five minutes old, and the time is just after noon. A red smoke grenade is thrown to conceal the retreat. One by one, the American vehicles egress at a high rate of speed.

But in the chaos, three Green Berets are left behind. Staff Sergeants Dustin Wright, Jeremiah Johnson, and Bryan Black are pinned down, taking cover behind their black SUV. Wright is a former football player from the small town of Santa Claus, Georgia. Johnson is a specialist in chemical warfare from Springboro, Ohio. Sergeant Black is a nationally ranked chess player from Washington State who actually planned his own memorial service before going to Africa—just in case—asking that the Irish folk song "Finnegan's Wake" be played.

All three soldiers now work together to survive, determined not to die on the desolate desert sands of Niger.

Sergeant Wright drives while the other two jog along the far side, shielded from terrorist gunfire. Every man wears a helmet cam, so the events soon to play out will be clearly visible: the dust, sound of gunfire, and hand signals are recorded.

Help *is* on the way. Realizing their mistake after making a successful exit, the other Green Berets return to the battlefield. But though they kill more than a dozen terrorists, they cannot get through to their three trapped comrades. In the attempt, a simple mistake will cost Sergeant La David Johnson his life—he also becomes separated from the team. Sergeant Johnson and two Nigerien soldiers are quickly surrounded by the ISIS attackers. They are a half mile from the original ambush site. Before long, the three are shot to death.

And it looks like there will be no escape for any of the Green Berets. They are surrounded, spread out over a square mile of desert and scrub. Puffs of red from smoke grenades waft through the air. The afternoon is hot and windy.

On one part of the battlefield, Sergeants Wright, Johnson, and Black are finally overwhelmed and shot dead. They fight until the very end. ISIS fighters approach the bodies and mutilate them. The gruesome footage of the Americans' final moments will be placed on the internet as an Islamic State recruiting tool.

The surviving seven Green Berets are now fighting desperately. With their trucks bogged down, they are now on foot. The Americans and twenty Nigeriens form a defensive perimeter, tending to their wounded. A final radio call is made back to headquarters, stating that they are surrounded. Then the radios are destroyed so they will not fall into terrorist hands. The Nigeriens get on their knees and pray. The Americans use their private phones to message loved ones back home, saying good-bye.

But it is not all over. French Mirage fighter jets suddenly fly low over the battlefield. Within minutes, the terrorists flee. They leave behind twenty-one dead.

French Puma helicopters soon land to rescue the remaining Americans and Nigeriens and to evacuate the bodies of the dead. Sergeant La David Johnson of Miami Gardens, Florida, who was once known as "Wheelie" because as a teenager he traveled around the city on a bike with no front wheel, is nowhere to be found. It will be a week before children will come upon his remains and notify the Americans.

The fight makes Tongo Tongo the worst battlefield incident since the infamous Black Hawk down tragedy in Somalia more than twenty years ago.[*]

The slain Sergeant Jeremiah Johnson enjoyed being known as a man who did his job well and did not want glory. In fact, he left word with relatives that if tragedy should ever befall him on the battlefield, his name was not to be mentioned in the papers.

After the ambush in Tongo Tongo, a reporter calls his mother, asking for comment.

But Debbie Gannon will not go on the record.

"I'm going to honor his wishes," is all she will say.

✦ ✦ ✦

The date is June 28, 2021. The leader of the US Africa Command, General Stephen Townsend, is talking to reporters almost four years after the Tongo Tongo ambush. The USAC no longer speaks of defeating terror, preferring to use the term "containing." American troops are being pulled out of Africa, and US air strikes against terror groups have ceased altogether.[†]

At the same time, ISIS and al-Qaeda have recruited a new group of terrorists all across the African continent. Just three weeks ago, in the nation of Burkina Faso, which shares a border with the terror-troubled countries of Nigeria and Mali, 132 civilians were brutally murdered. Jihadists entered the village of Solhan late on a Friday night, burning homes and slaughtering innocent people.

The level of atrocity has grown so high across Africa that citizens are becoming desensitized to the threat. It is now common for

---

[*] The bloody Tongo Tongo encounter lasted three hours and resulted in the loss of four American lives, five Nigeriens, and twenty-one ISIS terrorists.

[†] President Joe Biden ordered a cessation of air strikes on African terror groups upon taking office in January 2021. No reason was given, nor was there any public announcement.

terrorists to intermarry into local tribes, insert themselves in local politics, and attempt to impose a caliphate.

The terrorists seem to be unstoppable. Nowhere in Africa is this more apparent than in Mozambique. On March 24, 2021, in the resort town of Palma on the Indian Ocean, terrorists invade by land and sea. Many are teenagers. They number two hundred. The group is called Ahl al-Sunnah wa al Jamma'ah—and has sworn loyalty to ISIS. The young terrorists rampage for days, killing indiscriminately, until local beaches and city sidewalks are covered in headless bodies.

The sophistication of the attack shows military precision. Banks, police stations, the local airfield, and an army barracks are destroyed. Palma is home to hundreds of foreigners working for a nearby French natural-gas plant, many of whom barricade themselves in a hotel for almost two days waiting for rescue—only to have terrorists enter the building and behead those they capture. Thousands of locals flee into forests and coastal mangroves to hide.

The Islamic State's news agency, Amaq, broadcasts the slaughter to the world. And though the terrorists leave Palma, their accomplishments are clear. The Mozambique government was unable to stop the raid. Just as in Syria and Iraq a decade ago, radical Muslim forces are now capable of terrorizing entire countries.

As General Townsend bluntly states: "ISIS and al-Qaeda are on the march. If ISIS can carve out a new caliphate, or al-Qaeda can, they will do it."*

---

* There are few news bureaus staffed by American journalists in sub-Saharan Africa because it is simply too dangerous to live there. In the countries of Kenya and South Africa there are freelance reporters.

CHAPTER TWENTY-SIX

"The Beast of the East" rides a Harley.

Rory Larkin spent ten years in the Middle East conducting hostage rescue missions. Every year on the Fourth of July, he receives thank-you texts from Americans he saved from beheading. Rory Larkin is not his real name. The ex–Navy SEAL prefers not to publicize his personal heroism, living by the code of Special Forces soldiers who defer always to "brothers" in the teams who have been killed in action.

Rory is a stickler for keeping his word and living by the code of honor he learned in the military. He is single, no kids, his lone marriage to a former *Playboy* model a casualty to constant deployments. He has a dog named for a popular Irish whiskey. The graying warrior, now in his fifties, also has a titanium ankle, a compression fracture in his lower spine, and constant back pain, all caused by injuries suffered while stalking terrorists.

Rory Larkin also has a "rage problem." He refers to his occasional fury as an "Irish wolfhound." He deals with the situation by contacting other military people who have shared experiences. It's kind of like Alcoholics Anonymous—when he feels his anger rising, he contacts someone to calm him down.

Larkin attended the United States Naval Academy and went straight to the navy's Basic Underwater Demolition/SEAL (BUD/S) training in Coronado, California, the first step in earning his trident. After completing training, the newly minted operator attended Army Ranger School at Fort Benning, Georgia. He doesn't hesitate about his motivation at the time. "When you make the choice to join Special Forces you know you're going to war. That's why most of us join—we want to defend our country. We want to be warriors. We want to be downrange."

But after ten years in uniform, Larkin chose to leave the service for precisely the same reason he joined: America was *not* at war. No amount of training could substitute for actually going into combat.

Then came 9/11.

On September 12, 2001, Larkin phoned a navy recruiter. Their initial conversation was brief: "I served as a Navy SEAL officer but resigned my commission four years ago. Can I return to the naval service?"

"How soon can you come to my office?" the recruiter replied.

"I can be there today."

One week later, Larkin formally returned to the military. Soon, he was in Iraq, working hostage rescue missions—and not just for missing Americans. Larkin's first operation was to rescue two Bulgarian truck drivers kidnapped in Baghdad, Iraq. He failed. The men were eventually beheaded by al-Qaeda and found floating in the Tigris River; the ransom demand for their return was not paid.

Rory Larkin is openly critical of the US State Department and, in particular, the FBI, which focused their efforts on Americans only. He claims he took "calculated risks" but, just to be sure, carried three guns at all times—a rifle, a pistol, and a small 10mm handgun hidden on his ankle—"so I had a gun if I was thrown into the trunk of a car."

Larkin constantly went "outside the wire"—secure US bases within Iraq and Afghanistan—with Special Forces teams to gather intelligence. "When SEALs or Green Berets go out at night, they are hunting," he says. "They believe their skills are the best. Special Forces go out because we want to be in the fight. We carried on our shoulders guilt and remorse when we *couldn't* be in the fight."

Larkin well remembers the morning he awakened to reports that a CIA "spy" was in the hands of al-Qaeda. The year was 2006. He opened a video link and saw an Iraqi local tied to a small chair. A sign with the handwritten letters "CIA" dangled from his neck by a string. The handheld footage was grainy, and the images wobbly. One captor held up a small brown identity card for the camera. At the bottom was a yellow strip, signifying that the man was allowed to enter the US Green Zone in Baghdad. In essence, the Iraqi was being accused of being a spy because he cleaned toilets for the Americans.

"This is for all of you," the terrorist captor said. A small group of jihadis stepped into the frame, gathering for a group photo around the terrified man tied to the chair. "Like it was a trophy hunt," Larkin remembers.

The lead terrorist then lifted a three-foot broadsword from a table behind him. Raising it high, he brought the sword down on the "spy's" neck.

While telling the story, Larkin's voice becomes measured but enraged. "The guy's head falls to the floor, and there's blood spraying everywhere, and these guys are dancing around in a frenzy, all of them chanting 'Allahu Akbar' and 'God is great.'"

Larkin, a Roman Catholic, finds these last moments of the five-minute video the hardest to watch. "I just don't understand how a religion can glorify murder."

In all, Rory Larkin worked 448 cases involving kidnapped hostages from all nations. "No day was normal; they were all different, but they usually started with a beheading video." He spent ten years in the Middle East before returning home, taking with him a case of post-traumatic stress disorder (PTSD) but leaving behind the "Beast of the East" nickname earned for his unstoppable work ethic.

After all his years in the field, Rory Larkin is reflective on the battle against terrorism.

"How we wage war and how the terrorists see it are completely different. It's about ideology and has everything to do with religion. These are hard-core fundamentalists. Their religion drives them to kill—they even murder people who share the same faith. Iraqi victims of this terror are in the tens of thousands since 2003. No one making US and coalition strategy in the Middle East wants to say this, but religion is the difference.

"Let's put it this way: those brothers of mine who carried out the bin Laden raid and got al-Baghdadi are the baddest MFers on the planet. No one badder. Every time they get on a bird to fly into a mission, they know there's a good chance they could die. But we were willing to die for our cause; [the terrorists] *wanted* to die for theirs."

Larkin chooses his next words carefully.

"The Special Forces fighting terror carry the burden of the greatest generation, which was our grandfathers in World War II. They fought with honor, and their victory was decisive. We strive to uphold the standards of our forefathers in Vietnam—and I have yet to meet a Special Forces operator from that war who was not successful on every mission.

"We always held ourselves to those high moral and ethical standards. No matter how bad a situation gets on a mission, my brothers would never dream of strapping on a suicide vest to kill."

✦ ✦ ✦

After six years, torment remains for Carl and Marsha Mueller, the parents of Kayla. They still live in the same house on the hill where she grew up. Both are retired. They make it a point to stay busy. Their son, twenty-nine-year-old Eric, lives nearby. Carl is still active in the Prescott, Arizona, Kiwanis Club. But all his activities are shrouded by images of Kayla.

"Around here there's not a day goes by when I don't think of her. I truly suffer because I couldn't get her home," Carl explains. He is gray-haired and lean, still uncomfortable talking about his daughter's death. "I just feel like a failure. It's hard to lose her, and every day I think of that. It's not the retirement we expected.

"We're taking things one day at a time. We go on because Kayla would want us to go on."

Time has not softened Carl and Marsha's anger over Kayla's murder. They believe her death was preventable and are now more openly critical of the US government's handling of Kayla's disappearance than they were before. Both are patriotic and, before Kayla's abduction, not the sort of people to question the government. But that has changed.

"Kayla and the other hostages were the first Americans that illuminated the terrible nuisance of terrorism to the world," Carl Mueller told the authors of this book. "The way the hostages suffered and the way the government handled it was all just a real debacle. America should have done what other countries do—get their people home."

It is obvious that Kayla's father replays the horror constantly. He is haunted by what happened. "I think we had eleven or twelve emails back and forth with ISIS. They wanted to get rid of Kayla. They wanted to send her home. But the Obama administration stopped us at every turn. They said they were doing everything they could to bring the American hostages home. We heard that from the FBI, we heard that from Lisa Monaco at Homeland Security, we heard that from President Obama.

"But they weren't."

Marsha Mueller adds this: "My faith in our government, my belief in everything they told us, changed. Because I realized Carl had been right all along. He would get mad at me because I had such belief in our government. He would tell me that politicians and bureaucrats weren't going to bring Kayla home. But I believed those people when they told me they would. It's heartbreaking when I go back to that. A parent should be there for their child. But the government was after al-Baghdadi, and Kayla was their ticket to him. They just wouldn't say so."

✦ ✦ ✦

Carl and Marsha Mueller did not see caution flags when Kayla first chose to work in the Middle East. It was their daughter's nature to help people in need, a pursuit that gave her life purpose and joy. Marsha remembers that her daughter's passion for helping others began in high school, where she received silver and gold presidential awards for volunteer service. After securing a $500 prize for being named Yavapai County Student of the Year, she immediately donated the money to the home for troubled youth where she was working. While at Northern Arizona University, Kayla traveled to Guatemala with the Christian youth ministry and became so determined to help others that she returned to school and graduated in two and a half years—so that she might quickly go out into the world.

Kayla Mueller endured typhoid in India, learned French because many aid agencies require the language, and wrote poems about the Israeli-Palestinian conflict in a journal her parents would not discover until after her death.

"Our country gives so much to so many other countries because we have so much money," Kayla's mother says. "These young American kids are encouraged—and they were especially encouraged by the Obama administration—to go into the world and volunteer. But yet, when they do, and something happens to them, there's no one there to help them. They're all alone. And there's no place for parents to go for help when this happens. That's wrong. There needs to be some way. We just can't leave them out there all alone."

Marsha continues: "I'd always say to her, Kayla, just remember, put the oxygen mask on yourself before you put it on others. But she always gave someone help before she did anything for herself."

Marsha also remembers a conversation with Kayla the last time she came home for a visit, Christmas 2012. "She had this mindset of, 'What are we doing? Why can't we get along? Why can't we agree to disagree and just figure out some way to make something for the good of everyone instead of just destruction, destruction?'"

✦ ✦ ✦

The Muellers' frustration with America's handling of the hostage situation began shortly after Kayla's kidnapping, in August 2013. President Obama would not initially meet with the Muellers and the other parents of hostages. "The administration had blinders on and did not believe that ISIS was a threat," says Kayla's father. "They just thought they were powerless thugs, and they called them 'the JV team.' And because of that, and because they didn't act, thousands and thousands of people were killed. Thousands of young Yazidi girls in Iraq were raped and sold from one soldier to the next."

Marsha adds: "President Obama wouldn't see us in the spring of 2014, when Kayla had already been held for six months. Even as we negotiated with ISIS through the FBI, the administration slammed the door on us at every turn."*

✦ ✦ ✦

Having no alternative, the Muellers continued working with government officials to secure their daughter's release. But, increasingly, they became frustrated and bitter—especially with ISIS taunting them on social media.

Then, a turning point in July 2014: the Special Forces raid on a suspected ISIS hideout in Syria came up empty.† But the rescue attempt infuriated the ISIS captors. And they stepped up their threats against Kayla.

Carl Mueller remembers: "When they did this raid, on the Fourth of July in real life, which we were not informed about, ISIS sent us an email on the eleventh or twelfth, stating that 'because of what your *arrogant government* has done, Kayla has just thirty days to live.'"

The anger in Carl Mueller's voice rises. "I called the FBI negotiator and asked him about the raid. I don't believe he had any idea what I was talking about. But the administration continued to deny that the raid ever took place, even after Jim Foley was beheaded one month later. So, in order to save face, we finally got a call from the Obama administration, saying the news of the raid had just leaked and they wanted us to know ahead of time.

"This is how we were treated."‡

✦ ✦ ✦

---

* In August 2014, President Obama stated that his administration was doing "everything that we can to protect our people and the timeless values that we stand for" but avoided referring to Kayla by name. The Obama administration did not publicly confirm Kayla Mueller's kidnapping until February 2015, at which time the president reiterated that he was "deploying all the assets that we can, working with all the coalition allies that we can, to identify her location, and we are in very close contact with the family, trying to keep them updated."

† That incident is portrayed on page 47 in this book.

‡ It has been American policy since 9/11 to classify all covert antiterror action.

Month after month, the Muellers continued to suffer, knowing their only daughter was in mortal danger. There was no relief, no rest. Carl Mueller defines the situation:

"I think it was September nineteenth of 2014 we got an email from ISIS saying that Kayla's release was still obtainable. This would have probably been right before she was removed from the prison a day or two later and sent to the home where al-Baghdadi visited. The FBI saw that email, and I'm positive President Obama received a copy, too. But right after that, he started bombing within Syria, and all communication stopped."

Kayla's father then recalled the moment he heard on his car radio that the United States Senate had released a study about the torture of captured terrorist suspects. Immediately, Carl thought that put Kayla's life in danger. "It was two years in the making. Senator Feinstein released it. I have since found out that President Obama had to sign off on it before it was released. I'll never forget that day. I was heading into town. Shocked me so much. I pulled off to the side of the road. I had Senator John McCain's cell number in my phone, and I called him. I said, 'Senator, what's Feinstein doing? Doesn't she realize that my daughter is being held by the very comrades of the people she says we torture? Can you imagine what those hostages are enduring from those people now that this report has been released?'"*

✦ ✦ ✦

Finally, staying in Arizona was too painful for the Muellers. They spent the rest of 2014 traveling the world at their own expense in a desperate attempt to save their daughter: Washington, Turkey, and Qatar. The purpose of their journey was to arrange a ransom for Kayla. They traveled as private citizens, not involving the American government. Along the way, they heard that ISIS was anxious to get rid of Kayla. She represented a liability and put them at high risk.

"We heard they just wanted to get rid of her," remembers Marsha. "And whether it's Mexico or the Middle East, they don't call

---

* John McCain said he would look into whether or not Kayla was being held by the same group being tortured at Guantánamo Bay prison. "Carl never got a response back," Marsha Mueller remembers. "We didn't really expect to. Carl made his point."

it ransom, they call it barter. That's the way they do a deal. They barter. And we were being told the US didn't pay ransom to terrorists,
when in fact, it has been going on all along. The US government
doesn't want to admit it, but they always paid ransom or had somebody pay it for them. That's why we were in Qatar—to find someone
to do it for *us*.

"We traveled to Qatar to try and save our daughter," says Carl.
"We did it without the government's consent. They told us they
couldn't protect us and that we were on our own. We met with several officials in the Qatar government. The last important individual
we met was their foreign minister. He came into the room and introduced himself. And he said that before the meeting, he wanted to
let me know he just got off the phone with Secretary of State John
Kerry.

"He informed me that Qatar would *not* help us pay ransom."

✦ ✦ ✦

That shocking statement almost caused Marsha Mueller to collapse.
She couldn't speak. The Muellers both believed that somehow John
Kerry had intruded on any deal.

Marsha adds one final disturbing statement: "The government
knew who it was that took Kayla out of the prison and was raping
her. But they didn't tell us that. Instead, they led us to believe that
they had a proof of life and that she was *relatively* okay.

"I remember asking the FBI agent who used those words, what
exactly did he mean by 'relatively'? And the person answered: 'poor
choice of words.'"*

✦ ✦ ✦

---

* President Obama called the Muellers soon after Kayla's death. A short time later, he issued a statement about his administration's dedication of "enormous resources to freeing captives or hostages anywhere in the world." He also reiterated his determination
not to pay ransom to terrorist kidnappers. "It's as tough as anything that I do—having
conversations with parents who understandably want, by any means necessary, for their
children to be safe. We will do everything we can short of providing an incentive for
future Americans to be caught."

Then came the dreaded outcome. Kayla Mueller was murdered in February 2015.

Her parents changed their focus from rescuing Kayla to bringing her body home. There was little activity for the next two years. However, in January 2017, the Muellers gained access to the new Trump administration. They met with Vice President Mike Pence, CIA Director (and later secretary of state) Mike Pompeo, Attorney General Jeff Sessions, National Security Adviser Robert O'Brien, and, eventually, President Trump himself.

"I truly believe that if they would have been in power when Kayla was first taken, she would be here. I truly believe that," says Carl.

✦ ✦ ✦

The search for Kayla Mueller's body is ongoing. COVID-19 has hindered overseas travel, but the Muellers remain determined to find their daughter. They also continue to be mired in an unending tragedy—unable to close the terror-induced nightmare.

To ease their pain, Carl and Marsha Mueller are now campaigning for new laws. They want the world to unite against terror: "There are no laws that pertain to what these terrorists are doing, and they know it. They use our legal system against us, they use our morals against us, and they reveled not only in holding our daughter and making her life miserable but making *us* miserable as well. From those [ISIS] emails, I could tell they just enjoy having Americans in the palm of their hand and squeezing them."

Interview complete, Carl adds one final word. "Most people go through life with blinders on. They care only about what color their next SUV is going to be. Or their next house. Or whatever else. They don't want to know about ISIS."

Then, Kayla Mueller's father shared with the authors a very personal piece of wisdom from his daughter. It came in a poem she wrote before going to the Middle East.

"If we can't handle learning about the darkest places in the world, they will turn into the darkest places in ourselves."

Carl and Marsha Mueller, whose daughter, Kayla, was taken hostage and murdered by ISIS, make remarks during the fourth and final day of the Republican National Convention on Thursday, August 27, 2020.

EPILOGUE

AUGUST 26, 2021
KABUL, AFGHANISTAN
5:48 P.M.

ISIS is about to murder Americans.

United States marines guard the Abbey Gate entrance to Hamid Karzai International Airport, one mile from the city center. Hundreds of frantic Afghan citizens crowd the entrance, desperate to flee the return of repressive Taliban rule in their homeland. The temperature is more than ninety degrees and the air smells of human waste from a nearby sewage canal. Some of the desperate people even stand knee-deep in the fetid wastewater to cool themselves on this scorching summer evening.

The evacuation process has gone on for days and these Afghans have mostly waited with patience, knowing that one hundred thousand of their fellow citizens have already been flown out in the last two weeks. When their time comes to walk through the Abbey Gate, each man, woman, and child will be asked to show identification documents and be searched for weapons. The crowd is peaceful, full of hope that their lives will soon be changed forever.

Which will happen. But not in the way these folks imagine.

The coming disaster will be engineered by a man who does not want to leave Afghanistan.

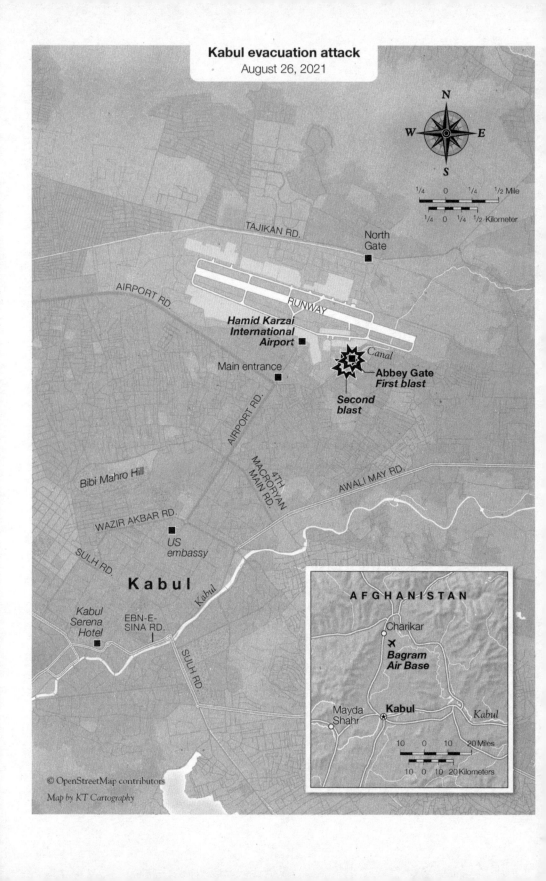

Kabul evacuation attack
August 26, 2021

His name is Abdul Rahman Al Logari, a young member of the radical group Islamic State–Khorasan—ISIS-K, as they call themselves.* Al Logari is a former engineering student who has been known to the Central Intelligence Agency to have had terrorist ties since at least 2017. At that time, he was plotting a suicide bombing in New Delhi, India. Tipped by the CIA, Indian officials arrested Al Logari and turned him over to the United States. He remained in American custody until Kabul fell. Now the man stands just fifteen feet from the nearest marine. The terrorist wears a knee-length kurta tunic, lightweight pajama pants, and weathered leather shoes. Al Logari hates the United States, having only recently escaped American custody at Bagram Air Base. ISIS-K is made up of Iraqis, Pakistanis, and Afghans. They consider themselves an elite unit, targeting foreigners, journalists, and high-profile targets like the Karzai airport. Afghans who favor Western ways are considered "collaborators" by ISIS-K, and even the Taliban are suspect.

Al Logari waits in line like all the other would-be refugees. But concealed beneath his robe is one of the most lethal suicide vests imaginable. At twenty-five pounds, it is unusually large and bulky for an explosive device. Should he detonate the weapon perfectly, everyone within his line of sight—Americans and Afghans alike—will either be killed or horribly mutilated. The terrorist accepted his assignment yesterday from Shahab al-Muhajir, the leader of ISIS-K.

The marines know the terrorist is here. But they don't know what he looks like. They have been warned by the Taliban that there is a significant chance of a terror attack. Although there are two other entrance gates to Karzai International, the possibility of a bombing has closed them for today. Also, the United States, Great Britain, and Australia have all directed their citizens still remaining in Afghanistan to stay away from the airport. Instead, they are told to meet a nearby hotel, where they are flown in a military CH-47 helicopter to the runway. That order was given four days ago as thousands of ISIS prisoners

---

* Khorasan is a region comprising parts of Iran, Afghanistan, and Turkmenistan that played a large role in the early history of Islam. The group chose this name because they deny that modern nations exist, preferring the symbolic power of invoking a time when the ancient Islamic caliphate was at the height of its power.

were released from detention in nearby Bagram. The directive came from the US State Department, which somehow did not calibrate the possibility that Abdul Raman al Logari and others would immediately turn to mayhem.

Some of the danger could have been avoided when President Joe Biden ordered the withdrawal of American forces from Afghanistan after twenty years of war. Bagram would have been a far more secure option for evacuations. The base, forty-five miles north of Kabul, is ringed with antiterror devices. It is much harder to penetrate than the Kabul airport.

In just a few hours, President Biden will feel the repercussions of his decision to abandon Bagram in the middle of the night.

✦ ✦ ✦

Al Logari moves forward in line, unbothered. He can clearly see the faces of the young marines near him. They are friendly, smiling, weary after a long day. Some are even women, a fact which offends al Logari's religious beliefs because women should remain subservient to men. So to see them here, carrying a weapon and telling men what to do, is a violation of all that is sacred to the terrorist.

The American military presence is everywhere. But it doesn't prevent al Logari from easily assimilating into the crowd. There is no pre-security screening. And while the Taliban has stepped in from time to time to prevent refugees from behaving in an unruly manner, its focus is elsewhere. Not on ISIS-K.

The terrorist now steps close enough to smell the breath of the nearest marine. It is not his turn to enter the gate, but he does not want to take a chance. He has made his decision.

The suicide vest is made of thick plates of explosives, over which a fragmentation jacket filled with pieces of steel is fitted. In effect, al Logari is a walking land mine. A simple detonator is attached, meaning all he has to do is push the button that will stimulate an electrical charge. The bomb will then detonate.

Al Logari, age and origin unknown, well knows that his body will be instantly torn to pieces, even as his head is wrenched from its torso and flies away intact.

No matter. He presses the button.

Everyone within a thirty-foot radius feels the ground give way as the massive explosion rocks the crowd. Arms and legs are torn from bodies and fly through the air. The percussion blast destroys the hearing of those who still live. Hundreds are dead or wounded, among them eleven United States marines, one army sergeant, and one navy medic. Eighteen other Americans are wounded.

✦ ✦ ✦

From Washington, DC, President Biden soon addresses the nation about the loss: "We will not forgive. We will not forget. We will hunt you down and make you pay . . .

"We will respond with force and precision at our time, at the place we choose and the moment of our choosing," says Biden. "Here's what you need to know: these ISIS terrorists will not win."

✦ ✦ ✦

The murders of the thirteen US service people and 169 others at the Kabul airport shocks the world. Immediately, anti-Biden brigades on social media blame the president himself. Those paid to defend him struggle to present a cogent argument. Bagram was secure—but it was abandoned. Why?

There is no logical answer forthcoming.

In the weeks to come, ISIS-K will quickly gather strength, coalescing in eastern Afghanistan. Yes, it is a sworn enemy of the Taliban. But *the* most desirable target for the new terror threat is the West.

Especially the United States of America.

IN MEMORIAM

Navy Corpsman
Maxton "Max" W. Soviak,
22, of Berlin Heights,
Ohio

Army Staff Sergeant
Ryan C. Knauss, 23,
of Corryton,
Tennessee

Marine Corps
Staff Sergeant
Darin T. Hoover Jr., 31,
of Salt Lake City, Utah

Marine Corps Sergeant
Johanny Rosario
Pichardo, 25, of Lawrence,
Massachusetts

Marine Corps Sergeant
Nicole L. Gee, 23,
of Sacramento, California

Marine Corps Lance
Corporal Kareem
M. Nikoui, 20,
of Norco, California

Marine Corps Lance
Corporal Dylan R. Merola,
20, of Rancho Cucamonga,
California

Marine Corps Lance
Corporal
Rylee J. McCollum, 20,
of Jackson, Wyoming

Marine Corps Lance
Corporal Jared
M. Schmitz, 20,
of St. Charles, Missouri

Marine Corps Lance
Corporal
David L Espinoza, 20,
of Bravo, Texas

Marine Corps Corporal
Humberto L. Sanchez, 22,
of Logansport, Indiana

Marine Corps Corporal
Daegan W. Page, 23,
Omaha, Nebraska

Marine Corps Corporal
Hunter Lopez, 22,
of Indio, California

KILLING THE KILLERS: TERROR SNAPSHOT

Terrorism's global reach can best be understood by this overview of terror incidents during the two-year period of 2016 through 2017. This snapshot of terror details incidents not recorded in this book, many of which did not attract major-media attention.

2016

January 1: Six car bombs explode in Baghdad.

August 7: ISIS suicide bombers attack a US-backed Syrian rebel base. Several people are killed.

August 18: ISIS suicide bombers kill at least twelve Syrian fighters.

August 29: ISIS kills fifty-four in a suicide attack on army recruits in Aden, Yemen.

August 30: ISIS spokesman Abu Muhammad al-Adnani is killed in a US air strike.

September 9: Three French women connected with ISIS are arrested for planning to attack the Gare de Lyon train station in Paris.

September 9: Suicide bombers attack the al-Nakheel Mall in Baghdad, killing twelve people and injuring more than forty.

September 11: Three women connected with ISIS attack a police station in Mombasa, Kenya. One officer is stabbed and the building is set on fire.

September 17–18: Nine people are stabbed by a lone man affiliated with ISIS at the Crossroads Center mall in Saint Cloud, Minnesota.

September 26: ISIS militants murder five individuals in Egypt for allegedly collaborating with the Egyptian army.

October 14: ISIS militants kill twelve Egyptian soldiers at a checkpoint in the Sinai Peninsula.

October 24: Suicide bombers murder sixty-one sleeping police cadets at a training academy in Pakistan.

October 27–29: A Kenyan police officer is attacked by a lone man with a knife outside the US embassy in Nairobi.

November 4: ISIS kills eight people with a car bomb in southern Turkey.

November 12: ISIS claims responsibility for a bomb blast at Shah Noorani shrine in Baluchistan province, Pakistan, that kills more than fifty people.

November 19: ISIS militia kills five police officers in an attack south of Mosul, Iraq.

November 21: ISIS claims responsibility for an attack on the Shia Baqir ul-Uloom mosque in Kabul. Thirty people die.

November 25: ISIS claims responsibility for an attack on an Egyptian military checkpoint in the Sinai Peninsula. Twelve soldiers die.

November 27: ISIS fires at Israeli troops patrolling the Golan Heights. Four of the gunmen are then killed in an Israeli air strike.

December 11–13: An ISIS suicide bomber attacks Cairo's largest Coptic cathedral, killing at least twenty-five people.

December 18: An ISIS suicide bomber kills at least seven in an attack on Libyan forces in Benghazi.

December 18: ISIS suicide bombers kill forty-eight Yemeni security officials and wound dozens in the southern port of Aden.

December 18–20: Gunmen lay siege to Karak Castle in southern Jordan, killing nine and injuring twenty-nine more in gunfire exchanges with security forces. Jordan declares an end to the siege after all four gunmen are eventually killed. The Islamic State claims responsibility for the attack.

December 22: ISIS detonates three car bombs that kill at least twenty-three, including eight police officers, in Mosul.

2017

January 1: ISIS kills seven police officers at an Iraqi police checkpoint near Najaf.

January 1–2: An ISIS gunman kills thirty-nine people in a mass shooting at a nightclub in Istanbul.

January 2: ISIS claims responsibility for a car bomb that kills twenty-four in Baghdad. ISIS militants also kill seven police officers in a related attack.

January 5: ISIS kills fourteen people in a Baghdad car bomb attack.

January 6: ISIS kills four Iraqi soldiers in Tikrit, Iraq.

January 7: A fuel truck detonates in a town in northern Syria, killing dozens.

January 8: ISIS detonates a car bomb at a vegetable market in Baghdad. Thirteen people are killed.

January 9–10: A suicide bomber attacks a security post in the city of el-Arish, Egypt, killing ten and wounding twenty-two.

January 19: ISIS executes twelve people in Palmyra, Syria.

January 20: An ISIS car bomb kills five Turkish soldiers and injures nine near the northern Syrian town of al-Bab.

February 7–8: A suicide bomber attacks Afghanistan's Supreme Court in Kabul, killing twenty and injuring another forty-one.

February 8: ISIS gunmen attack the International Village Hotel in Somalia, killing four guards.

February 10: An ISIS suicide bomber attacks a restaurant in Mosul, killing four.

February 16: An ISIS suicide bomber attacks a Sufi shrine Pakistan. At least seventy-two people are killed, including thirty children.

February 24: An ISIS car bomb kills more than fifty people in the village of Sousian, Syria.

February 26–27: An ISIS bomber attacking a police station in Algeria is shot and killed before he can enter the building.

March 8: ISIS gunmen dressed as medics attack a hospital in Kabul, killing more than thirty.

March 24: An ISIS suicide bomber attacks security forces near an airport in Bangladesh. Two police officers are injured.

March 24: ISIS militants attack a military base in Chechnya, killing six Russian soldiers.

March 25: ISIS bombings in Bangladesh result in six deaths and more than forty wounded.

March 29: ISIS in Egypt beheads two men for practicing witchcraft and sorcery.

April 7: ISIS fighters kill dozens of civilians attempting to flee Mosul.

April 9: ISIS bombs two Catholic churches in Egypt on Palm Sunday. Sixty-five worshippers are murdered.

April 12: An ISIS suicide bomber kills at least five people in an attack near the Afghan Defense Ministry in Kabul.

April 18: ISIS gunmen attack Egyptian security forces near St. Catherine's Monastery on the Sinai Peninsula. One police officer is killed and four more wounded.

April 18–20: An ISIS gunman kills a Paris police officer.

April 21: An ISIS gunman kills two in an attack on a regional Russian Federal Security Service office.

April 28: An ISIS car bomb kills four Iraqi traffic officers in Baghdad.

April 29: ISIS murders senior Afghan Taliban official Maulvi Daud in Peshawar, Pakistan.

April 30: ISIS fighters kill three Iraqi soldiers and wound eight in an attack near the Syrian border.

May 2: ISIS militants attack the Rajm al-Salibi refugee camp in Syria, killing thirty-eight people.

May 3: An ISIS suicide bomber kills eight civilians after attacking a NATO convoy in Kabul.

May 7: ISIS suicide bombers kill two and injure six after attacking a military base home to US military advisers in northern Iraq.

May 12: An ISIS bomb kills twenty-five and injures thirty-five more in Pakistan.

May 15: ISIS claims responsibility for two car bombs that kill at least six people near a refugee camp along the Syria-Jordan border.

May 17: Four ISIS gunmen and one suicide bomber kill six and injure at least nineteen people in Afghanistan.

May 18: Islamic State militants kill twenty people near Aleppo, Syria.

May 19: An ISIS suicide car bomber murders several civilians near Basra.

May 20: ISIS fighters kill almost two dozen, including two children, in a village outside of Deir ez-Zor.

May 23: A car bomb kills four and injures thirty-two in Homs, Syria.

May 24–25: ISIS suicide bombers kill three Indonesian police officers in two blasts near a bus station in Jakarta.

May 26–27: ISIS gunmen attack a bus carrying Coptic Christians in Egypt, killing at least twenty-eight people.

May 30: An ISIS car bomb kills thirteen people and injures thirty in Baghdad.

May 31–June 1: ISIS gunmen attack an Algerian military patrol unit south of Algiers. Four soldiers are wounded.

June 5: An ISIS gunman holds a woman hostage in Melbourne. Three officers are injured in the resulting stand-off before Australian authorities shoot the terrorist dead.

June 8: ISIS admits to murdering two Chinese teachers kidnapped in Pakistan.

June 9: An ISIS female suicide bomber kills at least thirty-one people and injures thirty-five at an Iraqi market in Al-Musayab.

July 7: ISIS suicide car bombs kill at least twenty-three Egyptian soldiers and injure another twenty-six at two military checkpoints in the Sinai Peninsula.

July 10: A US Army sergeant stationed in Hawaii is arrested for attempting to provide drone aircraft and combat training instructions to the Islamic State.

July 17: An ISIS car bomb kills four people at a security checkpoint in northeast Syria.

August 9: ISIS kills four Egyptian police officers in an attack on a patrol car in the Sinai Peninsula.

August 14: A suspected ISIS militant stabs and kills a Turkish police officer while being taken into custody.

August 17–22: ISIS claims responsibility for an attack by a man driving a van through a crowded pedestrian area in Barcelona. At least thirteen people are dead and more than eighty injured.

August 19: A man inspired by ISIS attacks several people with a knife in the Siberian city of Surgut, Russia. There are no fatalities.

August 25: ISIS fighters attack the Shia Imam Zamin mosque in Kabul during Friday prayers. Thirty worshippers are killed.

August 25–26: An ISIS-inspired man carrying a knife attacks two soldiers in Brussels. The attacker is shot dead.

August 28: An ISIS car bomb kills at least eight people and injures twenty-five in an attack at a vegetable market in a Shia district of Baghdad.

August 30: ISIS claims responsibility for a suicide attack in Jalalabad on the home of the deputy speaker of the Afghan parliament.

August 31: ISIS murders two police officers in a suicide attack on a police station in western Algeria.

September 2: ISIS suicide bombers attack a power station north of Baghdad, killing seven people.

September 14: ISIS militants attack a police checkpoint and two other targets in southern Iraq. At least sixty people are killed.

September 29: ISIS kills one and injures five in a suicide attack near the Shia Hussainya mosque in Kabul, Afghanistan.

October 1: An ISIS fighter shouting "Allahu Akbar" stabs two women to death in a knife attack in the southern French port city of Marseille.

October 1–2: ISIS murders more than sixty civilians in central Syria.

October 2–3: Two ISIS suicide bombers attack a police station in Damascus, killing at least ten.

October 3: ISIS releases a video showing two captured Russian soldiers in Deir ez-Zor, Syria. Russia denies that any troops have been taken prisoner.

October 4: ISIS gunmen kill at least four and injure another forty in a suicide attack in Libya.

October 5: An ISIS suicide bomber kills eighteen people in southwest Pakistan.

October 11: ISIS suicide bombers attack police in Damascus, killing two and injuring six.

October 12: ISIS kills at least fifty people in three car bomb attacks in northeast Syria.

October 13: ISIS murders six Egyptian soldiers in an attack on a military post in the Sinai Peninsula.

October 15: ISIS militants attack security outposts in the Sinai Peninsula, killing six soldiers and injuring more than twenty.

October 20: ISIS suicide bombers kill seventy-two people in attacks on two mosques in Afghanistan.

October 24–26: ISIS murders eight soldiers and one civilian in northeast Nigeria.

November 5: An ISIS suicide car bomber kills fifteen and injures twenty in south Yemen.

November 7: ISIS gunmen disguised as police kill two at a television station in Kabul.

November 14: An ISIS car bomb kills at least six people in Aden.

November 16: An ISIS suicide bomber kills nine in Kabul, Afghanistan.

November 17: An ISIS-planted car bomb kills twenty people and injures another thirty in Syria.

November 24: ISIS militants attack a Sufi mosque on the Sinai Peninsula, killing 305 people and injuring at least 128 others.

NOTE ON SOURCES

Writing a book on terrorism is a unique research challenge. The key players live in a clandestine world, whether it be the terrorists themselves, the intelligence agencies who shadow them, or the Special Forces operators who do the hunting. In a world of TikTok and YouTube, where it seems like everyone is trying to be famous, these men and women do their best to remain almost completely out of the limelight.

But the information is out there. Not all of it—there are some events in this book that will not be fully revealed to the public for years. In those instances, we opted for as much detail as the research allowed, only writing in specifics when facts could be verified. The rest—all the stuff that's still top secret—we did not even try to guess about and chose to let those details remain vague.

We were helped to an extreme amount by five wise men whose names shall remain off the record. They spoke on background, under the condition of anonymity. Very often the interviews veered into a level of confidentiality, whereupon the authors were politely told, "I can't answer that question." But for the data that could be discussed, these gentlemen provided opinions and details. Their wealth of experience and in-depth knowledge of the subject matter is formidable, and all thanks go to them for being patient and kind in answering what must to them have felt like very basic questions.

In addition to the hurdle of writing about a topic that is still highly classified, there was the issue of travel. A normal part of writing a *Killing* book is going to the locations being described, whether that be walking one of Crazy Horse's battlefields or visiting the site of a gangland slaying. Nothing beats studying the land to provide context while trying to set a scene.

But COVID and terrorism made travel a no-go for this book. Other than a long layover in Istanbul, there were no visits to the Middle East during the writing process. Most locations are off-limits or war zones. Instead, we made great use of satellite imagery to see the color of soil, the density of a forest, the width of roads, and a thousand other details that seem minor until you start trying to describe something.

The same should also be said about the plethora of video footage now available online, allowing the same view of a location or event as if we had been there ourselves.

Not surprisingly, online newspaper databases are an enormous help in researching terror. Google an event, and the same day in history will be described in dozens of different newspapers. We leaned on papers from New York, Tehran, Paris, London, and cities across Asia and Africa. Some depend upon the wire services, which is obvious when the exact same article is run in big-city newspapers around the world. The trick is finding the newspapers that do their own reporting, digging deep into a happening to provide specifics other writers don't put in their stories: the caliber of a weapon, temperature, local color, and many other tiny details for which researchers like us are truly thankful.

It is a common practice to mine the bibliographies of well-researched books on a topic. This is a road map into the data hunt. But while those books on terror are definitely out there, we didn't lean on them. Most events we describe are too recent for books to offer the sort of perspective that can be found by looking back on an event thirty or fifty years later. But there were a few we consulted, mostly about the bin Laden raid or General Soleimani. A great thanks to those authors for their expertise and attention to detail.

And finally, an enormous thanks to the family of Kayla Mueller.

ACKNOWLEDGMENTS

Much of this book is based on primary sources. That means eyewitnesses to what actually happened. Martin Dugard and I were fortunate enough to gain the trust of five high-ranking US intelligence officials. Their service spans a twenty-year period.

As with all honest reporting, we verified as much as we could with other sources. We believe all the information in this book is accurate. There is no speculation or embellishment.

The five intel guys we spoke with remain in physical danger from terrorists, so we are obviously not going to name them. All had or have top secret clearance.

Our deep gratitude goes to these patriots who protected us. They all wanted the truth about terrorism to be told.

And so it has been.

BILL O'REILLY
MARTIN DUGARD

ILLUSTRATION CREDITS

INDEX

Note: Page numbers in italics indicate figures.

ABOUT THE AUTHORS

Bill O'Reilly is a trailblazing TV journalist who has experienced unprecedented success on cable news and in writing seventeen national number-one bestselling nonfiction books. There are more than eighteen million books in the *Killing* series in print. He lives on Long Island.

Martin Dugard is the *New York Times* bestselling author of several books of history, among them the *Killing* series, *Into Africa*, and *Taking Paris*. He and his wife live in Southern California.